François Frederic Roget

# First Steps in French History, Literature and Philology

For Candidates for the Scotch Leaving-Certificate Examination, etc.

François Frederic Roget

**First Steps in French History, Literature and Philology**
*For Candidates for the Scotch Leaving-Certificate Examination, etc.*

ISBN/EAN: 9783337205430

Printed in Europe, USA, Canada, Australia, Japan

Cover: Foto ©Thomas Meinert / pixelio.de

More available books at **www.hansebooks.com**

# FIRST STEPS

IN

# FRENCH HISTORY, LITERATURE AND PHILOLOGY

# FIRST STEPS

IN

# FRENCH HISTORY LITERATURE AND PHILOLOGY

*FOR CANDIDATES FOR THE SCOTCH LEAVING-CERTIFICATE EXAMINATION,*
*THE VARIOUS UNIVERSITIES' LOCAL EXAMINATIONS,*
*THE UNIVERSITY ENTRANCE EXAMINATIONS*
*AND THE ARMY EXAMINATIONS*

BY

## F. F. ROGET

GRADUATE OF GENEVA UNIVERSITY, EDINBURGH UNIVERSITY EXTENSION LECTURER,
LECTURER IN THE FREE CHURCH OF SCOTLAND TRAINING COLLEGE, LECTURER
ON FOREIGN LITERATURE AND TUTOR FOR COMPARATIVE PHILOLOGY,
ST. GEORGE'S CLASSES, LECTURER IN THE ST. GEORGE'S
TRAINING COLLEGE, SENIOR ASSISTANT-MASTER
AT FETTES COLLEGE, ETC.

## WILLIAMS AND NORGATE

14 HENRIETTA STREET, COVENT GARDEN, LONDON
20 SOUTH FREDERICK STREET, EDINBURGH
AND 7 BROAD STREET, OXFORD

1896

# PREFACE

THIS compilation has been prepared in order to bring together, in one volume and in a small compass, as large a portion of the French subjects lying beyond the province of ordinary grammar as students, preparing for the Scotch Leaving Certificate, for the University Entrance Examinations, for the University Local Examinations, and for the Army, can, in the light of our experience, be expected to acquire.

It has also been our aim to provide a faithful introduction to the easier and more generally known works of specialists in the field of advanced French studies.

We trust that our Manual is so written that those who would master its contents may receive some valuable intellectual impressions; for it is our desire that this book may help to alter the trivial spirit in which French is often taught.

We are sure that the application of the historical method to the study of French can alone raise it to its proper place in the sphere of educative, mind-stimulating pursuits.

F. F. R.

*July* 1892.

# CONTENTS

## FRENCH LITERATURE



## CHAPTER I.



## CHAPTER II.

# CHAPTER III.



# CHAPTER IV.

### *Dramatic Poetry*



### *Prose.*



# CHAPTER V.



### *Lyric Poetry.*



### *Dramatic Poetry.*



### *Prose.*

## CHAPTER VI.



## CHAPTER VII.

## CHAPTER VIII.

## CHAPTER IX.



---

# FRENCH LANGUAGE.

## CHAPTER X.



## CHAPTER XI.



## CHAPTER XII.

# CHAPTER XIII.

xvi                    *Contents*

## CHAPTER XIV.



## CHAPTER XV.

# FRENCH LITERATURE

## CHAPTER I.

### INTRODUCTORY.

IN Cambridge University, a very few years ago, when it was proposed that French should be raised to the circle of the 'artes humaniores,' one of the weightiest objections was that French is of no use except to diplomatists, waiters, and couriers. In the mind of its propounders this pithy argument was sweeping enough to embrace all modern languages in a peremptory condemnation. Yet contempt showed itself powerless to impede reform. Modern languages are fast making good in Great Britain their claim to rank with Greek and Latin as instruments and vehicles of the highest culture.

If a schoolmaster were freed in his appreciation of the comparative value of languages from all irrelevant but yet binding considerations, such as the future profession of his pupils, the state of public opinion, the demands of examining boards, he would place himself in succession at three different standpoints, in order to gauge in quality and quantity the profit accruing from linguistic studies. These points are : (1) the mental exercise offered, (2) the light thrown on language in general by the particular language under scrutiny, (3) the contents of the literature opened up by a knowledge of the language. On behalf of French the case would appear very much as follows :—

## 1. MENTAL EXERCISE OFFERED.

An acquaintance with French formerly served superficial purposes only. It was studied as an accomplishment; it gave to the gentleman and the courtier credentials for polish, refinement, and wit. During the period of French literary supremacy in Europe, the aristocratic circles in every country represented almost the whole of society. Then French taste and French manners reigned supreme in strictly defined areas. This lasted till the national spirit, in Germany and in England especially, gave birth to an independent literature, and to a spontaneous culture, so overwhelming by their intensity, and by the numbers of their followers, that the Frenchified circles were thrown into the shade. French, it is true, was never driven from high places. It remained also in good repute as an international tongue, and it gained what it had not before, the appreciation of those men to whom the development of their own national literature brought some culture and taste.

Still, the company it kept was too fashionable; the master of French and the master of deportment were too closely allied not to bring some contempt upon the language, when under the stress of commercial necessities, in spite of national and political prejudices, it was generally recognised as an instrument of education in British secondary schools. A doubt lingered whether French had a right to any such position at all, and the rooted predilection of the universities for Latin and Greek stood out against it with might. It must be said in excuse of its opponents that the way and the manner in which French had introduced itself were little to its credit. Its advocates, till the middle of this century, put it to uses and claimed for it capabilities that are not of the best kind in request among pedagogues. The French life, manners, tastes, and literary achievements of the seventeenth century used to be the grounds on which French studies recommended themselves, not only to foreigners, but also to the French educational world. Those grounds are insufficient, and British educationists who believe still that there are no better ones cannot be blamed for resisting them. By so doing they show much good sense, but also great ignorance. In this they are no worse than Voltaire, who, like them, knew not that the French language has growth, and that its literature has a history.

It is through its growth and through its history that French has its best claim to the student's attention. Thanks to them, it offers an excellent field for mental exercise. Without them it would still have distinctive merit, such as the vivacity of its style, the directness and precision of its expressions, the nicety and delicacy of its syntax, the elaborateness of its rhetoric, its logic, lucidity, penetration, and alertness; but these qualities are not superlative, and they are better perceived and turned to more account by mature minds than by minds under training.  History and growth, on the contrary, to the growing mind are picturesque and wonderful: they interest, develop, and enlarge it.  When a teacher of botany wishes to give a first lesson on plant-life, he does not choose his examples in distant foreign parts, but he seeks out a kind familiar to the student's eye, and he takes care that the student has access to the soil in which it grows.  Then he seeks out the best specimen of that kind for anatomical and physiological study.  So will a teacher of language, if he is wise, be at pains as great to choose a language whose life is traceable by descent and determinable by comparison, without assuming the student's acquaintance with lands unknown to him.

Of all languages accessible to the ordinary student, French is the best to impart a sense of genesis in language, and by analogy and parallelism in almost everything else.  It is the best specimen of its kind, because the decomposed soil from which it springs—Latin—is school property; because the successive states it has gone through are visibly marked on its material and in its significance; because its line of development, diverted from Roman culture, lies across the richest historical ground.  Of other languages, two classical ones take their rise in periods lying beyond the compass of secondary studies; two modern ones, German and English, lead back, with Anglo-Saxon, Gothic, etc., to semi-savage regions, in obscure times. Though they may be more curious, they are less normal than French—hence their pedagogical inferiority. Mental training by means of languages is best served by the most perfect living specimen of language that is accessible.

Next to the growth of the language, the history of its literature comes to be considered. French literature has proved itself of late to be a much more imposing affair than was dreamt of in the seventeenth and eighteenth centuries. To its progress, since the Renaissance, it owes the sort of credit which still colours visibly both the esteem and the disfavour in which it is generally held. But its long development through the Middle Ages, now brought to light for the first time, will lead to a more liberal appreciation of French literature. It used to be currently stated that French literature had its roots in the Augustan age of Latin culture, and that the Hellenism of the Renaissance was the air in which it grew. The mythological apparel of French poetry and the classical rhetoric do admittedly proceed from that source. But hearts beat and imagination wove its fancies in France ages before scholars imported the literary finery of Greece and Rome. Mediæval productions, enormous in bulk, genuine in subject and in treatment, influential beyond compare in Western Europe, are now revealing themselves as the natural trunk of French literature, if not of French letters. Henceforth the competent learner will no longer turn French literature to account exclusively for the study of the formal art of writing.  He will avail himself of an unbroken literature of about one thousand years to inquire how a literature can closely reflect a nationality and yet be possessed of an interest more generally human than any other.  English, German, Greek, and Latin show to smaller advantage the same spectacle.  The latter have the misfortune of being dead, the former offer less historical continuity, and their vitality is more spasmodic.

## 2. The Light Thrown on Language in General.

To explain the general laws of comparative philology by a reference to French and the Romance tongues, all living, is a task as pleasant as it is fruitful.  French is an analytic tongue with many synthetic constructions, its phonetics are most regular and varied, its processes of word-formation are of the richest.  Interest never flags.  Instead of consisting of words painfully raked together, like pebbles, from mysterious places out of reach, the material for illustration may at every turn be taken out of the student's mouth.  French is typical for the laws of language, for the elements of speech, and for the joint elaboration of sound, sign, and significance into an instrument of high perfection.  With students who know Latin, French philology is a pursuit as legitimate as Sanskrit philology at the Universities.

## 3. The Contents of French Literature.

In a very well-conceived series of papers on language-teaching in the *Journal of Education* (the best periodical by far in British pedagogical circles), a German scholar is quoted, who, when asked whether Homer was poetry to him, or whether it was all roots, replied, with a melancholy air of delight, 'It is all roots.' That man was clearly no better than the life he led. We can see him from here, seated at his desk in his dressing-gown, smoking his long pipe, and hugging books—totally unfit to be a teacher. Every act of study must be an act of life, kindling in the mind a proportionate vital effort. The philological explanation of words must quicken the spirit of inquiry ; the merest grammatical remark must aim at the stimulation of energy and curiosity. The contents of speech, the network of intertwined ideas, sentiments, and reasoning running from word to word, as blood runs in our body, must not be ousted from consideration. The highest life of the mind that can be communicated through language is deposited in literature and poetry. There it lies, as in a chest, accumulated, ready by passing into the slowly maturing brain to profoundly affect psychological growth. No doubt the cultivation of the mind by literature falls for the most part into a period to which specific teaching does not extend. Juvenile readers are omnivorous, not critical. It is rightly urged also that the study of literature in a foreign tongue is uninviting, because the language itself stands as a barrier to literary perception. Nevertheless, the practice of reducing humanities to grammatical and syntactical drill is absurd, and, little able as youth is to appreciate masterpieces, to give it a language without its literature would be like offering to a man in the dark a candlestick without a candle. To educate the mind by literature is to put the crown on mental training by language. The custom of teaching several languages, and of reaching finality in none, cannot be too severely condemned. If a choice is to be made among the foreign languages in order that one may be selected for the excellence of its literature, the British pedagogue cannot long remain in suspense. The literature that has influenced all others, and has hardly been influenced by any, whose development is unbroken and even, whose form is most artistic, and whose substance is most varied, rich in tone, deep in thought— the typical modern literature, in one word, is the French. Not that it is altogether free from drawbacks: its poetry, for instance, is weak. Owing to its lucidity, to its tendency to abstraction, to the rigidity of its syntax, to the poverty of its versification, and to a bad poetical faculty inherited from Latin, French is rather unsuited to lyrical inspiration. The morbid strain by which the psychological analysis of many contemporary French novelists is marred is a bad disorder indeed. However, these are mere specks upon an almost faultless picture. A reviewer is struck by the general manliness of French literature; more than its rivals, it has art, substance, solidity, fecundity. It stands forth in an attitude of intellectual and moral conquest; it breathes the triumph of man over the conditions of life. It abhorred till recently what is sickly, pessimistic, sentimental, and mysterious. It is the expression of society rather than of nature. Its strength lies exactly wherein English literature is weak; and what could be better than to seek in its liberal and idealistic tone the complement of a sterling British education in the things that go to make worth?

# CHAPTER II.

## SUMMARY NOTES ON FRENCH HISTORY.[1]

GAUL. The Celts inhabiting the country now known as France came into contact with civilisation when a colony of Greeks from Asia - Minor was formed at Massilia (Marseille), 600 B.C. Then came the Romans, who extended their dominion over the southern part of the Valley of the Rhône, and called it Provincia (Provence). Julius Cæsar, in his conquest of the remaining parts of Gaul (58 B.C. to 51 B.C.), used Provence as a basis for his operations, which took him as far north as the present Belgium and across the English Channel. The conquered Gauls adopted the *Lingua Romana* (or spoken dialect) of their victors, and for several centuries kept acquiring Roman civilisation and increasing in prosperity.

The FRANKS. These were a Teutonic tribe, occupying from the third century after Christ the eastern banks of the Rhine, approximately from Mainz to its mouth. A large number of them passed into Gaul in the fifth century. These founded the Frankish kingdom, which

[1] See, in the new edition of Chambers's *Encyclopædia*, under FRANCE, the article on this subject.

10

was at first under the sway of the Merovingian kings.
The Frankish kingdom under Clovis was greatly en-
larged by successful warfare, till under his successors
it extended over both banks of the Rhine, so as to
comprise the larger part of modern France, Thuringia
and Bavaria; but it was soon broken up into three
divisions—the kingdoms of Austrasia, of Neustria, and
of Burgundy.  In 613 the three kingdoms were united
again under one sceptre.  From the seventh century
the Masters of the Royal Household superseded by
degrees the authority of the Merovingian kings, till three
of them, Pepin d'Héristal, Charles Martel, and Pepin
le Bref, having established by successful warfare and
administrative capacity a title to the throne, the latter
was called to it by the military class.  This was the
beginning of the Carlovingian dynasty (752).  Under
them the Frankish kingdom became the greatest
European power; Charlemagne extended its boundaries
to the Eider in the north, the Ebro in the south-west,
Northern Italy in the south-east, the Saale in the east,
and was anointed successor to the Roman Emperors by
the Pope in 799.  After his death this vast military
monarchy was divided once for all by the Treaty signed
at Verdun between three of his descendants (843).
From that moment the history of the original Frankish
kingdom ceases, and that of France on one side, and of
Germany on another side, begins.  Charles the Bald
was the first king of France properly so called.  He
ruled over the lands to the west of the Rhône and
Scheldt.  Under his successors, France was exposed to

the raids of the Norsemen in the north, and of the Saracens in the south. Rollo, the leader of the former, became, in 911, Duke of Normandy. By degrees the feudal system developed itself in the land, and the power of the vassals was such as to reduce to a mere shadow the authority of the kings. By the accession to the throne of the House of Hugo Capet, Count of Paris and of Orleans, and Duke of Francia (Île de France), whose descendants were to continue as kings of France down to 1792, the foundation was established of an unbroken monarchical tradition, round which grew French nationality.

The CAPETIAN KINGS. The conquest of England by the Normans was the first event of great magnitude under this dynasty. Louis VII. having repudiated his wife, Eleanor of Aquitaine, she married, in 1152, Henry Plantagenet, King of England and Duke of Normandy, and brought him as a dowry the whole of western France. The French kings were brought thereby into great straits. However, Philippe Auguste succeeded in taking away from the English, Normandy, Brittany, Maine, Touraine, Anjou, and Poitou. Provence and Languedoc were added to the Realm by Louis IX., commonly known as Saint Louis. He succeeded also in curbing the nobility, in protecting town-ships and the peasantry, in establishing a code of royal law, in regulating the taxes, in forming a body of civil servants, and in laying the foundation of a Gallican Church. In the next reigns, French nationality

was so far constituted that it was able to challenge the
power of the Popes.   The Papal See was for many
years transferred to Avignon in Provence.   In 1302
deputies from the townships were, for the first time,
added under the name of Third Estate (*Tiers Etat*) to
the deputies from the nobility and the clergy, who
already formed the national representative body known
under the name of States General (*Etats Généraux*).

VALOIS KINGS (1328-1589).   The direct heir to the
throne being a woman, the Salic law came into operation, and the House of Valois, indirectly connected
with the House of Capet, came to the throne in the
person of Philippe VI.   The prolonged wars with the
kings of England, consequent upon their setting up a
claim to the French Crown, began again under this
prince.   Edward III. of England obtained possession of
Calais after the victory at Crecy (1346).   Philippe VI.'s
successor, Jean le Bon, was beaten and taken a prisoner
at Maupertuis.   By the Treaty signed at Bretigny
(1360) he gave back to England the whole of Aquitaine,
something like nineteen departments of modern France.
On the other side, he took possession of Dauphiné; but
the establishment of a side branch of the Valois House
in the Dukedom of Burgundy threatened danger to the
Crown in a manner hitherto unexpected.   Under
Charles VI., who became insane, the question of the
successioin to the throne was in debate between the
rival branches of the Valois family, and reached an
acute stage.   Henry V. of England took advantage of

this civil war to invade France, and to enforce, if possible, his claim to the Crown of France over both branches of the Valois family.   He conquered at Agincourt (1415).   He formed an alliance with the Duke of Burgundy, who conquered Paris (1417), and he was recognised by Charles VI. as his successor to the French throne.   After the death of Henry V. of England, and of the insane Charles VL of France, the son of Henry was, in his turn, crowned King of France.   The eldest son of Charles VI., who bore the title of Dauphin, which, since the conquest of Dauphiné, whose dukedom was conferred upon them, has belonged to the direct heirs to the French Crown, withdrew south of the river Loire, and sustained, first as Regent and then as legitimate king, a long war against the English.   The calamities and disgrace of this long conflict roused among the lower classes a passionate patriotism.   The famous Jeanne D'Arc, springing from the people, with a heart full of national pride and appearing to obey higher powers, led the French armies to repeated victories, compelled the English to raise the siege of Orleans, led the Dauphin and Regent to be crowned at Reims as Charles VII., and gave her countrymen an advantage over the English which they never again lost.   These, beaten at Castillon, saw their hold on France reduced to Calais alone.   Louis XI., continuing the successes of his predecessor, was able to incorporate the dominions of the Burgundian Valois with his own realm.   Charles VIII. won Brittany for the Crown, and opened a series of campaigns in Italy which were continued by Louis XII., and which, under Francis I., led to the crushing defeat at Pavia (1525), in which the French were beaten by Charles V. of Spain, whose pretensions to Burgundy and Italy clashed with those of the French King. At that time France was being moulded more and more into the shape of an absolute monarchy. The functions belonging to the ancient parliaments were cut down, the clergy were made dependent on the Crown; Henry II. acquired Metz, Toul, and Verdun, and succeeded in turning the English out of Calais, their last foothold in France. Under his successor, the Catholic princes of the House of Lorraine (Duc de Guise) formed a reactionary political and religious party, which was as much directed against the king as against the Protestants. The princes of the House of Bourbon, the leaders of the Protestants and of the progressive political party, took up a definite position against them. The strain put on the religious and political unity of the French kingdom became so great that under the reign of Catherine de Medici there broke out the Huguenot wars or wars of religion. The frightful massacre of the Protestants on the famous night of St. Bartholomew in 1572, instead of bringing about the triumph of the House of Guise, resulted in the flight of the King, Henry III., to the camp of Henry of Bourbon, who is better known in history as Henri de Navarre. The French King was murdered by a fanatical monk in 1589, and with him died out the House of Valois.

The BOURBON KINGS. Henri de Navarre having

formally accepted the Roman Catholic faith, became king under the title of Henry IV. He passed the Edict of Nantes, whereby he granted to the Protestants sufficient liberty in the exercise of their religion to make them peaceful citizens. With the assistance of Sully he restored the finances, and organised a standing army. Under the minority of his successor the royal authority was again so undermined that the *Etats Généraux*, which used to be summoned to meet only when the Crown was in serious jeopardy, were called together in 1614; but Richelieu, having been put at the head of affairs by Louis XIII. in 1624, resumed with unrelenting energy the traditional policy of the French kings, namely, that of centralising all political and military power. The aim of his foreign policy was to humble the House of Austria, which alone stood in the way of the ascendancy of France on the Continent. He sided, therefore, with the Protestants in the Thirty Years' War. As a home minister he put down with a strong hand the rebellious leanings of the aristocracy, and stripped the Protestants of their particular political rights. After his death, Mazarin became Prime Minister, and developed consistently Richelieu's policy during the minority of Louis XIV. He won the day over the aristocracy in their last struggle for political power (the war of La Fronde), and obtained for France, by the Peace of Westphalia in 1648, Alsace, which belonged then to the House of Austria. When Louis XIV. attained his majority (1661), there stood at his disposal a well-ordered kingdom, with a powerful central administration, about to be headed by most capable ministers, such as Colbert and Louvois. The young and ambitious king adopted a broad and aggressive policy, with a view to crippling sooner or later the power of Spain. His attack upon the Low Countries dragged him into war with the first regular coalition against France known to history, the outcome of which was that Franche-Comté and a part of Flanders became French. After the victories of Condé in earlier wars, and of Turenne in Germany, the military power of France was paramount on the Continent. At home, also, the now fully developed monarchical system bore its best fruit. Literature, art, and science flourished at the Court of Versailles, and in Church matters Louis' authority stood higher than that of the Pope. Unfortunately, he subjected, in his riper years, the material prosperity of his country, the loyalty of a part of his subjects, and the military resources of his kingdom, to an excessive strain. The revocation of the Edict of Nantes in 1685 sent out of the country about half a million Protestants, who took away with them their industry, and put at the service of Prussia and England their force of character, their wealth, and their military talents. The French armies, employed again in aggressive wars against Germany, Holland, England, Spain, and Savoy, met with reverses, and the disasters brought to the French when they raised the war of the Spanish Succession were the natural result of Louis XIV.'s baneful policy from the moment he had fallen under the influence of Mme. De Maintenon. The victories of

Marlborough at Blenheim, and of Prince Eugene of Savoy at Turin, are the worst blots on the long and otherwise brilliant military record of France during that reign. The State was burdened with the enormous debt of two thousand million French livres. The son and the grandson of Louis died before him, so that during the minority of Louis xv. the Duke of Orleans was Regent. The profligacy and lavish expenditure of that prince at a moment when the greatest honesty in politics, ability in finance, and a sense of responsibility in private life were required to maintain the shaken loyalty to the kings, brought matters from bad to worse. Under Louis xv., who reigned till 1774, the external and internal prospects of France brightened up for a while during the premiership of Cardinal Fleury. Unfortunately, the demoralisation in all branches of the public service, and the unjustified ascendancy of disreputable women in the councils of the king, had gone so far that France was badly worsted in the War of the Austrian Succession and in the Seven Years' War. France had to abandon most of its colonies to England in 1773; as a set-off, full rights over Lorraine were obtained. Louis xvi. might have saved France from the approaching horrors of the Revolution if his power to mend matters and his political enlightenment as to the measures to adopt had been on a par with his good-will and philanthropic disposition. In 1777 the kingdom was in such financial straits that the liberal and energetic finance minister, Necker, was called in to ward off imminent bankruptcy.

In 1789 the States General, which had not been called together since 1614, were summoned to meet and consider the situation of the State. On Necker's proposal, the representation of the Tiers Etat on that body was doubled. The effective power began at once to pass from the hands of the king and his ministry to an assembly which had at its back public opinion. In the same year the deputies from the towns succeeded in winning among the representatives of the nobility and of the clergy support for their own views, and formed themselves into a constituent national assembly. This was the beginning of the Revolution.

The REVOLUTION (1789-1804). Every change in the relations between the King and this Assembly was reflected first in Paris and then in the whole of France. When the king collected his troops and dismissed Necker, the people of Paris replied by storming the Bastille. When the National Assembly put an end to class privileges, the people compelled the King to transfer his residence from Versailles to Paris. Mainly on account of the vacillation of Louis XVI., it became impossible to replace in the monarchy the absolute principle by the constitutional, and to go no further, as Mirabeau wished. The new constitution allowed the King but the very smallest powers, and put the government in the hands of elected representatives, substituting for the time-honoured division of France into provinces a totally artificial division into departments. Privileges were done away with, universal freedom in

matters of religion was introduced, the property of the
Church was confiscated, and ecclesiastics were called
upon to swear an oath of allegiance to the new constitution.  The King was unfortunate enough in June
1791 to make an attempt at flight, whereby the anger
of the people was increased; and when the majority of
the legislative National Assembly elected in that year
was found to belong to the Girondist party, who dis-
countenanced the maintenance of the monarchy, Louis
XVI. was unable to oppose the declaration of war against
Austria and Prussia, guilty of tolerating the warlike
designs of the French *émigrés*.  The French troops met
at first with some reverses, for which the mob sought
revenge on the royal family.  The royal residence in
the Tuileries was taken by storm; the King applied to
the National Assembly for protection.  He was deprived
of his royal status, and sovereign power passed for a
time into the hands of the Municipal Council of Paris,
and of the extreme radical party known as La Montagne.
A large number of royalists were put to death, after
which the monarchy was formally abolished and the
Republic proclaimed.  The National Assembly was
then dissolved, and the National Convention took its
place, in which the extreme party outnumbered the
comparatively moderate Girondists, and, finding a rest-
ing-point in the military organisation of the people of
Paris, brought about the judgment and execution of
the King (January 1793).  Then began a reign of
terror of the most horrible kind.  Thousands were
brought up before the revolutionary tribunal, among

them the Girondists, undoubted Republicans though they were, and they were sent to death along with clergymen and nobles. Some of the provincial towns having risen against the tyranny of the Paris political clubs, the Committee for Public Safety, formed in the spring of that year, put down the rising with frightful ferocity, and set about deliberately breaking every link with the ancient institutions of France by suppressing the Christian Church, by introducing a new calendar, by the introduction of a ten days' week, and by organising the public worship of reason. The Committee, extravagant in everything else, did, nevertheless, its duty in military affairs. All Frenchmen of an age to bear arms were called up. The Prussians were driven back across the Rhine, Belgium was conquered, the towns of Mainz and Frankfurt were held. Though badly beaten, the Austrians and Prussians resumed the field the next year, when a coalition of the European monarchies was formed with a view to stamping out the revolutionary practices and ideas before they could extend to other countries. The French War Minister, Carnot, replied to this challenge by putting no less than fourteen armies in the field. The French not only held their own on the battle-fields, but also occupied Holland. In 1795 a peace was signed at Bâle between France on the one side, and Prussia and Spain on the other. In the meanwhile the frenzied party leaders in Paris, after clearing the field of their joint opponents, took to rending one another. Robespierre sent to the *guillotine* (invented at that time for wholesale execution) those who had worked it before him, and was himself beheaded two or three months later. The moderate party was then able to resume the ascendancy. There was formed in the autumn of 1795 a Directory, with five members to wield the executive power and act as a cabinet. Then came the victories of General Bonaparte in Italy, followed by a treaty of peace with Austria, which secured for France Belgium and the left bank of the Rhine. Being unable, however, to recognise the new political order established in France, the powers formed a second coalition while Bonaparte was in Egypt. On his return he found himself in possession of such prestige that he was able to drive the Directorate from power and rule in its stead. For five years France was governed by three consuls, of whom he was the first, an arrangement whereby he practically became military dictator. He brought to an end the civil war in Vendée, re-organised the finances, prepared a code of civil law on the basis of the individual rights vouchsafed by the Revolution, and formed a powerful police to be the mainstay of his government. Then he entered upon a marvellous series of victories over the European coalition. The Austrians beaten at Marengo, the Prussians beaten at Hohen-Linden sued for peace, and agreed that the Rhine should be the eastern boundary of France. In 1802 Napoleon came to terms with England in the Amiens Treaty. The Roman Catholic Church was restored. In 1804 the French, exercising their right as to whether Bonaparte should become Emperor or not, agreed by a majority to be ruled by him, and as his power was thus grounded on the popular will, there was nothing to stand in his way.

The EMPIRE (1804-1815).  On being appointed to the Imperial dignity, Bonaparte took the title of Napoleon I., and while keeping a firm hand on the inner circumstances of France, he entered upon a course of European conquest.  Already in the following year he transformed the Cis-Alpine Republic into a kingdom of his own.  Then, when the European powers entered into a third coalition, it was he who reaped all the benefit from it.  He made himself king of Italy, set members of his own family as kings in Holland and in Naples, and united the princes of the Rhine Valley into a confederation under his guardianship.  Prussia was crushed in 1807, Portugal was occupied by French troops, the Bourbon branch was supplanted in Spain by one of his own brothers, and in 1809 he knocked Austria down for the fourth time.  The whole of the Continent of Europe with the exception of Russia and Turkey was then in subjection to Napoleon.  As for the boundaries of France proper, they were extended so far as to comprise Holland, the coasts of north-west Germany on to Lübeck, northern and middle Italy, including Illyria and the Ionian Isles.  Rome and Amsterdam were French towns.  The dark sides to this glorious picture were that the French navy since the disaster at Trafalgar had disappeared from the seas, that continental trade was greatly injured by Napoleon's interdiction of England, that the French people, although dazzled by their triumphant progress through Europe, began to reckon the price paid for so much military magnificence in the squandering of money and of blood. Had the Emperor kept his head, all might have been well with him yet. He committed very much the same mistakes as Louis XIV. in a somewhat similar position. Instead of stopping in time, he visited Russia with war in 1812 at the head of 600,000 men drawn from all parts of central and western Europe. This army was almost entirely destroyed in winter in its retreat from Moscow. Then Napoleon who had sown violence beyond endurance reaped at last the fruit of unrighteous ambition. Russia and Prussia, Austria, Sweden, and England united their arms against him in a supreme effort. He was beaten in the three days' battle at Leipsic in 1813. At the beginning of the next year the allied armies crossed the Rhine and drove back to Paris, step by step, the magnificent military leader, who had taught them by defeat the art of winning battles. In the spring of 1814, the Senate, which Napoleon had preserved beside him as a figure-head of Parliamentary institutions, called the Bourbon family back to France. Their head, the Duke of Provence, began to reign under the title of Louis XVIII., but less than a year later Napoleon left the island of Elba, to which he had been confined by the Powers, landed on the French coast, marched to Paris with an army recruited from among his old brothers in arms, and resumed possession of his Imperial throne. At once the allies were again in the field against him.  He conquered at Ligny on the 16th of June 1815, but was beaten at Waterloo on the eighteenth.  For the second time the allied armies entered Paris, Napoleon was taken away to St. Helena, and the boundaries of France were brought back to where they stood in 1790.

The CONSTITUTIONAL MONARCHY.  Louis XVIII. granted a Charter to the French people guaranteeing the political rights won in the more moderate period of the Revolution.  The French noblemen, however, who returned to France with him, endeavoured to counteract the effect of his liberal dispositions, and felt themselves supported in this by some outbreaks which occurred in the south, and which were directed against the Bonapartists and the Protestants.  Louis XVIII. was ill-advised enough to yield a good deal to them.  His brother, whose accession to the throne under the title of Charles X. took place in 1824, continued the same unwise policy, and followed out more and more in political affairs the wishes of the clergy.  The liberty of the Press was grossly interfered with, a narrow legislation irritated laymen against the Church, and those nobles, known under the name of *émigrés*, who had returned to France since the restoration of the monarchy, were granted an indemnity amounting to one thousand million francs. In consequence, opposition grew in breadth and depth; in vain did the king endeavour to stem the tide by a change in his home policy, and in 1830 by beginning the conquest of Algeria.  In the same year the Chamber of Deputies became so threatening that Charles x. endeavoured to curb it by having recourse to arbitrary measures and by consenting to its dissolution. A Revolutionary movement broke out in Paris in the last days of July. Anticipating any further steps that the people might take, the French Deputies acting in concert with the House of Peers appointed Louis-Philippe, Duke of Orleans, to the office of Lieutenant-General of the kingdom. Thereupon Charles x. abdicated, made his way to the coast almost alone and took refuge in England. The Charter was altered so as to include the all-might of the people and to confer upon the Houses the right of initiating legislation; but the body of electors remained limited to 200,000. The amended Charter having been accepted on oath by the newly appointed Lieutenant-General, he ascended the throne in the style of Louis-Philippe i., King of the French. Louis-Philippe i. (1830-1848) had been long enough in the school of adversity, and had seen enough of the practical working of politics, to realise that his government must be liberal if it was to last. He began by being an advocate of peace abroad; he sought at home to conciliate the middle classes (bourgeoisie), while accepting the hostility of the extreme parties, whether they were Republicans, Bonapartists, or Retrograde-monarchists. But with him and his supporters from the middle class, liberalism did not mean democracy. The lower classes were bent on the latter; a far-reaching socialistic agitation was set afoot; the mishaps which, whatever the form of government, spring from the very nature of human affairs, were taken advantage of to assail his policy both at home and abroad. Louis-Philippe fell into the same relation to his people as had brought about the doom of Charles x. In February 1848, Revolution broke out afresh in Paris. The King yielded then, but too late, the points in debate between him and the people. He was compelled to flee, and left his kingdom in the hands of a second Republic under the Presidency of Lamartine. This improvised Republican Government ran through its stages in four years, and, like the first Republic, ended in the appointment of a Dictator in the shape of Prince Louis-Napoleon, who was borne up to power by a temporary union of Royalists, Bonapartists, and Democrats, which secured for him five and a half million votes. As in the case of the first Napoleon, the authority of the Prince President, which the Republic was renewing in the person of his nephew, being founded on the duly expressed will of the great majority of French electors, escaped from the control of the Parliamentary Assembly. The famous *coup d'état* on the 2nd of December 1851 rid him of a legislative assembly which was bent on re-introducing limited suffrage, while he was the anointed of universal suffrage.

The SECOND EMPIRE (1852-1870). Louis-Napoleon took the opinion of the people on his *coup d'état* in 1852, and was whitewashed by an enormous majority. The Second Empire was at once proclaimed, and was accompanied by the same semblance of a Parliamentary Government as the first. The same people who had risen against the far less autocratic government of Charles x. and of Louis-Philippe accepted for eighteen years the rule of the 'small' Napoleon, as Victor Hugo dubbed him.  He ruled with great brilliancy, undertook mighty works to develop the material resources of the country, and flattered the lurking Imperial instincts of the French people by an active foreign policy.  He joined England in the Crimean War with such success that after the treaty of Paris France was the leading power on the continent.  He had, however, committed the same mistake as his predecessors in allowing too much influence to the clergy.  When he entered on the Italian Campaign against Austria in 1859, it took all the glory of the victories he won at Magenta and Solferino to keep up his already waning credit with the masses. The conclusion of a commercial treaty with England on a Free Trade basis in 1860 was a wise enough measure, but not so the undertaking of an expedition in Mexico, which ended disastrously.  On the other side of the Rhine the power of Prussia was growing, and a basis for uniting Germany under its leadership was obtained by the defeat of Austria (1866).  From that moment Napoleon found himself struggling in a network of embarrassments which seemed to paralyse his faculties and to strike him with political blindness at a moment when energy and judgment were most needed.  He made lame attempts at re-organising the military so as to be ready to check the progress of Prussia, and, like his predecessors, bethought himself too late of rallying the French Electorate by liberal and democratic measures. So, driven to extremity, he had recourse to the favourite Napoleonic device—foreign war. There was a question of selecting a Prince of the ruling House of Prussia to be King of Spain. At the same time it entered into the plans of the Prussian Statesman, Bismarck, to take the first opportunity of fighting the French. Napoleon III. played into his hands by declaring that he could not allow a Hohenzollern prince to rule Spain; and on the 19th of July 1870, the French declared war upon Prussia. The South Germans sided with the Prussians. The German armies being in a better state of preparation than the French found but little difficulty in compelling to a hasty retreat the French troops that had collected in Alsace. The battles about Metz were of a more serious kind, but the French commander Bazaine, having failed to do his duty as a tactician and as a patriot, about 200,000 Frenchmen were driven back into that city and surrounded on all sides. Marshal Macmahon, who at the head of another army was barring the direct road to Paris, suddenly altered his course and turned northwards, intending to double back on the Germans and to join hands with Bazaine at Metz. This plan was baffled by the presence of mind of the head of the German general staff, General Von Moltke. Macmahon was followed up in the north and caught as in a trap at Sedan. After two days' fighting, Napoleon, who was nominally in command of the French armies, surrendered himself into the hands of the King of Prussia. After this disaster, France was almost bare of regular troops. The exasperation of the people against the Emperor, who was now a prisoner of war, made it easy for the Republican chiefs to proclaim the Third Republic in Paris on the 4th of September.

The THIRD REPUBLIC. The new Government set about the work of national resistance to the German invasion. The war, hitherto the affair of the military class and of the standing army, became the affair of every citizen. Paris prepared to endure a siege, and when it was about to be surrounded by the German armies, the Republican Ministry, calling itself the Government of National Defence, was transferred to Tours, and when the German armies overran the valley of the Loire, Bordeaux became the official headquarters. Gambetta and De Freycinet improvised armies whose devotion to military duty in a most trying winter campaign saved at least the honour of France if they failed to make much impression upon the enemy. The troops in Metz surrendered in the last days of October; the French fortresses fell one after another into the hands of the Prussians; a whole army was driven to seek refuge in Switzerland; Paris surrendered at the end of January; and preliminaries of peace were signed at Versailles in the next month. These were finally ratified in May and embodied in the Treaty of Frankfurt. Yielding to the stress of the moment the French agreed to give up Alsace and the larger part of Lorraine, and to pay five thousand million francs as a war indemnity. Whatever that war may have cost the French, it is not at all clear, when viewed from

the year 1892, that it did them more harm than good.
The whole government and administration of the
country has been, since then, set on a better footing;
parliamentary institutions seem at last to have secured
a sure hold, and the whole military organisation, put
on the basis of compulsory universal service, has
become truly formidable. As might be expected in
such an inflammable political centre as Paris, the transition from the exciting period of the siege to that of
peace and order was troublesome. The extreme socialistic and communistic party set an insurrectionary
movement agoing on the 18th of March, which was not
got under till the end of May (1871). For several years
it was doubtful whether a return to the constitutional
monarchy would not take place; but thanks to the ex-
ceedingly wise policy of Thiers, the first president of
the new Republic, nothing was done to interfere with
the natural development of political events. In 1875
the Republic was definitely accepted as the form of the
French State. The bulk of Frenchmen rallied steadily
round the flag of Parliamentary Republicanism, upheld
by Gambetta at the critical general election of 1877.
Macmahon, who had succeeded Thiers in the Presidency of the Republic, resigned in 1879, and was
succeeded by Grévy, who, in 1887, resigned his office
into the hands of Congress, when the present President
Carnot, a descendant of the great Carnot of the revolutionary period, was appointed. The premature death
of Gambetta on the 1st of January 1883, deprived the
French of their best orator and strongest leader. Owing

to the fickleness of the parliamentary majority, the short life of French ministers under the Third Republic has become proverbial, but their stability could hardly be expected when the way to a political settlement was being sought. Of late years the very transient character of General Boulanger's popularity was like an after-ring of the old Napoleonic infatuation. The failure of the French to follow him to the end afforded an excellent measure of the progress they had made in political wisdom.

# CHAPTER III.

## CHRONOLOGICAL TABLE OF THE HISTORY OF FRENCH LITERATURE IN THE MIDDLE AGES.[1]

### *Oldest Epic and Lyric Poetry.*

In the South—Troubadours (langue d'oc): canzones, tensons, plaints, sirventes.

In the North—Trouvères (langue d'oïl): *Chansons de geste*, romans, fableaux, lais.

Carlovingian or Royal Cycle—*Chanson de Roland*, eleventh century. Sung by Taillefer at the battle of Hastings, and attributed by some to Turold, who was probably only a reciter of it.

Notes.—The influence of the French epos on the poetry of the neighbouring nations was very great. It found another home in England, where it was brought by the Normans. Many French poems were translated into English and into the Gaelic dialects. The *Chanson de Roland* was translated into German in the twelfth century and later; Wolfram of Eschenbach put in German verse the poem of Aleschans. The Norwegians became acquainted with the *chansons de geste* through the English from the beginning of the thirteenth century. The Spaniards drew inspiration

---

[1] See, for the material used in this chapter, *La littérature française au Moyen Age*, by Gaston Paris, passim.

C

from French poems before singing their Cid, and some parts of the *cantares de gesta* are based on French romances connected with the Carlovingian Cycle. The fortunes of the French epos were most remarkable in Italy. It was early introduced into the north; then it was worked up into poems written in an artificial language formed from French, but much influenced by the northern dialects. At the time of the Renaissance, especially in Tuscany, French epic matter was dressed in Italian prose and in Italian poetry. Pulci, Boiardo, Ariosto, built up on the foundation of the *Reali di Francia* their famous poems. In this fashion the Carlovingian Cycle, after dying out in France, obtained a fresh lease of life in Italy. It received there an artistic treatment which, modernising it, enabled it to rank thereafter as classical literature.

The *chansons de geste* passed by degrees from the province of serious literature into that of humour, satire, and parody, as is indicated by the modern meaning of the English word 'jest.'

CHANSON DE ROLAND. In 778, the rearguard of the army of Charles, King of the Franks (Charlemagne), returning from a successful expedition in Spain, was attacked in the Valley of Roncevaux by the Basque tribes inhabiting the Pyrenees. The baggage of the army was plundered and its guardians killed, with Roland, who had been put in command of the rearguard. The imagination of the people in France was struck by this disaster. It was made the subject of

song.   By degrees a regular legend of considerable
scope was built up on this historical foundation, in a
manner that reminds one of the gradual formation of
the Homeric poems.   The Basques were replaced by
Saracens representing the Mussulman world.   Instead
of Charles, King of the Franks, who could only be
thirty-six years old at the date of the battle, the legend
introduced by. anticipation the figure of the fully-
developed Charlemagne, holy Roman Emperor, and
champion of Christendom.   Instead of being, like the
Basques, a handful, the Saracens were represented as
having outnumbered the Frankish warriors by thousands, as having attacked them after suing for peace,
and at the instigation of a Frankish traitor, Ganelon.
Ganelon was made out to be a personal enemy of
Roland, who was no longer the Count of Brittany, but
Charlemagne's nephew, and one of the twelve peers, and
to have arranged with Marsile, the chief of the pagan
host, that Roland should be put in command of the
rearguard that he might be killed in the projected attack.
The battle known to history had taken place in the Pyrenees :  so popular tradition in the flat countries, where
the legend was formed, kept floating before it a vision
of gigantic mountains, of black rocks, and óf wonderful
steepnesses as the scene of the tremendous fight.   The
Basques and the Franks had fought on foot ; the legend
put both parties on horseback and clad them in heavy
armour.   In reality, the disaster suffered at Roncevaux
was never avenged, for when Charles retraced his steps
to punish the mountaineers, they had already with-

drawn to their fastnesses.  In the epos, Charlemagne returns with the whole of his army, summoned to the scene of the fray by the long-echoing calls of Roland's horn.  God lengthened the span of that day that he might cut up the remains of the pagan army.  The Emperor rode down to the plains of Zaragoza, took it, and met in a last battle the head of heathendom, who was defeated in single combat.  Then Ganelon was brought to judgment, and received the reward due to his crime.  There appears at Roland's side his faithful companion Oliver, brother of the handsome maiden Alde, whom Roland is to marry on his return; but instead of beholding again the knight she loves, she receives the tidings of his death and falls into her last sleep at Charlemagne's feet.


### BRETON CYCLE OF KING ARTHUR'S TABLE ROUND.

CHRESTIEN DE TROYES (twelfth century) : *Perceval le Gallois, Lancelot du Lac, Chevalier au Lion.*

NOTES.—The Conquest of England by William of Normandy was fraught with important consequences in literary history.  The Normans were soon interested in the past of the island, and wished to know its history as far back as they could.  The Welsh, through dislike of the Anglo-Saxons, were their natural assistants. Geoffrey, surnamed Arturus, born in Monmouth, and who died a Bishop of St. Asaph, wrote in Latin a so-called history of British kings, which he, no doubt, partly invented.  He relates the wonderful birth of

King Arthur, who rid the island of the Saxons, as he says, and conquered Scotland, Ireland, the Orkneys, Norway and Gaul. Then the king gathered about his person the leading knights in the world, gained a victory over the Romans, and was about to conquer Rome when he was summoned back to Britain by the treachery of his nephew, Modred. There ensues a battle, in which Modred is killed. Arthur, wounded to death, is carried away into the island of Avalon. (This island is the Paradise or Elysium of British legends.)

Geoffrey of Monmouth succeeded in bringing the Celtic legends into general interest. By his brilliant description of Arthur's court he gave them a chivalrous stamp, which at first was foreign to them. His book was quickly turned into French—we know some renderings of it in the twelfth century. One of them is by the Anglo-Norman, Geoffrey Gaimar, another is by 'Robert' Wace; this latter is called *Brut*, a name which represents the ancient British race. The Knights of the Table Round appear in Wace's version, not in Geoffrey's.

The Celtic stories, when once they were free of their national character, penetrated into France, thanks to the singers and story-tellers of Brittany. Hence they were carried almost all over Europe. Breton musicians are often mentioned in that age as visitors at the English court, and later at the French court. They relieved with snatches of music the setting forth of their subject. The adventure described was usually romantic, and in French the name of *lai* was given to the whole production. This name appears to be borrowed from the English word 'lay.' The more important subjects of the lays were soon related at greater length in French poems. About fifteen such poems were the work of a common woman, Mary by name, who was born in France, and came to settle in England. Having acquired the Breton dialect, or at any rate the English language, in which these lays were translated, probably, she related their contents in her own simple way under the reign of Henry II. We find in her work stories of love and of adventure, in which often appear fairies, marvellous events, and wonderful transformations. The island of Avalon, that land of immortality to which the fairies lead the heroes, is mentioned more than once, and so are Arthur, his court, and Tristan, of whom we are about to speak. These are mostly remains of an ancient mythology. The personages of the ancient Celtic tales appear as knights, and there reigns over all that tender and melancholy atmosphere which is best described by the word ' romantic,' if it be taken in the sense given to it by Madame de Staël and the writers of her class.

The poems on Tristan stand in a close relation to some lays which have been lost. The scattered stories dealing with Tristan (Tristram) and Iseult were collected in one poem, in the twelfth century, by an Anglo-Norman writer. A little later there was a German version, but the more important of these poems are those of Chrestien de Troyes. His Tristan, however, has been lost. About 1170, an Anglo-Norman poet, called Thomas, gave a Tristan, in which he quotes a Breton story-teller, Breri, who indeed was famous in the twelfth century among the Welsh. Only fragments of this poem have come down to us, but we are helped out of our difficulty by recourse to its German, Norwegian, and English renderings.

The Anglo-Norman poets who first treated of Tristan brought him into connection with King Arthur and the Round Table. From this connection there arose in England many Arthurian poems towards the middle of the twelfth century. These Anglo-Norman poems are almost all lost. They are known by English, Gaelic, and especially by French imitations. They were early introduced into France, either in manuscript shape or by word of mouth. Relations between England and France were then very intimate, partly on account of Henry II.'s possessions on the Continent, partly on account of the ties which united the royal families.

Chrestien de Troyes is the most famous of the Frenchmen who have treated of the *Matière de Bretagne*, as the subjects of the Breton Cycle are called. His romances are derived from Anglo-Norman stories, whether written or spoken, whether in prose or in verse. He wrote often from bad material. His great merit is his style. His works offer the best example of twelfth century French. He worked up his matter to such a pitch of contemporary realism, that the aristocratic classes in the twelfth century may well be considered to be mirrored in his poems. This applies to his *Perceval le Gallois*, but still more to his *Lancelot du Lac*, in which is painted the polite and courtly love fancied by the noble ladies forming the company of Marie de Champagne, his protectress.   He professes to owe to her, not only the subject he wrote about, but also the spirit in which he wrote.   In the *Lancelot* the chivalrous ideal of the Provençal *Cours d'Amour* is fused with the inherited character of the Breton romances with such excellence that they were never again separated.

The Anglo-Norman tales are mostly the romantic biography of one of the heroes of the Round Table. There arrives generally at the court of King Arthur an unknown young knight; then some adventure, held to be impracticable, tempts his courage.   He leaves the court, does the impossible deed, and marries in the end a maiden, who is mixed up with it somehow, and brings him a kingdom as her dowry.   Chrestien's *Chevalier au Lion* is a good example of the poems derived from that plot.   It was translated into German, Norwegian, and English.   Other poems of his are forthcoming in Gaelic, in Dutch, and in Italian renderings.

One of the Anglo-Norman tales was about a Welsh knight called Perceval.   A small English poem of the fourteenth century gives a very fair idea of the original Perceval.   He is brought up by his mother, a widow, without any knowledge of chivalry.   He acquires it by chance; soon he excels in it; then he kills his father's murderer, discovers his mother, who had been lost in the interval, and marries a young girl  whom he has rescued from her enemies, and from whom he has been parted by various adventures. In Chrestien's poem on that subject there is added an adventure, the purport and issue of which are not very clear. Perceval is to put a certain question about a mysterious *graal* which he has seen in a castle during his wanderings. But he fails to put the question. This graal, that is, a 'dish,' exists in the Gaelic rendering of the story of Perceval, whose Gaelic name is Peredur. Chrestien did not finish his poem, yet it had an immense success, and was continued in various ways by Wolfram of Eschenbach among others, who not only finished it, but wrote also a huge introduction to it. The story of Perceval was resumed by several Frenchmen at the point where Chrestien had left it.

A poet from Franche-Comté, Robert de Boron, at the beginning of the thirteenth century set about connecting Joseph of Arimathæa with the Breton Cycle, the graal becoming the cup in which was gathered the blood of the crucified Christ. Other poets followed up this clue and further extended the story, so that Lancelot became involved in it. Lancelot of the Lake, so called because he was brought up by a fairy, or 'lady of the lake,' was one of the best-known heroes of the Table Round. His adventures and his marriage were the subject of a biographical Anglo-Norman poem, which was reproduced in German before 1200, from a copy taken to Vienna by one of the lords who were hostages for Richard Cœur de Lion. This Lancelot, the older one, was very much altered later, and made to fit into

the *Quête du saint graal* in which Galahad is the hero.
The second treatment dates from 1220 approximately.
The altered or second Lancelot has been assigned to
Walter Map, Archdeacon in Oxford, who died before
the end of the twelfth century. However, Map appears
to have really written nothing in the Arthurian Cycle.
The alterations are more probably French.

This Cycle, containing an enormous amount of matter,
was completed before the middle of the thirteenth
century. An Italian, Rusticino of Pisa, gave a summary of it in 1270, using a manuscript which belonged
to Edward, the son of Henry III. of England. Rusticino's summary met with great popularity. It was
turned into Italian (even Italians wrote then in French
rather than in their native language). Many Italian
poems are derived from that source. The Lancelot was
turned into Dutch as well, and later into German prose.
Other romances of the same class were translated into
Italian, Spanish, Portuguese, and English. In the
English 'Arthur,' by Sir Thomas Malory, we have a
compilation reminding one of Rusticino's, and written
in the fifteenth century from French originals, now
partly lost. The *Perceforest*, written in the fourteenth century, and the *Amadis*, which appears in
the fifteenth and sixteenth centuries, in a Portuguese,
and then in a Spanish, shape, are imitations of these
great prose romances. The original poems were universally admired. Dante claimed on their account the
first place in Europe for the French tongue as a narrative instrument, and Brunetto Latino bears him out.

### *Romantic Poetry.*

ROBERT WACE (twelfth century) : *Romans de Brut et de Rou.*
GUILLAUME DE LORRIS (reign of Louis IX.) : *Roman de la Rose.*
JEAN DE MEUNG (reign of Philippe-le-Bel) : *Roman de la Rose.*
RUTEBEUF (reign of Louis IX.) : Trouvère, author of *Fableaux.*
MARIE DE FRANCE, authoress of *Lais.*
The Authors of the *Roman de Renart.*
JACQUEMART GELEE DE LILLE (reign of Philippe-le-Bel), author of
    *Renart le Nouvel.*

### *Old French Lyrics properly so called.*

QUESNES DE BETHUNE (time of the fourth crusade).
THIBAUT DE CHAMPAGNE (1201-1259), Imitator of the troubadours.
GUILLAUME DE MACHAULT (d. 1377) : Lais, virelais, ballades, ron-
    deaux.
EUSTACHE DESCHAMPS (1340-1410) : Ballades, rondeaux.
CHRISTINE DE PISAN (d. 1431) : Ballades.
CHARLES D'ORLEANS (1391-1465) : Ballades, rondeaux.
VILLON (1431-1500) : *Le Grand Testament.*

The Rhyming Measures used by these poets found imitators
in foreign parts, may be among the early Scottish poets.

### *Dramatic Poetry.*

Mystères and Miracles performed by the CONFRÉRIES. Privileges
    granted in 1402 by Charles VI. to the Confrérie de la Passion.
Moralités, farces and soties performed by the BASOCHIENS and the
    ENFANTS SANS SOUCI.
La farce de Pathelin (end of the fifteenth century), ascribed to
    Pierre Blanchet, the best dramatic production in the Middle
    Ages, modernised in 1706 by Brueys.

### *Prose Chroniclers.*

VILLEHARDOUIN (1160-1213) : *Histoire de la Conquête de Con-
    stantinople.*
JOINVILLE (1223-1319) : *Histoire de Saint Louis.*
FROISSART (1333-1410), *Chronique de France, d'Angleterre et d'Ecosse.*
    He travelled partly at the expense of Philippa de Hainaut,
    wife of Edward III. of England. He is a neutral beholder of
    the Hundred Years' War. His description of the battle of
    Poictiers is a masterpiece.
COMMINES (1447-1509) : *Chronique et Histoire du règne de Louis XI.*

NOTES.—As in epic poetry, the points of contact with England and other countries are numerous in lyrics, in the drama, and in chronicles. For instance, French versions of King Horn, Havelok the Dane, Guy of Warwick, and Aaluf were borrowed from Anglo-Saxon. The patriotic feeling raised in the Hundred Years' War found an outlet in the *Combat des Trente* (1351), a poem describing an episode made famous by Froissart. Many stories rhymed in France in the twelfth and thirteenth centuries appear somewhat later in the literatures of other peoples, mostly in Italy and in England. It is beyond doubt that Boccaccio and Chaucer imitated often French fableaux, but it is by no means certain that they always did so. The contents of those fableaux were a treasure common to all Europe. They are found in sermons and in books of piety, and they may have been picked up independently by the poets and novel-writers in different countries.

Once formed in the crusading period, the art of writing history in the common French tongue was developed first in England, under the patronage of the Dukes of Normandy. On account of the existence in England of an Anglo-Saxon dialect, looked upon by the Norman kings as unworthy, French took early in the new kingdom a place which did not belong to it in France itself, and it was used in serious literature. The lords, and especially the ladies, of the Anglo-Norman aristocracy were particularly fond of history. It appears certain that from the beginning of the twelfth century there existed in England some works on history written in French, most likely in verse. We know that Aelis de Louvain, Henry I.'s widow, had ordered from a poet called David a life of her husband. This life is lost, but it was in the shape of a *chanson de geste*, and could be sung. We find that piece of information in Geoffrey Gaimar, author of an *Histoire des Anglais*, which he wrote about the middle of the twelfth century. His history is a proof of the speed with which the Norman conquerors had made themselves at home in Britain, and of the liberal spirit in which they understood English history. Gaimar gives in eight-syllabled French lines the whole history of the island, beginning with the expedition of the Argonauts, passing on to the arrival in Britain of the Trojan Brutus, then translating from Geoffrey of Monmouth for the next part, then taking the history of the Anglo-Saxons, mentioning very shortly the events following the Norman Conquest, and ending with the death of William Rufus. What we have of this enormous poem has little literary value, but is not without historical interest, though the contemporary history is sadly curtailed.

Wace wrote shortly after Gaimar. He was born at Guernsey in the year 1100 or thereabouts, a scholar in Paris, a cleric at Caen, a canon at Bayeux. He died about 1175, after writing two great historical poems: the *Geste des Bretons*, or *Brut*, which he translated from Geoffrey of Monmouth, and, later, the *Geste des Normands*, or *Roman de Rou*. Here again the most interesting part has not been written. He was to write up to his own times, but he was discouraged on hearing that

Henry II., who had commanded him to write the history
of the Dukes of Normandy, had entrusted Benoit de
Sainte-More with the same office. Wace is a translator mostly. Here and there he brings in some popular stories or some special facts which he knows from
tradition. His French is excellent. His competitor,
Benoit de Sainte-More, whom Henry II. had no doubt
selected on account of his previously written romances
of *Troie* and *Eneas*, did not complete his task, having
been disturbed in it by the wars and troubles in the
second half of Henry's reign.

There has been handed down to us a poem in a very
personal style, composed by an Anglo-Norman cleric, a
scholar at the University of Paris, Jourdain Fantosme,
on the war waged by Henry II. upon the King of Scotland in 1173. This is at last a document of contemporary history. There is a poem on the conquest of
Ireland by the same Henry, which was written, no
doubt, shortly after. This also is of importance in
history, but it is very obscurely written, and the only
manuscript we have has been very much spoilt. The
most noteworthy of the Anglo-Norman histories in
verse is the *Vie de Guillaume le Marechal*, Earl of
Pembroke and Regent of England during the minority
of Henry III. This poem was composed shortly after
the Earl's death by a native of one of the French
Provinces belonging to the English Crown. The writer
is evidently thoroughly well informed, his style is
fluent, graceful, full of life and animation. He has
many interesting bits about the young King Henry
and his brother Richard; in fact, this poem, only lately

discovered, and published as yet only in fragments, is assuredly one of the most important documents we have on the history, the manners, the habits, the life, the modes of thought and of speech in the twelfth and thirteenth centuries. From the thirteenth century onwards history ceases in England to be written in French. Pierre de Langtoft, at the beginning of the fourteenth century, is almost the only exception. The language is already very corrupt. When, in the fourteenth century, the English kings, with whom French was still the preferred language, wished for writers of history, they sent to Flanders for such men as Froissart and Jean de Wavrin. French remained the language of Acts of Parliament till the end of the fifteenth century, and of the law courts much longer.

In Normandy and in Norman England the literature of knowledge makes an early appearance. As in the case of history, we have at the beginning productions of a fantastic stamp, like the *Bestiaires*, which are collections of wonderful stories about animals, taken from Latin sources, and even of Eastern importation. The most ancient *Bestiaire* is that of Philippe de Thaon, an Anglo-Norman priest, who dedicated his work to the Queen Aelis de Louvain. For him the nature and habits of animals furnish apt illustrations of Christian doctrine and Christian life. The same Philippe de Thaon has a poem in six-syllabled lines on the ecclesiastic computum[1] and the calendar, a strange topic for treatment in verse, but remarkable because this book, written before 1119 for priests only, is in

---

[1] A method of ascertaining Easter.

French, showing what part French played then in the
education of the Anglo-Norman clergy. We may
mention in the same category of works the *Lumière
des Laïques*, by Pierre de Peckham; the *Petite Philosophie*, also Anglo-Norman; the *Secret des Secrets*, by
Geoffrey of Waterford, who is also the author of a
French translation of Eutropius. The most remarkable
production in the literature of knowledge is the *Trésor*,
which the Florentine Brunetto Latino composed in
French prose during his exile, because, says he, French
is the more delightful language, and the better known
of all people.

There is a kind of old French literature which is
found nowhere but in England, namely, treatises
written in French with a view to teaching French to
foreigners, or, may be, to Anglo-Normans who were
forgetting the language. Such a work is the one compiled by Walter of Bibelesworth, which throws light on
the ignorance of the French language prevailing in
England about the beginning of the thirteenth century.
Some other treatises dealing with spelling were made
by Englishmen.

Moral subjects are treated in verse by Elijah of
Winchester and Everard of Kirkham in the twelfth
century, by Simon de Fraisne, who translated the
*Consolation of Philosophy*, and by others. Among books
dealing with the manners of the day, an Anglo-Norman
poem, the *Ditié* (in English, 'Say') *d'Urbain*, has been
falsely assigned to King Henry I.

Satire could not fail to play a part in the alternatives

of good-fellowship and enmity that mark Anglo-French relations in the Middle Ages. As both parties really spoke the same tongue, when they laid down arms they fought on with the pen. The satires exchanged during the Third Crusade between Richard Cœur de Lion and the French have not been handed down to us, though we know of the part attributed to Blondel de Nesle in the famous legend about the King's escape from prison. At the beginning of the thirteenth century, before Normandy was annexed to the French realm, André de Coutances replied in his *Roman des Français* to the satirical onslaughts of the '*Français de France.*' In pieces of a genuinely comic character the French poked fun at their neighbours beyond the Channel. They mocked the bad pronunciation of the Anglo-Normans in such satires as the *Paix aux Anglais*, the *Charte aux Anglais*, the *Deux Anglais*. The last blows aimed from the French side in this wordy warfare are the *Dit de la Rébellion d'Angleterre*, at the beginning of the fourteenth century, and the few pointed stanzas directed by a Norman monk against Edward I.

The *Roman de la Rose* enjoyed a greater popularity than any other mediæval piece of work. It was told in Dutch verse by Henri Van Aken. Chaucer put it into English; his translation was lost, however, and another by an unknown writer took its place. In Italian the *Roman de la Rose* appeared in a series of sonnets, which have come to light quite lately. Petrarch was accustomed to point to the *Roman* as the most important work in French literature.

D

In Biblical and sacred literature we have a large number of works to mention as the Anglo-Norman contribution to that class of writing. There are several Anglo-Norman poems, dating from the twelfth century, in which parts of the Bible are translated or reproduced. Robert de Gretham issued in the thirteenth century some fragments of the Lessons as read in the Churches. Wace wrote about the patron saint of school-boys, and about Saint Margaret; Sister Clementia of Barking wrote of Saint Catherine; an unknown poet wrote of the Saints Barlaam and Joasaph. The legend underlying his narrative is of the greatest interest, because it can be followed to Greek sources, and even to a Syrian shape, in which it was put by a monk who had travelled in India, and had heard there the story of Buddha. Saint Joasaph stands for no other than Buddha. Some fine Buddistic parables are worked into the life of the saint, and made to look unmistakeably Christian. We can seldom trace so clearly a story from Indian sources through successive Syrian, Greek, and Latin shapes to its ultimate Anglo-Norman or French rendering. Yet there is no doubt that a great many stories in our inherited European stock underwent a similar experience. Some saints were contemporaries of their biographers. This was the case of Thomas a Becket, whose life immediately after his murder was written by clerics, laymen, monks, and even women, both in Latin and in French. A budget of theology for the use of laymen was written by Robert of Gretham, and was called by him the

*Corset.* In the preceding century, namely, the twelfth, there had come out a capital Anglo-Norman version of Solomon's Proverbs, with allegorical comments. The English Franciscan monk, Nicole Bozon, compiled a collection of examples or illustrations from Scripture, in a simple style, which would be pleasant reading enough if the Anglo-Norman of the writer was not so barbarous.

The tendency of the Middle Ages towards allegorising reached its height in the work of the Cistercian monk, Guillaume de Deguilleville. After reading the *Roman de la Rose,* he wrote his *Pèlerinage de la vie humaine* and his *Pèlerinage ·de l'âme.* Twenty years later he added the *Pèlerinage de Jésus-Christ.* These Christian allegories received a welcome from the very first; they were printed over and over again from the fifteenth century; Chaucer translated some lyrical pieces in them; and it may almost be said that John Bunyan's *Pilgrim's Progress* is not disconnected with the performance of the Cistercian.

The *Manuel des péchés,* by William of Waddington, is written in very poor Norman-French. It was turned into English by Robert de Brunne.

Anglo-Norman literature has plenty of sacred plays to show; so much so, that William of Waddington, just mentioned, inveighs against the passion with which the clerics sought out theatrical performances full of scandal, rather than of edification. Most of these plays are no longer forthcoming in their Anglo-Norman shape, but they still live in an English dress.

ROMAN DE LA ROSE.—We have here a systematisation of floating allegorical matter, due to Guillaume de Lorris in the first instance. The foundation of the story is laid in a dream of the poet, the maiden to be won being represented by a rose, which the lover is to pluck in a delightful garden. The actors in the love drama thus prepared are mostly personifications which seem to lose their allegorical character, and to fill parts like individuals. They favour or baffle the efforts of the lover to pluck the rose. The lover in his twentieth year enters the garden of love, a paradise surrounded by high walls, on which are painted externally, as being excluded from this abode of bliss, all ugly and sad things of life. He beholds with pleasure in a rose bush a blossom fresher and more beautiful than the others. At this moment the god of Love pierces his heart with an arrow. Henceforth it is the lover's express purpose to pluck the rose. To this end he swears fealty to Love and takes his commands. On approaching the rose, he meets Welcome, with whom he gets on very well; but Danger,[1] Evil-speaking, Shame, and Fear declare themselves his enemies. He is a little too prompt in asking leave to put the rose to his lips. Danger drives him away, and Welcome is lost to his sight. Then Reason comes down from her tower, and endeavours to turn him away from the pursuance of his passion. He converses next with Friend, who comforts him, and with Danger, who is ready to forgive

[1] The old French word *Danger* or *Dangier* here in question does not mean danger, risk. It betokens rather the authority of a guardian over his ward.

but not to relent. In the meanwhile Generosity and Pity soften Danger, and Welcome is again within sight of the lover. But soon he becomes over-bold once more, slumbering Danger is aroused by Shame and Fear, and the lover is once more turned back. Then Jealousy has a tower built, that it may shut up Welcome in it, and the lover, driven to despair, gives vent to his plaint in a monologue. Guillaume De Lorris broke off in the middle of the monologue, and, as we have said in another place, it was Jean De Meun who took up the thread, and brought the plot to its conclusion through endless complications.

Roman De Renard.—The many fables about animals treasured by the people in the Middle Ages found their way into this poem. Many stories were told about the rivalry between the wolf and the fox, in which the former, stronger but more stupid, is invariably outwitted by the latter. This rivalry was often represented as taking place at the court of the lion, the king of animals. Some French clerics wove together these fabulous elements, and completed them by working into them other stories of the same class. The final step was taken when the heroes of these stories were personified, and received proper names. There was no longer any question of the goings-on of some wolf with some fox, but all wolf and fox stories were worked up into the individuality of *the* wolf, who received the name of Ysengrin, and of *the* fox, who received the name of Renard, each being accompanied by his wife.

The rivalry of the two antagonists, obtained by the systematic ordering of the floating material already alluded to, reaches its consummation in the death of Ysengrin. A crowd of actors of inferior rank gather round the two champions, foremost among these being Noble, the lion, Chanteclair, the cock, etc. The systematisation took place at the beginning of the eleventh century.

The material for the foregoing notes was scattered in the special literature of the subject, and was of inconvenient access till it was put together in *La Littérature Française au Moyen Age*, by Gaston Paris, 1888, the very best and latest authority. For general information on this period, see the first chapters in the *Literature of France*, by Keene (John Murray's *University Extension Manuals*). See also the first chapters in the *Primer of French Literature*, and in the *Short History of French Literature*, by George Saintsbury. For the general aspect of French and English literary relations in the Middle Ages, read the third and fourth chapters in Professor Morley's *First Sketch of English Literature*.

We did not consider it as falling within our scope to give a systematic account of French literature in the Middle Ages. The young students, for whom this book is mostly written, cannot be expected to give much attention to a period so remote. But we could not resist the opportunity of showing how little of a dividing line the Channel was then, and how much more French and English held then in common than after the Hundred Years' War.

# CHAPTER IV.

## CHRONOLOGICAL TABLE OF THE RENAISSANCE AND REFORMATION PERIOD.[1]

### *Epic and Lyric Poetry.*

CLÉMENT MAROT (1495-1544) : Elégies, épitres, complaintes, ballades, rondeaux, chansons, épigrammes, psaumes.

PIERRE DE RONSARD (1525-1585) : Odes, hymnes, sonnets ; La Franciade, an epic.

LA PLÉIADE FRANÇAISE : Ronsard, Du Bellay (*Défense et Illustration de la langue française*), Baïf, Daurat, Belleau, Jodelle, Ponthus de Thiard.

DU BARTAS (1544-1590) : *La Semaine*, a descriptive poem.

AGRIPPA D'AUBIGNÉ (1551-1630) : *Les Tragiques*, satires.

MATHURIN RÉGNIER (1575-1613) : Satires, élégies.

### *Dramatic Poetry.*

The Performances of Mysteries forbidden in 1548.

Renewal of the classical theatre.

LARIVEY : Comedies on Italian and Latin models : Les esprits.

GARNIER : Tragedies (on Senecan models).

### *Prose.*

RABELAIS (1495-1553) : *Vie de Gargantua et de Pantagruel*, a satirical novel.

MARGUERITE DE VALOIS, queen of Navarre (1492-1549): *L'Heptaméron, Lettres* (to her brother Francis I.).

---

[1] For a rapid survey of the history of French Literature, with reference to French society and French nationality, see the article under FRANCE in the new edition of Chambers's *Encyclopædia*.

Calvin (1509-1564) : *Institution Chrétienne.*

Amyot (1513-1593) : *Traduction de Plutarque.*

La Boétie (1530-1563) : *De la servitude volontaire.*

Montaigne (1533-1592) : *Essais.*

The Authors of *La Satire Ménippée* (1593), so called after Menippos, a Cynic Philosopher.

Agrippa d'Aubigné : *Histoire Universelle.*

Blaise De Montluc (1501-1577) : *Commentaires.*

Till lately it was usual to look upon French literature as beginning at the Renaissance. This opinion rested on an imperfect acquaintance with the history of the Middle Ages, and is now recognised as false in its broader aspect. Yet, in a limited and different sense, it still holds good; for it is during the Renaissance that that was acquired which showed itself thereafter to be characteristic of French literature, more or less, for 200 years. In the Middle Ages the French *esprit littéraire* (or literary disposition of the French) was comparatively indefinite, unfixed, untutored. It was almost international, true in this to the general character of Europe in those times. From the Renaissance onwards, literature comes under the influence of a criticism which, though free at first, enslaves gradually modern literature to Latin and Greek models, and breaks up the undetermined realm of literature into strictly limited departments called kinds or *genres*. In spite of this, the Renaissance and Reformation ages are, generally speaking, times of free thinking, free utterance, and free convictions. It is only at the close of that period—that is to say, in the days of Malherbe

and of Balzac, that the *esprit français* becomes true to
the definition given of it by such critics as Nisard.[1]

The writings of most authors in this chapter are
strongly tinged with Humanism and Protestantism.
The king, Francis I., was their first patron. He founded
in 1529 the *Collège de France*, a home of learning free
from university trammels, and which could grow un-
hampered by the doctors of Sorbonne, to whose dismay
both Greek and Hebrew were taught in the new college.
The spread of Protestant doctrine was greatly helped
by it, though only in an indirect way.

CLÉMENT MAROT.[2] This poet has one foot in the
Middle Ages and the other in the Renaissance. He
remained a disciple of the old French poets, while
becoming a follower of Greek and Latin authors. He
was born at Cahors, came early to Paris, where he did
not distinguish himself as a student. Though he read
Horace and Virgil, his first writing was suggested by
the *Roman de la Rose*. After this attempt he gave up,
once for all, the allegorical style. In 1519 he was
attached to Marguerite de Valois. From 1523 his
talent shows itself in its originality, and is free from
imitation. He was wounded and made a prisoner at
the battle of Pavia, and while his King was still lan-
guishing in Madrid, Marot was, on returning to Paris,
accused of eating some bacon during Lent, which was

---

[1] *Histoire de la littérature française.*

[2] During the work of condensation and elimination, of which these
notices are the fruit, we had before us the *Histoire abrégée de la littérature
française*, by Charles Cottier, and *Leçons de littérature française*, by Petit
de Julleville.

held to be a sign of heresy.   He was put in prison, and owed his liberty to the King when the latter returned from Madrid.   Marot wrote during that time his *Enfer*, a bitter satire against judges, the horrors of lawsuits, and the cruelties of judicial torture.   At the end of 1526, Marot succeeded his father in the office of *valet de chambre du roi*.   Unfortunately he fell again into the hands of the Paris Parliament, whereupon he wrote an *Epître au roy pour estre délivré*, which is a model of respectful familiarity, playful temper, and satirical point.   Marot was then at the height of his talent and of his favour with the King; but there came from Geneva a bundle of bills adverse to Catholicism.   Some of these were pasted up on the door of the King's room. The King swore he would stamp out heresy.   Marot, who was then at Blois, on hearing that his papers had been seized, took refuge, after a while, at Ferrara under the protection of Renée de France, Duchess of Este. Ferrara becoming unsafe, Marot fled to Venice.   He succeeded in obtaining there leave to return to France. In 1539 he published thirty psalms, with an epistle to the King and another to the ladies of France.   He offered his collection to Charles v. of Spain, when this emperor crossed France on his way to punish the burghers of Ghent.   The emperor rewarded the poet, and ordered from him a translation of the 107th psalm. A new edition containing fifty psalms came out in 1543.   The success of this publication was extra-ordinary, though it is in many ways open to criticism. The Sorbonne condemned it as heretical, forbade its sale, and compelled the author to flee.  He went to Geneva, hoping to find there the natural home for a psalmist: but he gambled on Sunday and was, therefore, reprimanded by the Presbytery.  He then took refuge in Turin, where he died.

Marot's strong point is the familiar epistle.  He shows in it a refined, keen, clever wit, a charming simplicity and a graceful ease.  His epigrams are often indecent, but many of them are brimful of moral force and terseness.  Marot's *Enfer* can, as a satire, bear comparison with the best work of Régnier.  We cannot say so much of his *Coq-à-l'âne*, which stands between the *fatrasie* of the preceding century and the *amphigouri* of the next.  He did not invent new forms of verse.  It is his merit that he handled with skill and perfect ease the ten-syllabled line.  He is seldom better inspired than when he tells us about himself in the sprightly tone natural to him.  But for a few words that are now antiquated, his writings might pass for modern.  The poems of his youth are known collectively as the *Adolescence Clémentine*.

RONSARD AND THE PLÉIADE.  The attempt at literary reform of which Ronsard was the leader was the result of the intellectual activity which turned most minds towards classical studies.  Some young men, informed by Jean Daurat, the principal of the *Collège Coqueret* at Paris, held in contemptuous opinion the work of preceding poets, and convinced themselves that the French language could be put to higher and nobler uses. They rushed forward upon the path of innovation. Of these young men the most distinguished were Ronsard and Joachim Du Bellay. Acknowledging the former as their chief, the others gathered round him to form the Pléiade, including their common master, Daurat.

The Pléiade issued a Manifesto, written by Du Bellay, and published under the title of 'Défense et Illustration de la Langue Française.' It is the complaint of the author that scholars neglect the French tongue and use Latin only. The French tongue, he admits, is but a poor instrument, yet it may be improved by culture. As the Romans improved theirs by a wise imitation of the masterpieces of Greece, so the intending French poet may draw from the reading of Ancient, Italian and Spanish authors a form of poetry more exquisite than hitherto. 'So read,' he exclaims, 'and read again by day and by night, the Greek and Latin models. Let alone that old stock of French poetry, roundels, ballads, royal songs, and other such trash. Cause to ring in my ears those beautiful sonnets of cunning and sweet Italian invention. Give me odes instead of songs, satires instead of literary puzzles, comedies and tragedies instead of farces and moralisings.' Du Bellay did not advocate a slavish imitation, but the kind of labour recommended by Erasmus in acquiring the spirit, not the manner, of ancient writers.

Pierre de Ronsard belonged to a family of Hungarian origin. He was born in his father's castle in the country of Vendôme. Disliking the discipline of the

public school, he became a page in the household of the
Duc d'Orléans.  Then he spent two years and a half
in Scotland at the Court of James v., and was in
England for six months.  Deafness interrupted his
travels, and compelled him to adopt a sedentary occupation.  For seven years he studied unremittingly the
ancient authors in the *Collège Coqueret.*  His fellows
also had prepared themselves for a literary career by
assiduous toil, so that they were ready to take their
flight with Du Bellay when this herald of the new
school invited the poets of his day to rise to higher
regions than Marot and his forerunners had traversed.
Ronsard published his first collection of poems shortly
after the issue of the Manifesto.  He was severely
criticised by the old school, but, both parties having
agreed to come to terms, nothing stood any longer in
Ronsard's way.  He gained favour with Henry II. of
France, then with Charles IX., with Queen Elizabeth,
and with Mary, Queen of Scots.  After publishing
some Pindaric Odes, some hymns, and some elegies,
Ronsard wished to try his hand at epic poetry.  He
published the first four books of his *Franciade*, a work
which he never brought to a conclusion.  He says that
the death of Charles IX. discouraged him, but the likely
cause is the lack of interest in the work, the absence
in it of every historical foundation.  'I wrote my
Franciade,' says he himself, 'without minding whether
it was true or not, whether our kings are Trojans or
Germans, Scythians or Arabians, whether Francus
came to France or not.'  Under the reign of Henry III.

Ronsard, idolised beyond measure by men of letters and kings, withdrew himself into the solitude of one of his church livings, and died in the neighbourhood of Tours. His funeral was an apotheosis.

But his name soared too high to soar long. Malherbe was soon to cut down the excess of the praise given to him. Malherbe even went too far in apportioning the blame due to Ronsard, and Boileau went further still. Now-a-days, however, Ronsard has received justice at the hands of critics. There was nothing wrong in his notion that the imitation of the ancients might raise the dignity of language. His mistake was that he forgot what good judges of literature the people may be, and that they are the true moulders of language. He endeavoured to substitute his own art and his own language for that of his times. He despised the people, and thereby rose above the level of popularity. The scholars were on his side, and filled the air with his praise. But half a century later his language was old-fashioned, and his glory was gone. For all that, there remains of his work a small budget which will escape oblivion. Ronsard, when he is grave and simple, falls in with the mediæval poets, who, continued by Villon and Marot at the Renaissance, wrote in the true French vein. He had fancied that he would become immortal by imitating Pindar and Horace. This was a mere dream. The strange adjectives he coined, the undigested Latin words, the Greek terms which he thrust into the language—all this was tinsel that could not live. But the literary reform in which he failed was too ingrained in the spirit of the age to be abandoned. It was resumed with full success when the language had been perfected by grammarians, and when the first wild enthusiasm for antiquity had cooled down. The Pléiade re-introduced into France the sonnet which had been taken to Italy from Provence by Petrarch.

Du Bartas. This poet, a staunch Huguenot, was, in his lifetime, almost as famous as Ronsard. He was a native of the south-west of France, and was no untried hand at poetry when he published his *Semaine* or *Création du Monde.* His purpose was to sing the praise of the Creator. From the outset he appears as a Christian poet, delighting in the work of the Almighty. He seems overpowered with a holy dread, and after describing creation in the same order as Genesis, he makes on the seventh day vows for the peace of France. The subject was inspiring, and Du Bartas did not fall short of it. Though his often bombastic style and his descriptions of fabulous animals may bring a smile to our lips, his poem is none the less stamped with a sincere faith that commands respect. His contemporaries devoured in six years thirty editions of the book, and it was translated into almost every European language. Milton is under some obligation to him. He gives one the impression of having overstrained his talent, and if he had been more measured in the use of his gifts, he would have come nearer perfection. Like Ronsard, he delights in adjectives of his own coining, and, for the sake of rhetorical effect, falls into the mistake of duplicating the stem-syllable of verbs: saying, for instance, *flots bou-bouillonnants*, which is as if an English poet should speak of a *bo-boiling flood*. During the wars of religion Henry IV. sent him to Germany, and, later, to Scotland (1588), as an ambassador. He died, in consequence of neglecting wounds received in warfare, at the age of forty-six.

D'AUBIGNÉ. This Huguenot can be separated from the former neither as a poet nor as a soldier; and, but for the difference in religion, Montluc might well be mentioned in the same strain. D'Aubigné, in an age of essentially vigorous and powerful natures, ranks among the very first. He was born in Saintonge, on the shores of the ocean. His mother died at his birth, and his father when he was twelve years old. His education was none the less carefully attended to. He learnt the ancient languages in his childhood. On his way to Paris with his father, in 1560, he passed the bridge at Amboise, and on beholding there the heads of the conspirators, which were planted on stakes, the father exclaimed: 'The wretches! they have cut off the very head of France!' Then, stretching forth his hand over his son, and pointing out to him those remains of the Huguenot chiefs, he said to him: 'My son, do not spare your head after mine in avenging these honourable chiefs. If you do spare your head, let my curse be upon you!' Shortly after the boy was arrested near Paris, and was told that he would be tied to the stake and burned, to which he replied: 'I am more afraid of the mass than of the stake.' His Catholic captors let him go. He spent two years in Geneva, where he was put under the tutelage of Théodore de Bèze. The old divine saw with an indulgent eye the pranks of this youth, which seemed to him to promise a spirited manhood. He was not wrong in this forecast; for when D'Aubigné had returned to his tutor's house at Montargis, he was overpowered with such a sense of dreariness that he escaped at night half-naked, and joined a passing company of Huguenot soldiers. This episode became with him a matter of joke. 'At any rate,' he said, 'I cannot say that I lost my clothes in war.' During the life of Henry IV. D'Aubigné sided with the opposition. He could not brook the apostasy of the King, who, to win a kingdom, professed himself a Catholic. He stood out against the Regency of Marie de Medici, till, being weary of a useless struggle, he withdrew to Geneva in 1620. Protestant ascendancy appeared to be an impossibility in France. D'Aubigné was well received in the Protestant Rome, and was put in command of the soldiery of the Republic. At Geneva he published his *Histoire Universelle*, which begins and ends with his own times, some memoirs, and two satires, directed against courtiers faithless in religion, and against the corruption prevailing amongst the aristocracy. Though Protestant in tone, the satires were too free in treatment to please the Church authorities in Geneva. Like Marot before him, like the printer and scholar, Etienne, he received shabby treatment from the small-minded ecclesiastical court.  These were, however, mere pin-thrusts, but a real grief was reserved for him in the misconduct and apostasy of his son.  This son became father to Madame de Maintenon.

D'Aubigné began to write his satires in 1577, surrounded by the uproar of battles and the excitement of camp-life.  They were, however, published only at the beginning of the seventeenth century, and the seven of them are known under the name of *Tragiques*. They afford a striking picture of the disorder of the times, of the horrors of civil war, of the wrong-doing of kings and nobles, of the vices of princes, of the duplicity of lawyers, of the tortures inflicted upon the Protestants, of the battles between Huguenots and Catholics, of the penalties meted out by God to His enemies, and of the final judgment passed on the guilty and the guiltless.  Nothing could equal the powerful rush and sweep of this poetry, in which indignation seems to have dictated every word.  There is hardly anywhere a soft or tender touch upon which the mind could rest for a while.

MATHURIN RÉGNIER, born at Chartres, was the nephew of a rich ecclesiastic, who had made most of his money by writing light poetry.  Yet Régnier's father did not wish to see his son become a poet, and prepared to secure at once for him a comfortable competency in the Church.  So Régnier took holy orders, and went to Rome as the chaplain of Cardinal de Joyeuse.  He stayed altogether for about ten years in

Italy, and became thereby well acquainted with Italian literature. After depending for some time on others for his living, he received, in 1606, a church pension. From that moment, he could follow his own poetic bent. Unfortunately he availed himself of his leisure to indulge also in excesses of various kinds. Hence there fell to his lot a premature old age and early death. Boileau described Régnier as having been a student and follower of the ancient authors. This is a mistake; for Régnier was, above all, his own follower. He even looked upon himself as the first French satirist, in ignorance of the numerous predecessors to whom he is undoubtedly kin. The general types of humanity which are the staple of his satire are, by him, individualised, and show themselves in personal aspects. Being a satirist, and a man who knew his own mind in literary matters, he set himself up in opposition to Malherbe, and upheld against him the ideas of Ronsard, from sheer love of contradiction. Every man of letters in France has recognised the merit of ' free ' Régnier. Boileau praises him for his vigour in depicting character and manners. Musset marks him as the forerunner of Molière. We may be satisfied in recognising in him one of the poets in whom the traditions of the *esprit français* are best preserved.

Larivey.—The best known comic writer of the sixteenth century is Pierre Larivey, a Florentine, who translated his name into French, but remained an Italian withal. He imitated in French the plays of his own country, and had recourse also to Latin playwrights. His best comedy is *Les Esprits*. His plays have the usual defects of Italian plays—they depend on the plot for interest, the characters are not worked out, and the comic element is derived from the situations in which the personages are placed. The language is often coarse.

The school of Ronsard had undertaken to renovate the French theâtre by imitating the ancients. In 1548, the Parliament of Paris having forbidden the acting of Biblical plays, the field was open for the *Pléiade*, and the youngest of its members undertook to occupy it. This was Jodelle. He was no more able than Ronsard to command the attention of the people. His plays were acted practically with closed doors before a select audience, and did not survive him. Garnier did better. He endeavoured to produce characters in keeping with history or tradition. He fell into the fault of imitating Seneca, and shares in his defects,—bombast, affectation, and declamation.

RABELAIS was born at Chinon in Touraine. He was handed over, very young, to the monks in the abbey of Seuilly. Near Angers, at La Basmette, whither he was sent next, he formed a friendship with the brothers Du Bellay. He became a monk in 1509, and studied zealously the ancient languages and several modern ones. His fellow-monks persecuted him for his knowledge. They were unable to forgive him his acquaintance with Greek. He tried to improve his position by passing into another monastic order.   He became a Benedictine this time.   Yet he was still so hampered, on all sides, that he fled from the convent.   Rabelais was clearly advancing towards heresy, but as he did not care to face persecution, he turned to the comparatively safe study of medicine.   He was busy with anatomy, with the reading of Galen and of Hippocrates, and with medical practice, till he published at Lyons, in 1533, the first book of the *Faicts et prouesses du très renommé Pantagruel*.   The ecclesiastical censors at the Sorbonne looked askance at this publication, so Jean . Du Bellay took Rabelais away with him to Rome very opportunely.   Two years later came out *Gargantua*. In 1536, Rabelais was again in Rome.   He obtained leave from the Pope to practise medicine, and to remain a priest at the same time, while the Cardinal, his protector, gave him a canonry.   The remaining books of *Pantagruel* came out after this at irregular intervals. The contents of his books exposing him again to ecclesiastical censure, he went to Metz, where he practised for a while the medical art.   Then he returned to Rome for the third time, and was successful enough to obtain from the royal favour, in 1550, the living at Meudon. Rabelais may have been prevented by personal considerations from himself fulfilling the duties of a parish priest.   He even appears to have resigned his office before publishing the fourth and last book of *Pantagruel*, containing the most violent attacks upon the Church. The Sorbonne forbade the book, but Francis I. stood up in its defence.   There is no reason to believe that

Rabelais on his death-bed made the flashy and unseemly remarks attributed to him by some writers.

In Rabelais' book, as it is now traditional to print it, the account of the childhood, education, and wars of Gargantua precedes that of the travels of his son Pantagruel. The fantastic element in the web of the story is derived from legends about the wonderful doings and sayings of certain giants, which were a common heirloom of the people in some parts of France. It is idle to look in Rabelais' book for a satire on chivalry written of set purpose. Considerations of that kind really apply to the Don Quixote of Cervantes, and need not be transferred from the elucidation of the Spanish author to that of the Frenchman. Nor is there a connected allegory in Rabelais, though transparent allusions are continually made to the men and things of the sixteenth century in a spirit of criticism that gives to the work much of its value. Rabelais is no reformer, but he knew full well where reform was needed. He is a moralist in word, in whom the courage or the will to be a moralist in deed was failing. It may be that he did not believe enough in human nature to see in its frailties anything more than a literary theme. The adventures of Gargantua and Pantagruel were written at intervals, and then put together somewhat loosely. Rabelais appears to have kept adding to his work almost throughout his life. After describing in his first chapters the birth and boyhood of Gargantua, he becomes all at once serious when he reaches the subject of that young giant's education. Rabelais is here ahead of his time.

He breaks with scholasticism and authority; he sketches
an education conceived in the spirit of the humanist,
and of the modern natural philosopher.  Later in the
work the subject of education is again touched upon in
a letter which Gargantua in his manhood writes to his
son Pantagruel.  Before Gargantua has had time to
complete his education in the University of Paris he is
summoned back by his father, who has been attacked
by his vicious and despotic neighbour King Picrochole.
The young man is put in command of his father's
armies, and defeats completely the aggressor.  In the
course of the campaign he receives assistance from
Friar Jean, a physically powerful and mentally health-
ful monk, whose manliness supplies a living satire on
the monastic orders.  Friar Jean becomes a faithful
companion of Gargantua's, who builds for him the
Abbey of Thelema, an ideal resort for gentlemen and
gentlewomen, where life is arranged on plans which are
in glaring contrast with every known monastic rule.
Then Rabelais passes on to describe the adventures of
Gargantua's son, Pantagruel.  He is educated very
much on the same lines as Gargantua had been.  In
the course of his travels in France, he meets with
Panurge, who fills in this second part of the work very
much the same office as Friar Jean in the first, though
in a somewhat different spirit.  Panurge can be
described as Friar Jean minus morality, and as a piece
of literary invention he stands on a par with the Fal-
staff of Shakespeare, the Sancho Pança of Cervantes,
and the Figaro of Beaumarchais.  Pantagruel and

Panurge set out on a long voyage in the search of truth, complicated by certain subsidiary questions as to whether Panurge should marry or not. The band of travellers pass from island to island, in each of which some faulty institutions, or the vices of some class of society, are allegorically represented. At last the Oracle of the Bottle is reached. Its high priest introduces to the goddess the party of truth-seekers, and she vouchsafes the answer, 'trink,' which word is interpreted as bearing the sense of the French word *bois*, or in English, 'drink.' It appears, therefore, that truth is not to be received into the mind by the channel of the ears, belonging properly to knowledge only, but that truth is to be absorbed directly into the substance of man, somewhat in the same way as a draught of good wine cheers the cockles of the heart. The moral philosophy of Rabelais is given in two maxims, engraved in the Temple of the Bottle, on two adamantine tables, namely, that all things move towards their ends, and that destiny leads by the hand the willing man, but drags along the unwilling.

The moral lessons taught by Rabelais are, therefore, three at least. There is the educational lesson which is thoroughly taken to heart now-a-days. The political esson condemning wars of conquest, and describing the king as the first servant of his people, has seen its wisdom theoretically accepted. In his social lesson he brands particularly the idle and wicked sloth of monks, the greed of lawyers, and the corruption of magistrates.

Viewed simply as a service to letters, the influence and usefulness of Rabelais cannot be over-estimated. French was in danger of being smothered under foreign and classical influence when he turned to the popular dialects of France, and brought their most effective words and drastic terms within the pale of literary language. Humorous writers, both in France and out of France, acknowledge a debt to him. La Fontaine borrowed from him many themes, and some most expressive names. Racine took from him the character of Dandin in the comedy entitled *Les Plaideurs*. Voltaire, in his onslaughts upon ecclesiastical abuses and against the theological spirit, borrowed some of his sharpest shafts from Rabelais. Docteur Pancrace in Molière's *Le Mariage Forcé* is to some extent descended from Panurge. Montesquieu describes the feather-headedness of the Parisians in words that bear the stamp of Rabelais' lighter irony. Pascal, who, as a moralist, may be excused for disowning Rabelais, learned surely from him the art of making his adversaries ridiculous, in those parts of his exposure of the Jesuits, where, by the accumulation of terms, he obtains striking ironical effects.

Rabelais had followers in Germany, and some of his warmest admirers are Germans. In England there is a humorous disposition in the national character which makes Rabelais appear almost a Briton. Bacon called him 'the great railer of France.' Robert Burton read him over and over again before writing his 'Anatomy of Melancholy.' There is many a page in Sterne's

*Tristram Shandy*, and in Swift's *Gulliver*, that Rabelais suggested; and it is evident to any reader of Southey's 'Doctor,' that the lakist knew his Rabelais well. The first English translator was Sir Thomas Urquhart. He has of late been translated again by Walter Besant, and extracts from his works have been repeatedly Englished. The ordinary accusation brought up against Rabelais is, that even in his gravest moods, he was never absolutely sincere; and the unbounded licence characterising many of his chapters is given in proof. The indecency is indeed undeniable, but there is nothing serious about it, and nothing could be more removed from a deliberate teaching of laxity in morals.

MARGUERITE DE VALOIS.—The placing of this lady next to Rabelais suggests a malicious comparison which would not be quite without foundation. She gathered about her a large number of literary men, who, strange to say, combined decided Protestant leanings in religion with the exercise of the most unruly vigour of life and poetic talent of a high order. She fought in her own way the fight for liberty of conscience. No blame can attach to her personal character; she was a steadfast friend, and to all appearance a blameless woman. Yet in literature she belongs to the school of Boccaccio and of Chaucer. Her wit as displayed in the *Heptaméron* is as good as French wit will ever be; but the subject matter of the stories in which it sparkles had been better left to masculine hands.

CALVIN.—This outstanding reformer could not bear

Rabelais, and the *Heptaméron* could find no more favour with him. In morals, as in literature, his part is that of a disciplinarian, he is always serious in purpose, always grave and sharp in manner, somewhat narrow-minded as a moralist, wonderfully strenuous as a church reformer, and wielded, to all appearance, a greater force in the history of the world than even Luther. He was born at Noyon, in Picardy. His father intended him to enter the Law. He studied at Paris in the famous Montaigu College, on the benches of which Ignatius Loyola and Erasmus sat. From the study of law he passed to that of divinity. The death of his father brought him back to Noyon for a time; hence he returned to Paris, and became the leader of a few young men who were groping in the dark after better spiritual things. The authorities at the Sorbonne[1] were not slow in noting him as a dangerous youth. He left France at a moment when the affair of the handbills, previously alluded to, was bringing trouble upon the unwary few who had shared in this attempt to emulate the posting of the theses by Luther. Calvin addressed from Bâle a formal and stirring epistle to the ' very Christian king, his prince and sovereign lord.' The epistle was reproduced in print in the following year at the beginning of the *Institution Chrétienne,* the master-work on which Calvin's reputation rests as a stylist, as a logician, and as a divine. There is nothing in the method of this book to remind one of scholastic philosophy, or of the intel-

---

[1] The theological college in the University of Paris.

lectual fabrics of the Middle Ages.  For Calvin, the
Christian religion is made for man, and nothing may
stand between it and the soul.  Theological ideas,
such as that of predestination, though they do come
within the scope of that work, diminish in no wise its
merit in setting forth a more human religion.  From
Bâle Calvin went to Ferrara, where he strengthened
Renée of France in the Protestant faith, and had occasion to meet Clément Marot.  When Ferrara became
unsafe for both, he turned his steps towards Geneva,
where his ideas on ecclesiastical discipline resulted in
his temporary exclusion from the city by the liberal
party.  But we find him again in the town in 1541,
and from that day he established himself firmly in the
city, as a reformer of church and morals.  His influence,
however, remained purely personal, and it is a mistake
to speak of him as having held in Geneva a formal
Dictatorship for twenty-three years.  From Geneva he
held in his hands the threads of the anti-Roman
agitation, which came near overwhelming the Popes.
In language, his work is exactly the counterpart of that
of Rabelais.  The mind of Calvin was, above all, a
logical and strict one.  He strove after putting an
argument in the most precise and simple way, and
brought it to its conclusion in the sharpest and most
direct manner.  His *Institution Chrétienne* was first
written by him in Latin, and then turned by his own
hand into French.  His intellect was nurtured on the
close binding processes of Latin syntax, and French
prose received thereby from him a drill in accuracy

which benefited it for all ensuing times.  Descartes and
Pascal wrote French after him with the same consciousness that Latin syntax was the natural ideal for
a French writer to keep in view.

AMYOT. — This writer is a Hellenist, very much
in the same sense as Calvin may be said to have
been a Latinist.  We are with him in presence of,
as it were, a third set of influences in the shaping of
the French language, and in the moulding of French
moral philosophy.  In Marot and Régnier we saw the
continuation of the sound French mediæval literary
traditions.  In Ronsard, in Rabelais, and in Calvin,
Latin is, on the whole, the nearest model.  Now, in
Amyot we see a writer who writes in a form that is
to become classical, and which was suggested by an
acquaintance with Greek, without being in any way an
imitation of that language.  In point of time Amyot
comes after Rabelais and Calvin, and in point of art
he introduces a style that is an improvement upon
both.  He was born at Melun, went to Paris to study,
and kept himself alive during that time by doing
menial work for his richer schoolfellows.  His mother
sent him from home much of the bread he ate, and he
made up for the lack of candle-light by reading his
authors before a coal fire.  At nineteen he was a
Master in Arts, then he studied the law, was a professor, an abbot, a kind of king's messenger at the
Council of Trent, the tutor of two royal princes, and,
last but not least, a persevering translator from Plu-

tarch.  While he was teaching Greek he wrote his
*Théagène et Chariclée*, a smooth and sweet rendering of
a Greek novel, which Racine read in his youth while
pacing to and fro under the trees at Port Royal des
Champs.  Another of his minor works is *Daphnis et
Chloé.*  The bulk of his labours and his most influential contribution to literature are found in his *Les vies
des hommes illustres grecs et romains, translatées du
grec en françois,* followed thirteen years later by his
translation of the Moral Essays of Plutarch.  We may
say that from this unique intercourse of Amyot with
Plutarch arose a fresh element in the literary evolution of France.   In the first place, since the great prose
works in the various European languages in the sixteenth century were epoch-making in the development
of their several literatures, it is of some interest to find
that while translations of the Bible determined the
prose style in Germany, England, and other northern
countries, this style was fixed in France partly by the
reproduction of Plutarch's works.  The results of this
peculiarity reached beyond the mere matter of form.
The moral attitude of Plutarch, his conception of the
affairs of life, the heroic examples of virtue and of self-
restraint contained in his parallel lives, were gradually
instilled into French society, and became implicitly a
part of the training given to French youth.  The easy-
going philosophy of life of the French has a great deal
to do with Plutarch, such as he was when elaborated
by Amyot and Montaigne to suit the predisposition of
the French.  Generations of French schoolboys have

received *Les vies des hommes illustres grecs et romains*
as prize-books, and J. J. Rousseau, when he put in the
hands of his typical pupil, Emile, the book of *Robinson
Crusoe*, that it might be to him as a finger-post towards
a life more conformable to nature, gave him also
Amyot's *Lives* as an antidote to the dangers and evils
of over-civilisation.

LA BOÉTIE is more famous for his friendship with
Montaigne than for his actual literary performance.
He was at an early age a councillor in the Parliament
of Bordeaux, a name which should not be taken in the
English sense of the word, but as defining a local board
of magistrates whose business it was to fix the provincial taxes and to transact other legal and administrative business. La Boétie's famous pamphlet is known
under two names, *La Servitude volontaire* and *Le Contr'un*.
As this latter name indicates, it is a protest against the
tyranny exercised over a whole people by any one man.
The occasion of it was a bloodthirsty revenge taken in
the name of Henry II. on a rebellious uprising in
Bordeaux against the imposition of a tax by the king.
The affection felt by Montaigne for him is recorded in
the essays of the latter.

MONTAIGNE was born in the castle of that name in
the Périgord. His father showed in the education of
his son how little he cared to countenance the prejudices of the aristocratic class. The boy was entrusted
to the care of a German tutor and sent away with him

to a farm, where Latin alone was spoken by master
and servants.   At that rate Montaigne reached the age
of six before knowing anything about his native tongue.
For a long time the child dwelt in the country among
the people, so that he might gain respect for them while
having the advantages of a natural and healthy mode of
living.   At the College of Guyenne, in Bordeaux, young
Montaigne may have sat at the feet of George Buchanau,
the famous Scotch humanist and reformer.   Though Latin
was the staple subject in the college, Montaigne managed
to pick up there some little French.   His friendship with
La Boétie was formed when he entered practical life in
the Parliament of Bordeaux.   In 1566 he married, not
from inclination as we may presume, since there is a
famous saying of his that he would have refused to
marry even wisdom, should wisdom have made him an
offer.   In 1570 he gave up his connection with the
legal profession that he might withdraw into his castle
to live and write there at his ease.   The *Essais* were
the outcome of ten years of meditation and solitary
reflection on the things of the world.   We have an
amusing account of a journey he took in Germany, in
Switzerland, and in Rome.   From 1581, a year after
the publication of the first edition of the *Essais*, and
immediately after the above-mentioned journey, he
was called to the office of Mayor in Bordeaux.   However, the plague broke out, and he turned his back on
it, in spite of his official duties.   During the Civil War
he sided with neither party, and was exposed to the
attacks of both.   He died a Roman Catholic, merely in

compliance with the religious habits in which he was
reared. The *Essais* of Montaigne were suggested to
him by reading Amyot's rendering of Plutarch's moral
works. They were the first of their kind in modern
literature, and after them that kind of writing became
fashionable among moralists far and wide. It must
be recognised that Montaigne's style is far from the
smoothness of his model, though in point of energy,
picturesqueness, and terseness, he far outreaches him.
In point of philosophy, Montaigne has been called the
wisest Frenchman that ever existed, an epithet which
should be taken in the Greek sense of the word, with
a less noble meaning than attaches to Sophos and a
worthier than is usually connected with Sophistes.
Montaigne treats of practical or applied morals as
an experienced and accommodating man of the
world might be expected to do if possessed of an
especial insight and of much versatility. The views
expressed by Montaigne bear so decisively on life that
one's first impulse on reading him is to grant that he is
right, but on proceeding to second thoughts it becomes
evident that his plausibility in dealing with the contradictory aspects presented by human affairs entails
powerlessness in practical life, and that no greatness
of soul can be reared on the basis afforded by him.
Montaigne has no method. He talks about this or
that topic, and passes from one to another without any
visible bond between them. He is in turn engaged
with the moods, passions, virtues, and vices of men.
He comments on the manners and customs of peoples;

F

he has his say on religion, politics, education; he gives us his own reflections and conclusions, the latter of which are usually inconclusive, along with quotations from ancient writers. If he has any object in his discursive meditation, it appears at first sight to be the study of himself; but it soon becomes evident, greatly to his credit, that self for him is a convenient name to betoken the average nature of men in general. Montaigne professes to hold that man is all vanity, all change and shiftiness. He is at war with every positive conception of man's place in nature and office on earth. You should never say 'I know,' you should never even say 'I do not know,' but you should limit yourself to saying, 'Do I know anything?' Such is his doctrine. If we turn our eyes from its paradoxical aspect, Montaigne's view amounts to this, that we should exert the greatest moderation, the best common sense, the truest reason, in judging of all things about us, that there is nothing in man or out-of man between heaven and earth, about which man is able to pronounce judgment without reservation. There is an undeniable modesty and humility in this mental position, repulsive as it may be to the less thoughtful and more decided temperaments of the race. On some particular points Montaigne is, indeed, very wise. He has greatly contributed to the formation of sound views in education. He objects to bulky and pedantic learning. The development of judgment and understanding should be entrusted to a tutor who is right-headed rather than a mere store-house of knowledge. Books are good, indeed, but things beheld in their natural aspects are the best teachers. Nor should a schoolmaster condescend to instruct his pupils from the height of his superior knowledge as from the top of a tower, but he should let himself down to the level of the mind he trains, and teach without continual recourse to authority, which is only another way of trading on the ignorance of the pupil. Those who have read and been delighted with Montaigne form in most countries a goodly number of followers. He was translated into English by an Italian, Giovanni Florio. To Samuel Daniel he appeared, in 1602, to be the prince or rather the king of thoughtful men, fond of an easy and practical wisdom. Florio's translation was revised by Cotton and again by Hazlitt. The copy of Montaigne which was thumbed by Shakespeare, and bears his notes, is still shown at the British Museum. Montaigne may well have stood as a link between Shakespeare and Plutarch.

# CHAPTER V.

## FIRST PERIOD OF THE SEVENTEENTH CENTURY, TILL THE MAJORITY OF LOUIS XIV. IN 1661.

### *Lyric Poetry.*

FRANÇOIS DE MALHERBE (1555-1628) : corrects the language and brings poetry under strict rules. Odes, stances, psaumes.

MAYNARD (1582-1646) : disciple of Malherbe.

RACAN (1589-1670) : Odes, stances, les Bergeries.

### *Dramatic Poetry.*

ROTROU (1609-1650) : tragedies, comedies, tragi-comedies.

SCARRON (1610-1660) : burlesque plays.

PIERRE CORNEILLE (1606-1684) :

    *Le Cid* (1636), a tragedy taken from Spanish history.

    *Horace* (1638), *Cinna* (1639), } tragedies taken from Roman history.

    *Polyeucte* (1640), a tragedy taken from early Christian history.

    *Le Menteur* (1642), a comedy of manners.

### *Prose.*

BALZAC (1594-1655) : Lettres.

VOITURE (1598-1648) : Lettres.

VAUGELAS (1585-1650) : *Remarques sur la langue française.*

DESCARTES (1596-1650).: *Discours de la Méthode* (1637).

PASCAL (1623-1662) : *Lettres provinciales* (1656). *Pensées*, published after his death.

ANTOINE ARNAULD (1612-1696), and the Gentlemen of Port Royal.

MÉZERAY (1610-1683) *Histoire de France.*

SCARRON : *Roman Comique.*

CYRANO DE BERGERAC (1620-1655) : *Romans fantastiques.*

Mlle. DE SCUDÉRY (1607-1701) : *Le grand Cyrus, Clélie.*

ACADÉMIE FRANÇAISE.

HÔTEL DE RAMBOUILLET.

MALHERBE, belonging to a noble family of Caen, studied in his native town, in Paris, in Bâle and in Heidelberg. When he was of age, he entered the service of a nobleman, and remained for ten years in Provence. After the death of his first patron he entered the army. In 1605, he came to settle in Paris, and entered the establishment of the Duc de Bellegarde. He gathered and indoctrinated his disciples in the little room which he occupied in that nobleman's house. He took up early the attitude of a critic, and his sharpness of tongue made him enemies. Régnier wrote one of his satires against him in which he compares him to a pedestrian poet without imagination, while tacitly reserving for himself the part of an inspired poet. Though Malherbe was really more of a critic than of a poet, he had no mean idea of his lyric talent—the two following lines tend to prove it :—

> **Les ouvrages communs durent quelques années ;**
> **Ce que Malherbe écrit, dure éternellement.**

In spite of the manifest exaggeration of his self-esteem, in which he was encouraged by Boileau, who hailed in him the first harmonious poet in France, he has certain qualities of a kind that could find greater recognition in the seventeenth century than we can give them now. He professed to expel from the language every foreign expression, and every phrase which was not in keeping with the purest national tendency in speech. For him, the best French was that spoken by the common people, though his odes are very far from being written in a popular strain.  Yet he made it his duty throughout his life, in prose style and in conversation, to enforce the use of accurate and precise terms.  He was a grammarian at heart.  Balzac called him the tyrant of words and of syllables, and, he added, 'I am moved to pity by a man who sees so much difference between 'pas' and 'point,' who discusses gerunds and participles as if they were two great and neighbourly countries engaged in hot debate over their boundaries.  After many years of toil he had not succeeded in freeing the Court from provincialisms.'

Malherbe was not a prolific poet.   In the best years of his life he composed on an average thirty lines a year. He spoilt large quantities of paper in building up and then in taking to pieces a single stanza.  He published his work only when he had nothing more to correct in it, and it was one of his sayings that after writing a hundred lines, a poet may take a rest for ten years.  There is more elevation and nobility in his strains than enthusiasm, more of the reasoning and critical faculty than of the poetic.  A most cautious writer, ever in distress about the rightness of his phrases, he could never attain to true freedom and spontaneous inspiration or to natural simplicity.  He offers the interesting spectacle of a man who had the greatest influence on his own age and the next, who claimed to derive inspiration from the best Greek and Latin models, who on the other hand saw well enough that he must not cut his language away from that of the people, yet, with all that, only succeeded in doing a negative kind of work; and in actually clipping the wings of French poetry for a very long time.

MAYNARD.   The foremost immediate disciples of Malherbe are Maynard, Racan and Balzac.  These three writers are all very much his inferiors.  Nevertheless, the first of them deserves more praise than he usually receives.  It was his bad fortune to be kept during his lifetime far from Paris in the discharge of various official duties in the provinces.  There is perhaps less classical and critical affectation in Maynard than in Malherbe. His lines are truer to life, because a little more remote from conscious art ; and they can be read now-a-days as easily as if they had been written but yesterday.

RACAN  lived with Malherbe for ten years.  He was a diligent and teachable pupil, even a grateful and respectful one.  For instance, while translating the Psalms (it is interesting to see how many poets without any real creative force followed Marot's example in translating or paraphrasing the Psalms), he would not try his hand on those which his master had already translated, and some of his best lines had for a canvas bits of prose by Malherbe.  The *Bergeries* of Racan belong to what is called pastoral poetry.  They are a tedious drama without any dramatic interest, in which townspeople, dressed up as shepherds for a holiday in the country, as it were, express affected sentiments.  Yet Racan, who spent most of his life in the country, who was genuinely fond of it, and able to realise its beauties

in a right spirit, could not but occasionally rise above
his own dull level. He sounds here and there a very
pure note, a note that is seldom met with in French
poetry, that of utter simplicity and of sheer naturalness
with a touch of discreet emotion. The faults of Malherbe and his followers are a very good example of the
weakness that affected the whole of the development of
French literature from that date. French men of letters
are extremely sensitive to criticism, they are prone to
write from critical standards rather than from their own
nature and instincts. On the other hand, this period
exemplifies also a corresponding quality: the intense
conscientiousness and devotion to an ideal distinct from
themselves, which raises French writers to a level of
continued excellence, and to a consistency in literary
methods less known and less cared for in other countries. Owing to their greater intellectual sensitiveness,
the French, in their standards of literature as in their
standards of morals and political activity, are most
amenable to authority, and as authority driven to extreme in any one direction brings about in due course
a revulsion from it to an equally extreme authority in
the opposite direction, they present in their history repeated swayings from one literary pole to another, and
from one political extreme to the opposite.

Rotrou was born at Dreux. He was brought to
Paris in early youth, and wrote his first poetry at
school. His first play was put on the stage when he
was nineteen years old. His words in its preface are

those of a modest and sensible young man.  'There are some excellent poets,' he wrote, 'but none are so at the age of twenty.'  He did his best work in the last years of his life, for he died in his prime.  His *Saint Genest*, a free imitation from the Spaniard, Lope De Vega, is his most original production, and may well be considered the most peculiar drama composed in that century.  It deals with an actor who, playing before Diocletian the part of a Christian martyr, is suddenly overpowered by the force of the sentiments he utters, declares his faith, and accepts martyrdom in earnest.  Another play entitled *Venceslas*, also traceable to a Spanish source, is less original and more conventionally perfect.  On the whole, Rotrou gives signs of discomfort under the heavy armour of outer, formal rules with which the critics, assisted by the social tone of the day, were burdening playwrights.  Although he has greatly imitated the ancients and the Spaniards, the personal turn of his talent gives a definite character to his work.  In France, in the seventeenth century literary individualism was becoming impossible, and an author's personality was necessarily kept under in the conscious effort to receive from others the work produced in any given *genre*, and carry on further the development of the tradition.  Rotrou had this honour, at least, of not being disowned.  He kept his place in the chain; Racine, Molière, Regnard, La Motte, gave him all the best acknowledgment they could give as upholders of the classical tradition.  They joined their work on to his by borrowing freely from him.  The death of Rotrou was that of a generous-minded and dutiful man. Though generally an absentee from his native town, he held there the office of lieutenant representing the king's authority. Dreux was plague-stricken in 1650; Rotrou repaired thither at once. A few days later, in the faithful discharge of his public office, he was struck down at the age of 41.

SCARRON belongs to the side-walks of French literature. He ranks with those second-rate authors who were extremely popular in Paris society before the classical ideal was definitely accepted, and whose fame was cut to the ground, not without justice, by Boileau, the second in date, and most enduringly powerful critic in matters poetical. Scarron, however, was more lucky than Chapelain, who succumbed to Boileau, after a dictatorship of forty years in the Paris drawing-rooms, especially at the Hôtel de Rambouillet, and in the new Académie Française, for which he criticised the *Cid* of Corneille, and sketched the first authoritative dictionary. Scarron was, at any rate, the upholder of a literary *genre* known under the name of *burlesque,* and only fell when this kind of production lost favour with the public. He was attacked with paralysis at the age of twenty-eight. Being compelled thereby to spend the remainder of his life in an arm-chair, he sought relief from his pains in such poetry as would remind him least of them; so he took to playing the literary fool on the most extensive scale. His burlesques are now quite forgotten, except as curiosities; but his *Roman comique,* written in prose, has obtained in our own day a favour which did not fall to its lot at the time of the writing of it; for it is written in the truest vein of nature, relating as it does the unvarnished adventures of a company of actors travelling in the provinces. For strict accuracy in description, for close observation of things, and knowledge of men as they are, Scarron is entitled to rank as forerunner of the so-called modern realistic school. The French burlesque epics were suggested by the Italian Renaissance epics of the same kind, and stand, through them, in relationship with the decayed *chansons de geste* that were written in the latest Middle Ages. They were but toys contrived in order to amuse fashionable society. The Paris drawing-rooms were then exerting a narrowing influence on the literary development of France, as they have done ever since. How could it be otherwise when Corneille and Racine sought for their plays the applause of the same people whom Scarron delighted, and from whom they were not strong enough to set themselves free?

CORNEILLE. The works of Corneille are a long compromise between the claims of the Paris salons and the native independence of his dramatic gifts. He was born at Rouen. His father was in the Civil Service of the State. Corneille studied in the Jesuit College at Rouen. He was an advocate at eighteen, and purchased shortly after two legal charges, in which he did his duty faithfully for twenty years. Rouen stood next to Paris in its appreciation of things theatrical. One day

Corneille brought to a Parisian actor passing through Rouen a newly-written comedy called *Mélite*. The play was acted in Paris, and attended by enormous success. Having thus become famous, Corneille was introduced to Richelieu. This cardinal and statesman boasted that he would be as good a performer on the theatrical stage as he actually was on the political. He brought together a few writers, whom he supplied with plans, and whom he expected to build up plays on these foundations. Corneille became one of those hired assistants. However, his independence of character broke out and raised Richelieu's anger. He gave up his place in the literary quintet, and came back to Rouen to write *Médée* in peace. This was his first tragedy, and he had gone to ancient authors for it. Unfortunately, his choice fell upon Seneca, a second-rate writer. Yet the study of this Latin model assisted Corneille in throwing off the bonds of spurious Italian art. He now parted company with the bombast, high-flown rhetoric, and uselessly complicated plots that had obtained a footing in France. *Médée* was perhaps written with too much literary purity and too straight-forwardly to find favour with the misguided taste of the public. At any rate, Corneille laid down for a while his tragic pen, and donned again the bells and cap of comedy. His *Illusion Comique* was his next work, a play which the present generation applauded when it was acted again at the Comédie Française in 1861. A few months after the *Illusion Comique* came *Le Cid*, which is reputed one of Corneille's very finest efforts.

The subject is taken from a Spanish writer, Guillem de Castro, but actual imitation goes for very little in this play, where Corneille's own inspiration shows itself more freely than in almost any other tragedy of his. Corneille puts in the *Cid* for the first time on the stage that conflict of duty and honour on the one side against passion on the other, which was to become his favourite psychological theme. To explain this, once for all, we may give an outline of this play in a very few words, and leaving out the proper names. A maiden, who is the daughter of a noble and exacting father, is in love with a young warrior. Unfortunately, in pursuance of the code of honour accepted among men of his class, the young warrior is called upon to kill in a duel the father of the woman he loves. The girl's sense of honour and of duty to her father stands henceforth between her and her love, between the young man and the bride he fain would have. Events belonging to the history of the times affect diversely the course and issue of the debate. In the *Cid* the maiden resists every temptation from within and from without in order that she may remain faithful to her standard of honour.

The other best plays of Corneille are variations on this theme. There was a moral novelty in this conception of the drama that speedily won the affections of the public. Corneille's rivals, who represented the classical tradition so far as it was already formed, were fairly entitled to look upon him as an innovator, and to form against him a league in self-defence. Richelieu used Chapelain to draw up a critical report on the *Cid*, and sent it to the Académie Française to be endorsed. The members of the Académie were all, more or less, in Richelieu's pay. Had they been willing to resist his demands on literary grounds, they could hardly have done so, compelled as they were to take into consideration less worthy motives. Besides, Richelieu had, on certain issues, a fair case to make out. The play breathed forth the pride and high honour of the Spanish, with whom France was then at war, whose armies had been on the point of over-running the country, and whose literary influence was threatening to make of Paris a satellite to Madrid. Then the point of honour upheld in the play found its satisfaction in the fighting of duels, a practice which Richelieu was then putting down in France with a stern and wise hand. In the *Sentiments de L'Académie sur le Cid*, the so-called classical tradition is strictly held. The play was declared to be against the rules, and from that date French plays were expected to be regular. This meant that playwrights were to comply with the rule of the so-called unities. The action was to be one and single throughout the play. Only such subjects were to be chosen as would, in the world of reality, work themselves out in one and the same place; and further, no subject was to be put on the stage whose enacting in reality should extend over a longer period than twenty-four hours. Aristotle's authority was claimed for these rules, but Aristotle nowhere expresses them with the rigidity given to them by the French. From that

moment Corneille lost some of his self-confidence.   He
made the mistake of taking seriously the Academic
apparatus of criticism.   He was frightened away from
indulging his natural bent by the fuss made about the
rules.   He dared no longer write anything without
wondering whether the Academy would approve of it,
and whether Aristotle would have thought well of it.

He found in Livy the theme of his next play, *Horace*.
His *Cinna* also originates in an episode of Roman
history, but in his *Polyeucte* he turns away from the
pagan world—as Racine did too at a certain crisis in
his life—and seeks dramatic inspiration in the martyrdom of the early Christians.   Shortly after he returned
to the comic vein, and gave *Le Menteur*, the first French
comedy of the classical school strictly so called.   In
the *Menteur* there is no depicting of individual character
in the well-known fashion of Shakespeare, but an invented personage, whose character is made to represent
fairly well one of the vices prevalent in mankind,
stands forth as the type of all his like.   Such a conception of comedy presents on the face of it a moral
and philosophic aspect, and it was reserved to the
French to excel in that kind of writing.   Thoroughly
French as the *Menteur* is, the canvas of the play is
taken from a Spanish poet, and *La suite du Menteur* is
also from Spanish sources.   Corneille came back to
tragedy in *Rodogune*, the last of the plays generally
acknowledged to be his best.   In 1647 his prestige had
become so great that the Academy, which had twice
closed its doors against him, threw them open at last

to this master playwright. The latter period of his
life was saddened by the decay of his dramatic faculty,
by the cares of poverty, and by the rising up of his
young rival Racine. It became evident in the edition
of his works which he published in 1660 that Corneille
had finally accepted the standards set up by the
Academic critics. A further proof of his surrender was
afforded in the praise given him by Boileau, whose
authority was fast placing itself beyond every possible
challenge. From that moment the three rules became
a matter of European importance, and made themselves
felt in the literature of other countries besides France.

Balzac subjected French prose to the same schooling
as Malherbe had applied to poetry. He was Malherbe's
disciple, of whom he used to say: ' That man made me
swear on his dogmas and on his maxims.' He was a
tasteful writer, and, as he reports in his Twentieth
Discourse, he was able to foresee and provide for the
literary likings of his time. What some were seeking
he found, namely, a certain skill in putting words
together, and in allotting them to their right places.
He was born at Angoulême, and went to Holland at the
age of seventeen, whereupon he wrote some *Discours
Politiques* on that country. Then he spent three years
in Rome, and on his return published his *Lettres.*
These were followed by several treatises: *Le Prince,
Aristippe,* and *Le Socrate Chrétien.* Having fallen into
a literary controversy with the Jesuits, and feeling that
Richelieu looked upon him with coolness, he withdrew

from Paris, although he was a member of the Academy, and ended his life on his own country estates. The book entitled *Le Prince* does not remind one of Fénelon's *Télémaque*, nor is it like Machiavelli's *Il Principe*. It is best described as a lengthy piece of flattery addressed to Louis XIII. Balzac shows truer feeling when he turns upon the Jesuits. There is a fore-glimmering of the *Provinciales* in some of his invectives. 'The Court has brought forward certain doctors who have found the means of uniting vice with virtue. Devices are nowadays provided whereby thieves of other people's property may conscientiously retain it.' The *Aristippe* is an empty rhetorical production. Balzac speaks in his best tones in the *Socrate Chrétien*, a name which he applies to Christ, giving on the Christian doctrine, on the beginnings of the Church, and on the reading of Holy Scripture some substantial reflections put in a tolerably plain setting. Balzac is, like Malherbe, a harmonious writer. He casts a mould for thoughts without filling it. His style is highly strung; he aims at being witty; he was in the habit of 'working out the harmony and the build of a sentence as if personal salvation were at stake.'

VOITURE is distinguished from Balzac by being decidedly over-witty, while the latter remained reasonable in using his wit. Balzac was a nobleman, Voiture was the son of a wealthy wine-merchant; but an accepted writer could not but move in the highest circles of society. He sought patronage and received it. The merest trifle laid the foundation for his reputation. He had occasion to send a copy of *Orlando Furioso* to a lady, whom he addressed in the following words: 'This, Madam, is the finest adventure Orlando ever had.' Thanks to the favour in which drawing-room wit of that kind was generally held, he soon found himself an inmate of the Hôtel de Rambouillet. His correspondence is all about nothing, the *Lettre sur la Conjonction Car* affording a very fair sample of his ability as a writer of pretty nonsense.

VAUGELAS. In this man the literary circles of Paris found the grammarian they wanted. He hailed from a French-speaking province, La Bresse, which was not as yet included in the Kingdom of France. A poor man and a thorough provincial at first, he came to move in the most brilliant society. He belonged to Madame de Rambouillet's circle. He knew Balzac, Voiture, and Chapelain. An Academician, he was entrusted with the preparation of the Academy's dictionary. On his death he left some debts, and his assets consisted mainly of his lexicological labours. The Academy, for its own sake, rescued the latter from the clutches of his creditors. The life of Vaugelas was that of a grammatical student and linguistic emendator. The tendency of the sixteenth century had all been towards increasing the stock of words and expressions, so as to make it co-extensive with the greatly developed requirements of civilised communities. The tendency of the seventeenth century was, as an offset, all towards restriction and selection. Malherbe had first set the fashion that way, then had come the Hôtel de Rambouillet, then the Académie Française, then Balzac, and now Vaugelas was to carry on the task. His *Remarques sur la Langue Française* were put before the public in 1647. Long before that moment, however, his authority in matters of grammar and right usage was unlimited. No grammarian in his age could well be expected to look at the historical side of his subject, so Vaugelas' utter failure in this direction cannot be fairly held to reduce his merit. He was a policeman of the language. He guarded it like a watch-dog against the intrusion of Italian and Spanish words, against the importation of provincialisms in Paris, and against coarse or extravagant phraseology. The *Dictionnaire de l'Académie*, produced in 1694, is composed throughout on the lines laid down by him, and ten years later the Academy put its own stamp on his ' Remarques ' by issuing an annotated edition of them. Vaugelas experienced how difficult it is to be a grammarian without passing into a pedant. Molière, hunting down nicety in language as in morals, names him five times in his *Femmes Savantes* disparagingly, thereby giving posterity a somewhat unfair idea of his character. Vaugelas was more of a gentleman than of a schoolmaster.

DESCARTES was born at La Haye (not in Holland, but in the centre of France). He was brought up by the Jesuits. He received from them the thorough

Latin and Church education which they knew so well
how to give.   But his intellectual wants were far from
being all satisfied.   When he left college, he had made
up his mind that he would seek for science nowhere
else than within himself, and in the  open book of
nature.   He set to one side the things appertaining to
faith as belonging to reaches in which reason was out-
stripped, and he submitted to a fresh examination all
he had been taught from childhood.   At the age of
eighteen he was a licentiate in law, then he led for six
years a military life in Holland and in Germany,
revolving in his mind philosophic matters all the
time.   In 1620, he caught the first glimpse of his
famous method, and in the ensuing nine years he
spent his time, according to his own testimony, in
wandering about the world endeavouring to be a looker-
on rather than a performer in its comedies.   He was in
Hungary, in Poland, in Switzerland, in Italy.   At last,
weary of trundling along  on all the highroads of
Europe, he' settled down in Amsterdam, hiding from
the crowd both the place of his abode and the subject
of his intellectual work, and bringing his life into
agreement with the maxim *bene vixit qui bene latuit*.
After spending eight years in meditation, he made up
his mind to allow some of his works to appear before
the public.   He gave out in 1637 the *Discours de la
méthode pour bien conduire sa raison et chercher la vérité
dans les sciences*.   Descartes remained in Holland till
1649, visiting France at intervals.   The Queen of
Sweden, Christina, was then urging him to visit her in

her kingdom. He yielded to her entreaties in the last-mentioned year, and died at Stockholm five months later from congestion of the lungs. His long residence abroad is not disconnected with the dangers threatening then in France free and independent thinkers. Descartes is the first metaphysician who used deliberately and on a large scale the French language for his disquisitions. The study of philosophy stepped along with him into the drawing-rooms and social resorts of men. 'I have intended,' says he, in one of his letters, 'to write a book which even women could understand.' That is why he wrote in French, the speech of his countrymen, in preference to Latin, the language of his teachers. He was almost a stranger to the purely literary or political activity of his day. Nurtured on mathematics and on the Latin writings of philosophers, his mind escaped from every smallness and paltriness. His influence on language and on ideas, beginning with the publication of his *Discours de la méthode*, was mainly felt in the second half of the century, and reached far beyond the boundary of France. Cartesianism, as his doctrine is called, whose cornerstone is the well-known aphorism, 'Je pense, donc je suis,' found general acceptance in Holland, in Germany, and in France. Out of France the views of Descartes came to be generally held in the universities. In France, where the older kind of metaphysics, still upheld by the Church and the Jesuits, stood in their way, they found their most congenial atmosphere in the societies of laymen, in the drawing-rooms of cultivated ladies, and in the bosom of comparatively independent writers, such as the Port-Royalists, Malebranche, Retz, Bossuet, Fénelon. The metaphysical side of abstract philosophic research is not what is most prominent in Descartes. There is to his doctrine a practical side, and it is established on positive affirmations which served as a counter check to the scepticism in morals that had been imported from Italy. The great writers of the seventeenth century are, in the main, moralists, and they are indebted partly to Descartes for the excellent philosophy of life breathed forth in almost all their work. Boileau, who laid it down that to be natural is to be rational, is, to that extent, in literature a disciple of Descartes. Whatever Descartes did for his country, he was not able to render to the cause of science in general so good service as Bacon. Descartes has no distinct method of studying the phenomena of the outer world. By failing to give to the senses their proper function in the study of nature, he further strengthened the tendency already established in France towards the abstract consideration of man, and of topics of the moral, the social, and the psychological order. French naturalists were long Cartesians, but in the fulness of time they were converted to the doctrines of Newton.

PASCAL.—We have alluded to the Gentlemen of Port-Royal as followers of Descartes in philosophic method. One of them, however, stood out. This was Pascal. The group of laymen who meditated on moral and theological problems, and educated a few dozen young gentlemen according to principles which are comparatively modern, and broadly Christian rather than ecclesiastical, had their principal home at Port-Royal Des Champs, near Paris. Pascal's first literary work was the result of his connection with them, and brought them the celebrity which befitted their singleness of purpose in education, the earnestness of their convictions, and the talent they displayed in many directions. Pascal mistrusted the reason of man as fully as Descartes put faith in it. The former was a seeker after Divine truth, the latter after philosophic certainty.

Pascal was born at Clermont-Ferrand. His father, himself a *savant* of a high order, found it necessary at an early stage to put a check on the wonderful intellectual energies of his son. Young Pascal showed himself so abnormally gifted in the handling of mathematical problems, that from sheer prudence it seemed necessary to refuse him access to that science for a while. By the age of twelve he had discovered anew several propositions of Euclid. At sixteen he was the author of a treatise on conic sections. Up to the age of thirty he continued to be taken up with scientific problems. He devised a reckoning machine. He repeated Torricelli's experiments in physics. Under the strain to which his intellectual ardour put his physical strength his health gave way gradually, and contributed, in the latter period of his life, to turn his meditations into new channels. Up to the age of thirty, Pascal was essentially an intellectualist, and also a man of the world. After that, concern with questions

of a spiritual order absorbed his faculties and determined the nature of his literary work.  That is the
time when he went to Port-Royal and became at second
hand a disciple of Bishop Jansenius.  At that time Pope
Innocent X. had just condemned a set of five theological
propositions which had been referred to him by the theological faculty of the University of Paris.  These propositions purported to be drawn from the *Augustinus*, a
work by Bishop Jansenius, published after his death.

The Abbé de Saint Cyran, who had known Jansenius
personally, had brought the doctrine of the Dutch Bishop
to Port-Royal as early as 1636, and many of Saint
Cyran's friends, both ecclesiastics and laymen, had
adopted after him Jansenistic views.  The Jansenists
were condemned by the Pope, though they argued that
the five incriminated propositions were not in Jansenius.
Antoine Arnauld, himself a priest, and a doctor of the
Faculty,[1] upheld the fairness of the defence set up by the
Port-Royalists.  He received as a reward his dismissal
from the Faculty, at the request of the Jesuits.  Pascal at
once took up the cudgels on behoof of Arnauld.  He
wrote his first *Lettre Provinciale* in January 1656, and
several more were spread over that year and the following.  Pascal withheld his name, but he was soon
detected.  The combined simplicity and power of the
letters was so characteristic of Pascal as his relations
and friends knew him, that the *Lettres Provinciales* had
hardly appeared when they were set down to him.  In
the first letters Pascal defends Arnauld.  In the fourth

---

[1] *Docteur en Sorbonne.*

he passes from a defensive attitude to a policy of aggression. Among the Jesuits, he first attacks the Casuists on account of their lax morality; then he takes to task the Jesuits themselves and all their works. Theological controversies had not hitherto been carried on in French. They had been reserved for treatment in the language of the Church only, that is to say, Latin. So Pascal popularised theological controversies much in the same way as Descartes had popularised philosophic controversies. The Jesuits never got over the blows dealt them by Pascal, though they took revenge on the Port-Royalists by inducing Louis XIV. to demolish their residence, to scatter their scholars, and to forbid their doctrines. Pascal had entered upon his Crusade against the Jesuits in a spirit of righteous indignation. 'If the Pope condemns me,' he said, 'what I condemn in my letters is surely condemned in heaven.' The *Provinciales* are a most ironical and powerful piece of special pleading. The manifold talent which they reveal has met with the widest appreciation. Voltaire sees in this book the first work of genius in the French language. According to Vinet,[1] the style of Pascal 'does not stand between his reader and his thought, for it is the thought itself,' unclad, unadorned, alternately broad and pointed, and always irresistible. After giving the *Provinciales* to the world, Pascal withdrew himself from the field of polemics in which he had shown himself a master for all time, and devoted himself more and more to intro-

---

[1] A greatly esteemed Swiss divine and critic.

spection.  He formed a plan of an apology for the Christian religion.  This unfinished work is known as his *Pensées*.  In the seventeenth and eighteenth centuries, owing to the nature of the questions then in debate, the *Provinciales* were held in the highest repute.  In our times, when the battle of toleration has been fought and won, and when the objectionable morals of the Jesuits are no longer pushed to the front by those who may still hold them, the *Pensées* command greater attention than the *Provinciales*.  For the subjects broached by Pascal in the *Pensées* are ever with us.  They flow from the very mystery in which our life and our destiny are wrapped.  The *Pensées* came only gradually to be known in their present shape.

Pascal died when he was thirty-nine years old, after many years of suffering, in which the regularity of his work was greatly interfered with.  When he was free from pain he took up his pen and wrote down in jottings the thoughts which he formed, and wished to preserve with a view to further elaboration.  It was found that the notes collected after his death almost all bore upon that work which Pascal proposed to write in defence of Christian truth.  The friends of his who published these fragments were alarmed at his freedom of thought, and also at their unsatisfactory literary condition.  They took upon themselves to cut out and alter many passages.  In our century only has Pascal been heard by all in the terms in which he spoke to himself on the irreducible contradictions of soul and mind which are at the same time the greatness and the bane of our kind.

CYRANO DE BERGERAC is the author of two fantastic romances, where, under pretence of describing the state of affairs in the moon and in the sun, he gives a satire on the manners and ideas of his times. Beyond his originality he has little to recommend him. His writing is most affected. The bad taste made fashionable in Italy by Marini, in Spain by Gongora, and which penetrated into England as euphuism, stamps him beyond all remedy. He seems to think that in literature all that glitters should be taken for gold.

MLLE DE SCUDÉRY. Two kinds of romances at least were cultivated in the first half of the seventeenth century. The pastoral or idyllic romance running into the heroic and chivalrous was at once conventional and idealistic and the most fashionable. Beside it we find some instances of a simple treatment of ordinary incidents of life. These we may almost call realistic novels. The name of Mlle de Scudéry is attached to the first class, which is also by far the largest. Her *Grand Cyrus* and her *Clélie* run up to ten volumes each, and represent in an outer framework borrowed from ancient history nothing else than the manners and the lovemaking of the fashionable classes in her time, with the addition of a touch of courtly heroism and refinement.

ACADÉMIE FRANÇAISE. This body was founded in

consequence of a general wish to improve the language, and to uphold definite standards in literary art. After Malherbe's death the men of letters who had been disciples of the old poet continued to meet together, in order to cultivate his traditions and his memory. It struck Richelieu that this literary society might be of some use to him, and that it would be a wise piece of state-craft to give it an official organisation. The Malherbists received from him a royal patent, in terms of which the office was entrusted to them of determining the use of words, of increasing the elegance of the language, and of giving it power to treat of all arts and all sciences. The Académie Française was registered as a public body in 1637, and henceforth played the part of a universally accepted authority in matters literary. This institution has been greatly admired by critics who care more for purity and distinction of style than for freedom of expression. Matthew Arnold has put before the English public the points which, to his mind, make in favour of such an institution. At the same time, it must be remembered that the usefulness of a check or drag may be exaggerated, and that many evils have accrued from the extravagant respect in which the Academy was held for a long period. Its first dictionary took half a century to prepare.

HÔTEL DE RAMBOUILLET. In this house congregated the noblemen and the ladies who were fond of discussing literary topics, and anxious to meet the men of letters, to whom it was fashionable to extend patronage.

Among the notabilities of France in the middle of the seventeenth century, Condé, La Rochefoucauld, the Marquise de La Fayette, Mme de Sévigné, Mlle de Scudéry, Voiture, Balzac, Racan, Ménage, Chapelain, Corneille, and young Bossuet could be met there. The visitors in Mme de Rambouillet's drawing-room who were not saved from affectation by their reason or genius formed a circle of exquisites, given to the small talk of gallantry in the Italian style, and responsible for the bad odour into which Molière brought the word *précieux*. The use of metaphors in and out of season, and with the most glaring absurdity, reached such a pitch at the Hôtel de Rambouillet that at last there was a revolt of common-sense against it.

# CHAPTER VI.

## AGE OF LOUIS XIV. (1661-1715.)

### *Miscellaneous Verse.*

LA FONTAINE (1621-1695): Twelve books of Fables.
BOILEAU (1636-1711):
   *Satires.*
   *Epîtres.*
   *L'Art Poétique.*
   *Le Lutrin*, a mock-heroic poem.

### *Dramatic Art.*

MOLIÈRE, JEAN BAPTISTE POQUELIN (1622-1673): Comedies—
   *Les Précieuses Ridicules.*
   *L'Ecole des Maris,*
   *L'Ecole des Femmes.*
   *Don Juan ; or, Le Festin de Pierre.*
   *Le Misanthrope.*
   *Le Tartuffe.*
   *George Dandin.*
   *L'Avare.*
   *Le Bourgeois Gentilhomme.*
   *Les Fourberies de Scapin.*
   *Les Femmes Savantes.*
   *Le Malade Imaginaire.*
JEAN RACINE (1639-1699): Tragedies—
   *Les Frères Ennemis ou la Thébaïde*, taken from Greek history.
   *Alexandre.*
   *Andromaque.*
   *Les Plaideurs*, a comedy after Aristophanes.
   *Britannicus*, taken from Roman history.
   *Bérénice,*            ,,              ,,

*Bajazet*, taken from Turkish history.
*Mithridate*, ,, Roman history.
*Iphigénie en Aulide*, taken from Greek history.
*Phèdre*, taken from Greek history.
*Esther*, ,, Scripture history.
*Athalie*, ,, ,,
REGNARD (1656-1709) : Comedies—
*Le Joueur.*
*Le Distrait.*
*Les Ménechmes.*
*Le Légataire Universel.*

## Didactic Writings, Philosophy.

LA ROCHEFOUCAULD (1613-1680) : *Maximes.*
BOSSUET (1627-1704) : *Discours sur l'histoire universelle.*
LA BRUYÈRE (1639-1696) : *Les Caractères ou les Mœurs de ce siècle.*
FÉNELON (1651-1715) : *Traité de l'éducation des filles. Dialogues des Morts. Traité de l'existence de Dieu.*

## Epistolary Composition.

MME DE SÉVIGNÉ (1626-1696) : Lettres (addressed to Mme de Grignan, etc.).
JEAN RACINE (1639-1699) : Lettres (addressed to his son, etc.).
MME DE MAINTENON (1635-1719) : Lettres.

## Oratory.

BOSSUET (1627-1704) : Oraisons funèbres.
FLÉCHIER (1632-1710) : Oraisons funèbres.
BOURDALOUE (1632-1704) : Sermons.

## Fiction.

MME DE LA FAYETTE (1634-1693) : Novels—
*La Princesse de Clèves.*
*La Comtesse de Montpensier, etc.*
PERRAULT (1628-1703) : *Contes de fées.*
FÉNELON (1651-1715) : *Aventures de Télémaque.*

LA FONTAINE. The personal influence of Louis XIV. on the literature of his century is undeniable. However pleasure-loving he was in the earlier part of his life, and fanatical in the latter part, he managed to exert on literature an influence that was at the same time liberal and conservative. The writers whom he patronised acquired gravity, moderation, rectitude, and seemliness. Yet the scope of his action must not be exaggerated. Before he could possibly affect literature in his surroundings, a certain number of men whose works are sometimes held to be characteristic of his influence were already producing their writings, among them, Pascal, Corneille, La Rochefoucauld, Mme de Sévigné and La Fontaine. This greatest of fabulists was born at Château-Thierry, a town which is now included in the department of Aisne. Almost alone among the great classical writers he took but little interest in the education given him. His father having placed him in a monastic establishment, to complete his greatly neglected studies, the young man emancipated himself altogether from all regular application. But he did a good deal of discursive reading of his own. For a while he was in danger of yielding himself to Malherbe. Fortunately he was saved from the risk of falling into bondage to any one model by the reading of Horace, of Virgil, of Ovid, and of Terence. He was lucky also in establishing connections with the older French writers, such as Villon, Marot, and Rabelais; among the Italians, Boccaccio and Ariosto were his favourites. His father tried again to bring him upon a regular path of life, by handing over to him the office which he held under the crown, and by providing him

with a wife at the age of twenty-six. But La Fontaine
was not the sort of man that could lie at anchor. He
turned out a bad husband, a bad father, and a spend-
thrift. He sold his office, he sold his lands, he left his
wife, and was happy to be rid of his son. Then he
began a roving life, in the course of which he passed
from the establishment of one nobleman to another.
He was first in the pay of Fouquet, the famous financier,
who fell into disgrace with Louis XIV., partly from dishonesty, but still more by a display of magnificence
that was offensive to the king. La Fontaine, who
could, at least, be grateful for services received, endeavoured to soften the anger of the king in the *Elégie
aux nymphes de Vaux*, one of his most genuine and truly
poetic pieces. But Fouquet was imprisoned, and La
Fontaine, obliged to seek protection elsewhere, found
a home after a while in the house of Mme de la
Sablière. He spent twenty years under her roof, and
addressed to her the tenth book of his fables. During
that period he was welcomed in the best circles, and
entered into close association with the leading men of
letters. Saint-Evremond, a famous French critic who
spent most of his life in banishment in London, asked
La Fontaine to join him. The fabulist did not go, and
when Mme de la Sablière made up her mind to enter
a nunnery, he found himself again shelterless. Monsieur
d'Hervart came across him in the streets of Paris at
this juncture. 'Come and stay with me,' he said. 'I
was on my way to you,' was the poet's reply. In 1693
he was taken ill. He fell then, for perhaps the first

time, into a very serious mood, and looking back upon his past life with all its moral blemishes, he wrote to an ecclesiastic among his friends. ' 'Tis nothing to die, my dear fellow, but think that I am about to appear before God. You know what my life has been.' La Fontaine, however, was spared two years longer, and it is to his credit that he remained true to the new departure he had made. In 1684, La Fontaine was wanted by the Academy as a new member, but Louis XIV., who looked very closely after such matters, opposed the election of the fabulist and recommended his more correct friend Boileau, who was duly appointed. Then the king objected no longer to the election of La Fontaine.

The Fables of La Fontaine were published at intervals from 1668 to 1694. The author describes them as—

> Une ample comédie à cent actes divers
> Et dont la scène est l'univers.

They contain, indeed, a selection of the different types that are found in society,—king, courtier, judge, priest, monk,—all are gathered there, with misers, flatterers, busy-bodies, knaves, and hypocrites. La Fontaine's animals are symbolic of men, and represent humanity in its different aspects. The first four books were dedicated to the Dauphin (the eldest son of the king of France), and their general title is unassuming. La Fontaine did not profess to have invented his fables; he had merely gathered up and put in verse the numerous stories hailing from Greek and Roman antiquity, or from the French Middle Ages, or from Oriental sources, in which human beings are depicted under the guise of beasts. In spite of this, La Fontaine's fables bear the stamp of the greatest originality and talent. They are miniature productions in which comedy, tragedy, and every kind of poetry are compressed. La Fontaine's most personal and striking quality is charm. As he says himself, he endeavoured to endow the wisdom stored up in the fables of mankind with freshness and gaiety, meaning by gaiety, not that which provokes merriment, but a certain charm, a certain pleasantness which may be given to all subjects, even to the gravest. The second collection of his fables issued ten years after the first, when the author was perhaps at his very best, presents still more variety and higher flights of poetry than the first books. La Fontaine has also written a kind of novel bearing the mythological title of *Psyché.* In spite of its title, this work is of the nature of an autobiography, in which we see with what receptivity the author looked on the world around him, including its men and women, and the beauties of nature, as well as the animals whose especial poet he was. The same man who failed so utterly in the individual relations of life, was capable of sympathy, provided that he might free himself from the obligations of duty. La Fontaine has left a record of the friendship which bound him with three of the greatest poets of the time: Molière, Boileau, and Racine. A great deal has been made of this friendship, though, as a matter of fact, it did not last very long. Racine fell out with Molière by sending one of his tragedies to be acted by a rival company. Boileau, who was on terms of the closest affection with Racine, remained faithful to him, and thereby caused a coolness between himself and Molière. As for La Fontaine, since we have said that he could be everybody's friend in general though the friend of nobody in particular, it was natural that he should follow his own courses, and remain independent of this fellowship without disowning it. The French used by La Fontaine is of a wider scope than that of his contemporaries. Being the Rabelais of his period in what concerns, at least, the tone of his writings, he gave hospitality in his fables to many dialectic and provincial phrases which were fast losing the credentials still theirs in the sixteenth century. Though La Fontaine's fables almost always bring a moral in their train, it would be a mistake to view him as a deliberate moralist. His purpose, if he had any, was simply to give a foreshortened representation of human life. Reality was his object.

Boileau is by no means a poet in the highest sense belonging to that word. He is a literary critic who wrote in verse, because he thought that this form of expression is more pithy and easier to remember than any other. In the name of reason and of good sense he undertook a mission among men of letters which is in almost every way a continuation of Malherbe's office. He attacked those writers who, when compared with his standards, and when measured by his taste, were found wanting. He set an example rigidly in keeping with his own doctrines, and published nothing that could not

have stood the inspection of another critic like himself.
Further, he earned the title of '*Législateur du Parnasse*.'
This name, in the mythological affectation of its word-
ing, affords in itself a sample of the dry formality with
which he wrote and expected others to express themselves. He was a Parisian by birth and sprung from
a line of lawyers. His childhood was saddened by
the early death of his mother and the neglect of his
brothers. After the usual course of studies in the law,
he was called to the Bar at the age of twenty-one, not
without giving evidence of his literary dispositions.
He began by the publication of *Satires*, a kind of
writing which he continued to cultivate at a later
stage, till he had produced twelve specimens. Some of
them are on moral subjects, for instance, on man and
woman, on honour; others are literary in their contents,
such as the one addressed to Molière on the subject
of rhyme, and the famous seventh satire against bad
writers. Others are about the merest trifles, such as
one on the unpleasantnesses of life in Paris, and another
on a bad dinner. Boileau's satires are not so biting as
those of Juvenal. In fact, compared with these, they are
placid and good-natured, with the exception, however, of
the seventh and the ninth, in which he draws into light
those of the profession of letters who did not come up
to his standards, and whom he branded for as long
a period as his authority lasted. The *Epîtres* were
written, so far as the bulk of them is concerned, at a
later period than the majority of the satires. They
deal with current moral or philosophic topics, the

delights of peace, false shame, happiness, the pleasures of country life, the praise of the true in the sense in which it is quoted along with the good and beautiful in æsthetic treatises. The seventh epistle was written to Racine, to raise his spirits after the failure that attended the acting of his *Phèdre*. In the twelfth, on the love of God, a vigorous onslaught is made on the teaching of the Jesuits. The *Art poétique*, over which Boileau spent the labour of five years, is an imitation of Horace's *Epistola ad Pisones*. The Latin poet treats of tragedy only, but Boileau extended the scope of his inquiry so as to bring within its compass rules for almost all poetical *genres*. The best lines in the *Art poétique* have become proverbial. When Boileau leaves out of epic poetry subjects belonging to religion or to national history, when he upholds the rule of the three unities, when he views an apparel of mythological phrases as a necessary adornment, and when he shows an utter ignorance of mediæval art, he simply affords conclusive proof that he took his colouring from the society in which he moved while giving it his standards in exchange. *Le Lutrin* relates a quarrel which divided the canons of the Sainte Chapelle. The object of it was the place to be given to a lectern in the Church. The humour here, for it is a piece of classical humour, consists in a manner borrowed from Italy of dealing in the tone of serious epics with a most trifling incident. Boileau held for a long time jointly with Racine the office of *historiographe du roi*. Gloom was cast upon his old age by the miseries of the time and

by deafness.  As a critic he knew thoroughly his own
mind, delivered himself of his judgments with the
utmost deliberation, with great honesty of purpose and
firmness of conviction.  He placed Molière in the first
rank, he upheld Racine's *Phèdre* at a moment when it
met with disfavour.  He declared the excellence of
*Athalie* when it was discredited by the public.  He
followed frankly and openly Descartes in philosophy,
he set the *Provinciales* above every other production,
whether ancient or modern.  He was never weary of
inveighing against exaggeration, against over-refine-
ment in wit, against the excessive adornment of style
and pomposity.

Molière was born in Paris.  He was the son of an
upholsterer, who sold furniture to the general public,
and, by special appointment, to the king.  Later, Molière
succeeded his father in that office, with the difference
that he had no commercial dealings with the public,
and looked after the royal furniture exclusively.  His
studies at the college of Clermont at Paris were most
thorough.  He studied philosophy under Gassendi, who
was a mathematician rather than a metaphysician, and
breathed into him a dislike of Descartes.  At Orleans
the young student took to the law.  At the age of
twenty-three he went off the lines laid down for him,
like so many other young men whose natural literary
propensities are inconsistent with a fixed professional
occupation.  With some money to spend, he turned
an actor, became soon the head of the company which

he joined, and appeared successfully on provincial
stages in the course of a nine years' tour.  When he
went on the stage he replaced his family name, which
was Poquelin, by the acting name under which he
earned his laurels.  His theatrical activity gave itself
vent in three directions at the same time.  He was a
stage actor, the manager of a company, and his own
playwright.  In Lyons he put on the stage *L'Etourdi*,
imitated from the Italian; at Béziers, the *Dépit amou-
reux*, which still bears in some of its parts a perfectly
modern aspect.  In 1658, Molière and his company
settled in Paris once for all.  The king took him under
his protection, may be from a wish to enlist Molière's
comic force as an auxiliary, in the task he had undertaken of correcting the demeanour of his courtiers, and
of the noblemen about his person.  Be this as it may,
Molière set with great fearlessness about the business
of casting ridicule wherever he saw a fair opening for
it.   In the *Précieuses Ridicules* he made a laughing-
stock of the Hôtel de Rambouillet.  In the *Ecole des
Maris*, imitated from the Adelphi of Terence, he puts a
wise and kind discipline in the family circle in contrast
with the evil effects of a stern and harsh one.  In the
*Ecole des Femmes* he shows that ignorance in women
need not mean either innocence or virtue.  In *Don Juan*,
he gives a fresh setting to an old Spanish legend, more
at home in romance than in comedy.  In the *Misanthrope*
he pictures the petty passions, unkindnesses, and back-
bitings of mundane circles.  In the *Tartuffe* he gives a
satire of hypocrisy in such a violent strain that for four
years and a half public performances had to be

suspended. In *George Dandin* he teaches that conjugal happiness cannot be built up on vanity. In *L'Avare* he shows how a miser's vice may undermine family life, and ruin all happiness. In the *Bourgeois Gentilhomme* he punishes the childish vanity of a tradesman who sets about aping his betters. In the *Fourberies de Scapin* he clothes with fresh interest the personage of the *Valet de Comédie*, transferred from Plautus to the modern theatre by the Italians. In *Les Femmes Savantes* he lashes pedantry in women. In the *Malade Imaginaire* he holds up to merriment the folly of malingerers, and dies, for he was on the stage filling the leading part in that last play of his, when he sickened with the illness that snatched him away a few days later from the scene of his triumphs. The Church refused to perform the burial rites over Molière owing to his being an actor. The Academy had not admitted him, and this injustice was not repaired till 1778, when Molière's bust was at last erected in its assembly room. The originality and superiority of Molière is that he was able to paint the men of his time in their true likeness, while setting forth as well the unvarying features of man. The playwright goes entirely out of sight; human nature alone, exhibited in its comic weakness, strikes the eye of the onlooker. He is undoubtedly a moral writer, and a few comic touches of a coarse order which mark his plays here and there should be viewed as forced upon him by theatrical necessities.

RACINE was born in the same part of the country as La Fontaine, was brought up at the College of Beau-

vais, then in the *Petites Ecoles* of Port-Royal, where he
learned Greek, which was better taught there than in
the public schools of the day.  His Jansenistic educators
imparted to him a more liberal training than he could
have received in a Jesuit College; but he did not in
every way do justice to them.  His first poetic attempts
are insignificant when compared with his later performance.  He owed it to Boileau that he was able to
strike without too much hesitation the line of literature
that would suit him best.  His first tragedy, which is
imitated from Euripides, from Seneca, and from Rotrou,
was acted in 1664.  At that time Racine was under the
influence of Corneille.  In his next play, the influence
of Corneille is still visible, and the fact that Racine
was not quite himself may account for the weakness of
those two plays.  At this juncture his bent to tragedy
was exposed to the attacks of his Port-Royal masters,
as well as to the criticism of Corneille.  Racine broke
away from the former, that he might assert his independence, and by throwing off the influence of the
latter he took possession of his own individuality.
From 1667, and in the course of ten years, he produced
seven plays, which are masterpieces of their kind.
*Andromaque*, the first, is full of associations with Homer,
Euripides, Seneca, and Virgil.  *Les Plaideurs*, Racine's
only comedy, is an after-ring of the *Wasps* of Aristophanes, and an amusing satire on judges, lawyers, and
the clients of both.  There is no depth in this comedy,
whereby it is distinguished from the work of Molière;
yet the lightness of its style, combined with the comic

touches, have made it deservedly popular. Racine returned to tragedy with *Britannicus*, in which a page of Roman history is re-written, and a few Roman characters are recast with an admirable combination of modernity and of fidelity to the historian Tacitus. *Bérénice* is usually compared with a play of the same title written by Corneille, at the request of Henrietta of England, who was anxious to see which of the two poets, once they should be at work on the same subject, would win the prize. The subject set by her was too thin to allow Corneille to display his grand manner.

In *Bajazet*, an adventure which had shortly before taken place in Constantinople, supplied the tragic theme. By availing himself of an episode in recent history, Racine was running counter to the classical code. He was driven to say in self-defence that the use in tragedy of events happening at a great distance was hardly less justified than the selection of subjects belonging to a remote period of the past. The same critics who were delighted when they heard his Romans or his Greeks express the sentiments of seventeenth century French nobles discovered that the Turks in *Bajazet* bore no likeness to the Turks of Turkey. This latter criticism is by no means unfair, and goes to show that if the leading playwrights had not so absolutely given in to the prejudices of their critics, and had been bold enough to choose more subjects from modern history, such men as Boileau might have been brought to see the error of their cramping regulations. The sources of *Mithridate* are Greek, like those of the following plays, *Iphigénie* and *Phèdre*, and the subjects which he was reserving for later treatment are Greek also. A part of the public still upheld Corneille as the only legitimate tragic playwright. They endeavoured to break the long line of Racine's triumphs by recommending to public applause the plays put on the stage by some very inferior men. On that account, at the moment when Racine was rising to his highest in *Phèdre*, he lost favour with theatrical audiences. Yielding also to some religious scruples about his right to bring to light again pagan sentiments, and pagan conceptions of the relations of life, he became more amenable to the reproaches with which the Gentlemen of Port-Royal were still pursuing him. He accepted their disapproval of theatrical entertainments. He married; he was less often seen at Court, and hid his shining light in the domestic circle. However, Mme de Maintenon, the grand-daughter of Agrippa d'Aubigné, who was not yet wrapped in the bigotry of her last years, but who was already engaged in bringing back to the Church of Rome the orphan daughters of Protestant noblemen, asked him to compose for her school at St Cyr some sacred plays that girls might act. *Esther* and *Athalie* were the answer to this request. The former of these plays is little more than a charming sketch; the latter is, as a biblical tragedy, for power and sustained beauty, the counterpart of *Phèdre* as a pagan play. Up to this point the favour of Louis XIV. had never failed either Racine or his friend Boileau. It was unfortunate for Racine that his eyes were not completely dazzled by the magnificence of the Court. He felt or saw the depths of misery hidden under the outer trappings of the kingdom, and dared to put before the king a memorandum on behalf of the poor. He had also returned latterly to the Jansenistic opinions impressed upon him in his youth, so that his last days were troubled by the unmistakeable coolness of his sovereign.

If we put on one side Racine's biblical plays, and consider the remaining ones only, he appears as the tragedian of human passions, and especially of the passion of love. He represents no longer, like Corneille, the opposition of the conscience and the heart, the one upholding the moral law, and the other setting up its own rights against it; but he depicts in a way that is interesting rather than elevating the emotional weaknesses of his heroes. The psychological truth attaching to his representation of the human character is universally acknowledged, especially when he depicts women; and however much one may repeat the hackneyed objection that his Greeks and Romans are Frenchmen in disguise, no great store should be set by this criticism. Such faults do not depend on a writer, —they are forced upon him by the people he writes for. Racine had to please a certain circle; he had but one audience to appeal to, and Shakespeare would have been as much out of place at the French Court in the palmy days of Louis XIV. as Racine would have been in

England under Elizabeth.   Taken up with the current ideas as to avoiding in the *style noble* words of ordinary everyday speech, he used periphrases to an extent that became an excess in his imitators.

REGNARD is the only one among Molière's successors who recalls to any great extent the qualities of the master.   His venturesome youth took him from Paris to Algiers, where he was a slave, and from Algiers to Lapland, where he stood on the North Cape.   Having become wealthy, he indulged in leisure, took a fancy to the theatre, and had some small pieces acted, which were well received.   Of his more ambitious flights the *Joueur*, autobiographical to some extent, and the *Légataire Universel* are the best.   In 1705 Regnard translated, with more or less fidelity, the *Ménechmes* of Plautus, a comedy of errors based on the likeness of twins.

LA ROCHEFOUCAULD.   This writer was a scion of one of the noblest families in France.   His high birth called him to a career of arms.   He was a soldier before his sixteenth year.   The earlier part of his life was spent in idle political intrigues.   He belonged to that part of the aristocracy which resisted the gradual formation of the king's autocratic power under the reign of Louis XIII., and during the minority of Louis XIV.   Having beheld the ruin of his cause in the not very serious civil war known as La Fronde, being himself ruined and unwell, and doomed to find no favour with the now absolute king, he hid himself away for ten years and wrote his *Mémoires.* When he was fifty years old he re-appeared in the world, in the drawing-rooms where some belated *précieuses* of a milder type than the set castigated by Molière were engaged in the coining of moral maxims as a means of whiling away their time and sharpening their wit. La Rochefoucauld was prepared by the bitterness of his personal experience and by his personal predisposition to play seriously his part in what was for the others an entertainment. During ten years he was at work on his *Maximes,* which he submitted in their various stages and shapes to the criticism of his exacting audience. The fundamental thought of this work is, that man, in his actions as well as in his feelings, is moved by the love of self, however self-sacrificing he may imagine himself to be. A fair clue to the tone of the whole book is given in the following maxim :—' Les vertus se perdent dans l'intérêt comme les fleuves dans l'océan.'

BOSSUET issued from a family of the *bourgeoisie* in Dijon, did not become a magistrate like his forebears, but became an ecclesiastic. He received a thorough education from the Jesuits in his native town, and was sent to the Navarre College in Paris, where he was ordained a priest. Then he spent five years in Metz, engaged in serious private study, and in mission work among the Protestants. He gave in his early youth fore-glimmerings of his talent as a preacher. The specimen sermon which he delivered at a late evening

party in the Hôtel de Rambouillet, without preparation,
is often alluded to. Most of his sermons were given
before the Court in the hearing of the king, but they
were not published during Bossuet's lifetime. Two
hundred sermons in the rough were found among his
manuscripts after his death. These are comparatively
early ones; later, Bossuet ceased even to write fresh
notes, and simply joined, during the process of actual
delivery, fresh thoughts to his stock of old material.
An obvious consequence of Bossuet's office as Court
preacher was that he delivered obituary addresses at
the death of persons of note. His most famous *Oraisons
funèbres* are on the Queen of England, Henrietta Maria,
who was the aunt of Louis XIV., on the daughter of
that Queen, known in France as Henriette d'Angleterre,
and on Condé. This last is his masterpiece, deriving
as it does, by most skilful artifice, its literary aspect
from the military life of that general, so that it may
fitly be characterised as a 'dead march,' giving to the
second word of this expression its fullest literal meaning. From 1670 to 1683 Bossuet's energies were mainly
taken up in educating the Dauphin, son of Louis XIV.
He wrote several works for that young man; he set
before him his views as to what the government of a
State and right kingship should be. Bossuet's ideas,
rooted in the close reading of Jewish history, fell in
with the well-known principle of the divine right of
kings. The *Discours sur l'Histoire Universelle*, too, is
an outcome of Bossuet's educational labours. It de-
velops the idea that the hand of God is ever present in

human affairs, and shows great power in the philosophical handling of historic matter, a method almost new to the times, and in which imagination is tightly curbed by reason. There are some things in Montesquieu's *Considérations sur les Causes de la Grandeur et de la Décadence des Romains* which are clearly related to Bossuet's *Histoire Universelle.* In spite of his commanding intellect the eminent tutor did not succeed in intellectualising the heir to the French Crown. As for an actual liberalising of the boy's mind, with a view to successful government in an age that was to be fond of liberalism, neither the king nor Bossuet entertained any such intention. The Dauphin preceded Louis XIV. into the grave. Whatever judgment we may pass on Bossuet's pedagogy, he was duly rewarded for it by the gift of a bishopric. His power ruled steadily in Church and in State. Some leading Protestants were brought back to Rome by the reading of his proselytising treatises. However, Bossuet was too good a patriot to be an unreserved papist. His name is connected with the claim for the liberties of the Church of France, and with the upholding of Cartesian philosophy against the Jesuits. He is also the author of some works of practical piety, tinged with mysticism. His *Histoire des Variations des Eglises Protestantes* belongs to the year 1688, and ranks high among his very numerous controversial works; for Bossuet, far from dwelling in a serene atmosphere, was hotly engaged in every dispute of importance. He began a long controversy with Fénelon in the matter of quietism (the name given to the doctrine that one may lose the consciousness of self in the possession of the love of God). The attitude taken up by Bossuet was grounded on reason and practical good sense. Unfortunately, he showed in this quarrel the intolerance which, added to his failure in education, to his adulation of the King, and to his countenancing extreme measures against the Protestant minority, proves him to have been less endowed with wisdom than with energy.

La Bruyère was a Parisian who obtained early some lucrative offices in the provinces, which he could hold without leaving Paris. He became the teacher of the grandson of Condé in the historical and philosophical branches of knowledge. Seventeen out of the twenty letters by him which have reached us were addressed to his pupil's father, and bear upon this educational trust. La Bruyère remained attached to the house of Condé. He moved about that household as a man of the world, and used to the full his opportunities for observation. The first indication of his aptitude for a literary caricature of manners and morals was given in a translation: *Les Caractères de Théophraste, avec les Caractères ou les Mœurs de ce Siècle.* The work was indeed in its first shape a discreet rendering of Theophrastus' moral sketches; but the temptation to develop it into a malicious portraiture of the men and women he met got the better of the writer, who, luckily for posterity, had it in him to do so in a masterly way. From the first edition to the eighth, La Bruyère's gallery of contemporary characters, somewhat generalised in the names given to them, and coloured beyond recognition by an excessive literary treatment, grew from 420 sketches till it contained 1120. An enormous success attended the publication of this work. Drawing-room folks in Paris and all over the provinces sought intently in it for the likenesses of their friends. 'I return to the public what the public lent me,' says La Bruyère in his preface. 'I have received from it alone the material for this work. It may now examine at leisure its own image taken from nature.'

FÉNELON is among the late comers in the generation which adorned the *Siècle de Louis Quatorze.* Bossuet's junior by twenty-four years, he was descended from a noble family in the south-west of France. He studied at Cahors, and then at Paris at the Duplessis College and in the Saint-Sulpice Seminary. His life runs in many respects counter or parallel to that of Bossuet. Like him, he looked after the souls of the Protestant dissenters in the earlier days of his priesthood, while writing for a lady his *Traité de l'Education des Filles.* in which he gives vent to some liberal ideas, though on the whole still encompassed with the prejudices of those times in the matter of the education of girls. His sermons, excellent though they were, have not been handed down to us like those of Bossuet, for he carried still further than his rival the practice of skeleton notes or no notes at all. In 1689 Fénelon was appointed tutor to the young Duc de Bourgogne,

grandson of Louis XIV., and son of Bossuet's pupil.  He
abandoned then the missionary work which he had been
carrying on in the south-west, in a more liberal spirit
than Bossuet would have approved of, but still with
none of the tolerance that public opinion would have
enforced in our days.  Fénelon's educational charge
was not so hopeless as that of Bossuet, who had to deal
with a dullard, while the faults of Fénelon's pupil were
of an exactly opposite kind.  The Duc de Bourgogne
did not require stimulating.  What he demanded was
the application of the curb with a firm and yet kind
hand, such as would be required in the case of a too
fiery steed.  Fénelon applied to him a watchful and
exclusively moral method, in which authority went for
very little and respect for a very great deal.  He wrote
for him among other works his *Télémaque*.  The book
is a string of noble moral lessons, stitched together
with a somewhat monotonous but truly Hellenic grace
on a canvas of romance.  The ideal king shadowed
forth in those pages casts a very severe side-light upon
Louis XIV., and Fénelon had soon to suffer for his conscientious boldness.  He was summarily removed to an
Archbishop's see in Cambrai before he had completed
the education of his pupil.  That was in 1695.  The
dispute already alluded to on the doctrine of the complete resignation of self to the love of God brought
Fénelon into further difficulty.  Some of the propositions upheld by the Archbishop of Cambrai in his
*Explication des Maximes des Saints* had been condemned
by the Holy See.  Bossuet started at once on the war-

path to check the revival under Fénelon's patronage of a heresy in mysticism. Fénelon disarmed the Pope by a formal surrender. Louis XIV. showed himself sterner, for the *Télémaque* came out of a Dutch press in a complete shape at a moment when Louis XIV.'s practice was more than ever different from Fénelon's presentment of the duty of kings. It was an evil fate indeed which appeared to pursue Fénelon. The Duc de Bourgogne, like his father, preceded his grandfather to the grave. Fénelon, whose hope of obtaining influence in the government centred in him, baffled in his last expectation, died three years later. One of his very last works had been a letter addressed to M. Dacier on the occupations of the French Academy. He bewailed therein the impoverishment of the language by the excessive weeding out of words; he sighed over the disrepute into which had fallen Marot and Amyot; he regretted that the heart of poetry had gone out of French verse, whose formalism dried up the springs of inspiration. He recommended that freedom to create new words should be restored by common consent, provided these words were clear in their meaning and harmonious in their ring. Fénelon's *Lettres Spirituelles* came to light only after his death. He sets therein the example of fresh coinage in the word *désappropriation*, whereby he defines the state of self-surrender to God that lay at the bottom of his doctrine on quietism. Fénelon, along with Racine and André Chénier, represents a pure stream, so far as poetical style is concerned, of sweet Greek inspiration. He was picked out by the philosophic writers of the latter part of the eighteenth century, and by some critics of so-called 'romantic' views as a harbinger of their theories.

MADAME DE SÉVIGNÉ was born in Paris. She was left an orphan when she reached her sixth year, and taken in charge by her grandfather, and later by her uncle. Ménage, who ranked with Vaugelas as a grammatical authority on language, taught her Spanish, Italian, and Latin. She was early presented at the Court of Louis XIV.'s mother, where her wit and personal accomplishments won general favour. She was married at eighteen to a nobleman, who fell in a duel seven years later. The early years of her widowhood were spent in educating her two children. Then she appeared once more at Court, and took up her literary headquarters at the Hôtel de Rambouillet. In 1669 her daughter was married to M. de Grignan, the King's Lord-lieutenant in Provence. For the ensuing twenty-seven years letters passed generally at the rate of one a week between the mother in Paris and the daughter in Provence. Madame de Sévigné's manner of letter-writing is a complete innovation on that of Voiture and Balzac. She does not write to show her quality of mind or her wit. She writes because she has to tell her daughter, whom she loves, something that will interest her. So the wit, coming into the bargain as it were, is of the most charming kind. Her letters are brimful of particulars on all passing events or incidents. She records impartially great and small things, and hands them down to us in all their freshness, with the additional light which her independent judgment throws upon them. Serious when gravity is becoming, playful in trifling matters, reasonable when reason is demanded, and almost always fair in her appreciations, she is, all the same, sometimes as cruel as a thoughtless woman of the world can be. Her leanings in philosophy and morals were towards the Jansenists and the Cartesians. Her fidelity to Fouquet in his disgrace, and her friendship with La Rochefoucauld, show that she did not always take her cue from the Court circles.

MADAME DE MAINTENON ranks in point of time next to Madame de Sévigné as a letter-writer. She was born in the prison in which her father, Constant d'Aubigné, son of Agrippa d'Aubigné, had been confined on an accusation of high-felony. His daughter followed him to La Martinique, in the French West Indies, on his release. Left an orphan at the age of six, she was taken away from her aunt and put in the hands of a zealous Roman Catholic lady. The priests set about converting her to Roman Catholicism. Being a girl of spirit, she gave them a deal of trouble, and said once with the impetuosity of a true grand-daughter of Agrippa d'Aubigné: 'You know more than I do, but here is a book' (pointing to the Bible) 'which knows better than you. This book does not say what you say, and that is why you won't let people read it.' At eighteen she found herself the unwilling bride of the sick and ailing Scarron, who was her elder by twenty-five years. Seven years later she was a widow, and, having gradually forgotten the associations of her youth, she was thought fit to be entrusted with the education of the children of the king in their tenderest years. She received as a reward the title of Marchioness. Then, after the death of the Queen Marie Thérèse, it fell to her lot, wonderful to say, to become the wife of the king of France himself. It is only too clear that not a shred of Protestantism had survived in her. She meddled disastrously with State affairs. The Edict of Nantes, granted by Henry IV. in favour of the Protestants, was not repealed without her full consent. With formalism in literature, there coincides with her queenly position at Court formalism in morals, consequent upon the vogue of formalism in manners. She founded in 1684, at the village of Saint-Cyr, her famous school for young girls of noble birth. But for the proselytising character of the education given there, the Saint-Cyr school could be described, without reservation, as an institution doing the greatest credit to its founder. The school was for many years her favourite occupation, object of affection, and retreat from the worries of Court life. Her letters are more substantial and less sprightly than Madame de Sévigné's. She writes in a tone of responsibility, and shows a concern about moral points that betokens a serious and reasonable disposition.

MADAME DE LA FAYETTE counted among her most faithful friends Madame de Sévigné, the Duc de La

Rochefoucauld, author of the *Maximes*, and the sister of
Charles II., Henrietta, known under the title of Madame,
Duchesse d'Orléans.   She did not sign her own writings,
but there is no doubt that the famous short novel *La
Princesse de Clèves* is her work.   It marks a new
departure in novel-writing, a change from the complica-
tion and affectation of Mademoiselle de Scudéry's style,
and an approach to the genuine simplicity, the unvarnished directness of expression, wanted to raise
novels to the level of the best literature of that time.

# CHAPTER VII.

## A CHRONOLOGICAL TABLE OF THE EIGHTEENTH CENTURY WRITERS.

As we have already done to some extent in the preceding chapters, we include in this Table a certain number of writers whose works rank in the history of the general development of French literature, but who are not sufficiently representative to receive a distinct notice of their own in a review of such a limited compass as this.

### *Miscellaneous Verse.*

JEAN-BAPTISTE ROUSSEAU (1670 - 1741): *Odes, cantates, épîtres, épigrammes.*

LOUIS RACINE (1692-1763), son of Jean Racine: *La Religion*, a didactic poem ; *odes, épîtres.*

VOLTAIRE (1694-1778): *La Henriade*, a formal epic. *Odes, épîtres, satires, épigrammes.*

GRESSET (1709-1777): *Vert-Vert*, a witty pleasantry in verse.

GILBERT (1751-1780): *Adieux du poète à la vie.*

ANDRIEUX (1759-1833): *Contes*, in verse (*Le Meunier de Sans Souci*).

ANDRÉ CHÉNIER (1762-1794): Lyrical poems.

JOSEPH CHÉNIER (1764-1811): *Odes, hymnes, épîtres, satires.*

## Dramatic Art.

PIRON (1689-1773) : *La Métromanie*, a comedy.

VOLTAIRE (1694-1778) :—

Tragedies –
  *Oedipe ; Brutus ; Zaïre ; Mahomet ; Mérope ; Sémiramis ; Oreste ; Rome sauvée ; Tancrède.*

Comedies—
  *Les Originaux ; Nanine.*

GRESSET (1709-1777) : *Le Méchant*, a comedy.

DIDEROT (1713-1784): Dramas—*Le Fils Naturel ; Le Père de famille.*

SEDAINE (1719-1797): Comedies—*Le Philosophe sans le savoir ; La Gageure imprévue.*

BEAUMARCHAIS (1732-1799): Comedies—*Le Barbier de Séville ; Le Mariage de Figaro.*

DUCIS (1733-1816): Tragedies after Shakespeare (*Hamlet, Roméo et Juliette, le Roi Lear, Macbeth, Othello*).


## History, Memoirs.

ROLLIN (1661-1741) : *Histoire ancienne ; Histoire romaine.*

SAINT-SIMON, DUC DE (1675-1755) : *Mémoires.*

MADEMOISELLE DELAUNAY (1693-1750): *Mémoires.*

VOLTAIRE (1694-1778): *Vie de Charles XII., Roi de Suède ; Siècle de Louis XIV. ; Histoire de la Russie sous Pierre I<sup>er</sup>.*

J.-J. ROUSSEAU (1712-1778): *Confessions.*

BEAUMARCHAIS (1732-1799): *Mémoires.*


## Fiction.

LE SAGE (1668-1747) : *Le Diable Boiteux*, a satirical novel ; *Histoire de Gil Blas de Santillane.*

MARIVAUX (1688-1763) : *Marianne*, a novel.

VOLTAIRE (1694-1778) : Novels ( *Zadig, Jeannot et Collin, etc.*)

PRÉVOST (1697-1763) : *Manon Lescaut*, a novel.

J.-J. ROUSSEAU (1712-1778) *La Nouvelle Héloïse*, a novel.

MARMONTEL (1723-1799) : *Bélisaire ; Contes moraux.*

BERNARDIN DE ST.-PIERRE (1737-1814) : *Paul et Virginie ; La Chaumière indienne.*

### Oratory.

MASSILLON (1663-1742) : *Sermons* (Petit Carême) ; *Oraisons funèbres.*

MIRABEAU (1749-1791) : *Discours* (in the Constituent Assembly).

### Politics, Philosophy, Science.

MONTESQUIEU (1689-1755) : *Lettres persanes,* a satirical work ; *Considérations sur les causes de la grandeur des Romains et de leur décadence ; Esprit des lois.*

VOLTAIRE (1694-1778) : *Essai sur les moeurs et l'esprit des nations ; Dictionnaire Philosophique.*

BUFFON (1707-1788) : *Epoques de la nature ; Histoire naturelle.*

J.-J. ROUSSEAU (1712-1778) : *Du Contrat social ; Emile.*

VAUVENARGUES (1715-1747) : *Maximes.*

DIDEROT (1713-1784) : *Pensées philosophiques ; Lettre sur les aveugles.*

*Les Philosophes*: DIDEROT and D'ALEMBERT (1717-1783), chief editors of the *Encyclopédie* ; with the assistance of Voltaire, Buffon, Montesquieu, Condillac, Duclos, Turgot, Helvétius, d'Holbach, Necker, Marmontel, Raynal, Grimm, etc.

*L'Encyclopédie.*

DUC DE SAINT-SIMON.—This writer of voluminous memoirs, whose life extended far into the eighteenth century, may be considered as a belated representative of Louis XIV.'s age, for his interest and his writings are totally disconnected from the subjects in debate in the bulk of the eighteenth century literature. His father had been made a Duke and a Peer of the Realm by Louis XIII., and filled his son with a sense of the great honour due to their common dignity. Saint-Simon distinguished himself in several campaigns, but having been neglected in the distribution of military honours in 1702,

he was so wounded in his vanity that he resigned his
commission. This instance of pride was the beginning
of his disgrace with Louis XIV., who, while treating him
with every consideration, did not entrust him with any
office either at Court or in public affairs. Saint-Simon's
pet grievance was, that the illegitimate sons of Louis
XIV. had come to rank as Princes of the blood, and took,
therefore, precedence of Dukes. His joy was boundless
when, after the death of Louis XIV., an Edict of the
*Parlement de Paris* cancelled their royal status. During
the minority of Louis XIV.'s successor, a six-year-old
child, he was a member of the Regent's Council, but his
stubbornness in upholding the rights of the aristocracy
to the Government of the State met with such successful opposition that he thought fit to leave for a
while the scene of his struggles, and accepted the office
of ambassador at the Court of Madrid. So far as his
political opinions are concerned, he might well have
been one of the French nobles, whose curbing required
the strong hand of Richelieu, or one of that comparatively liberal aristocracy to which, if Fénelon's
ideas had ever been carried out, the principal place
would have been granted in the Government of France.
One of his sayings is, 'Tout pour le peuple, mais rien
par le peuple.' Saint-Simon has his place marked in
that limited number of French noblemen who, from the
Renaissance to the brink of the Revolution, showed
themselves at once exclusive in temperament and
liberal in the disposition of their minds, and without
whose complicity the first steps towards the Revolution

could not have been taken.  After the death of the Regent in 1723, Saint-Simon withdrew from the Court, and spent the last thirty-two years of his life in putting together his Memoirs.  These became the property of the State at his death, and the general public did not obtain possession of them till 1856.  The Memoirs were personal at the outset; then they became a history of the Court of France, and of the times.  The style is that of a man who is in a great hurry to put into words what his passion dictates, so that they are wanting in method, in orderliness, and in every cool study of the facts. But, for dash of style, for flashes of light springing up suddenly as from a dark cloud of phraseology, Saint-Simon is inimitable.  He is sometimes compared with the Cardinal de Retz, who wrote, from a standpoint which would, no doubt, have been that of Saint-Simon himself, an account of the civil war, *La Fronde*, waged by the nobles against Mazarin.

MARIVAUX belonged to Normandy.  He wrote some comedies of a peculiar kind, and, in absence of a fit name in the language that could describe his manner, the word *Marivaudage* was coined in his honour.  It was after him applied to describe any style in comedy or novel-writing in which the analysis of sentiment in its most subtle and shadowy manifestations is the object of the writer.  Nearer to our days Alfred de Musset, in his *Proverbes*, revealed himself in this art as a master superior to Marivaux, for he was a man of deeper perception, and combined with the play of wit a simpler and more psychological art. Marivaux's novel, *Marianne*, is still better known than his comedies.

MLLE DELAUNAY has left some interesting *Mémoires* about herself. She never knew her father, who fled to England for political reasons. She was brought up in a convent at Rouen, and extended her studies privately beyond the compass filled by the instructions she received from the nuns. She entered the household of the Duchesse du Maine as chamber-maid, and won much attention by her wit and good-sense. She was shut up for two years in the famous Paris prison, La Bastille, under the accusation of being implicated in a political conspiracy. After refusing several suitors, she accepted as a husband the Baron de Staal, a Swiss officer. That is why she is known to literature also under the name of Madame de Staal-Delaunay, which causes her to be sometimes confused with the famous Madame de Staël-Holstein, who lived at a later period. Her Memoirs deal especially with the last years of the reign of Louis XIV., and she is at her best when she relates the episodes of her private life, and shows in an ironical light the social comedies acted around her. The portrait she draws of the governor of La Bastille, who died of love for her, shows her talent at its best.

LE SAGE, the novelist and playwright, born near the town of Vannes, and sometimes mistaken for a Genevese writer of the same name, was educated by the Jesuits. An orphan in early years, he suffered greatly

in his worldly estate through the dishonesty of his
guardian. For many years he kept poverty at bay by
hard work; and when he was in mature years, having
in the interval stored his mind with a thorough knowledge of the world, he used his acquaintance with
Spanish literature to gain an access to a theatrical
career. His first original composition was *Crispin
rival de son maître.* The *Diable boiteux* appeared in
the same year and met with a stupendous reception.
This is the first book of 'gibes, flouts, and sneers,'
aimed at the excesses, abuses and misrule of the time;
a kind of political satire which the popular favour
made it impossible for the State to suppress, and
which, in the hands of Beaumarchais, was to become
a formidable instrument. Le Sage's next work in the
same vein is *Turcaret,* a comedy in which there does
not appear a single honest man, and in which the
scandals of farming out taxes to gatherers are shown
up in the fiercest light, with but a thin veil thrown
over the identity of the personages alluded to. Le
Sage was stopped in his theatrical career by falling
out with the actors of the leading theatres. He turned
his back upon them to become again a novelist. His
masterpiece in this capacity is *L'Histoire de Gil Blas
de Santillane.* A satire on human nature, and more
particularly on French ways and manners, is the
purpose of this book. The scene of it is laid in
Spain, a favourite device with the Frenchmen who
wished to read their countrymen a moral lesson. The
hero starting from most humble beginnings is made to

rise through many adventures from office to office
and from place to place, till he is allowed to end his
life in comfortable retirement. *Gil Blas* stands in the
literary lineage from which Beaumarchais' *Figaro* is
descended.

PRÉVOST. This Abbé, who rejoiced in a passionate
and romantic imagination, stands in contrast to Le Sage,
the calm and almost judicial observer of human faults.
Prévost was alternately a soldier and a monk. From
the monastery he fled to Holland, thence to London,
where he made a living by writing. Seven years later
we find him again in holy orders, and chaplain to the
Prince de Conti. One day he fainted in the forest of
Chantilly. He was taken for dead, and the surgeons
set about cutting up his body. He awoke under the
knife, only in time to die from the wound he had
received. He translated into French the novels of
Richardson, a fact of some literary importance when
taken in connection with the vogue which Richardson
enjoyed in France. His best known production is the
short novel of *Manon Lescaut*, a love story of an irregular
kind, in which Richardson's influence accounts for certain features. *La Princesse de Clèves, Marianne*, and
*Manon Lescaut* are three important landmarks in the
history of the modern novel before Rousseau.

VAUVENARGUES. This sympathetic moralist, born at
Aix in Provence, died at the early age of thirty-two.
He returned broken in health from his campaigns in

Germany, and wished to exchange arms for diplomacy. Unluckily he was taken ill with smallpox, and his hopes of an official life vanished. There appeared one year before his death his *Introduction à la connaissance de l'esprit humain suivie de Réflexions et de Maximes.* This is a storehouse of personal observations and of detached thoughts on the faculties of the mind, on passions, virtues, and vices. A collection of over six hundred maxims follows. He appears to have taken up moral subjects in the consciousness that La Rochefoucauld had written before him, and that there was room, in the same field of thought, for some oppositional writing. 'Why should our virtues be only vices in disguise?' he exclaims; 'Is virtue less profitable because one enjoys practising it? Is it on that account of less value to the world, or less different from vice which is the ruin of the human kind? Does goodness change its nature and cease to be good from the moment I delight in it?' Vauvenargues is most unlike Voltaire. These two men were none the less fast friends, and when the younger one was cut off in his prime, before giving the full measure of his noble seriousness, Voltaire was loud in the praise of the moralist whom he loved, admired, and respected. Vauvenargues was not the object of much notice during his lifetime. His contemporaries, with minds steeped in materialism and scepticism, kept their backs turned upon this stoic and idealistic writer, who was wanting in the rhetorical power that might have called their attention to him.

GILBERT is a poet whom the critics of this century have fondly drawn to themselves from among the eighteenth century poets as the only example of a true lyrical inspiration. There is no doubt that the vicissitudes of his existence had a great deal to do with the colour of his work. Having failed in a poetical competition in 1772, a pre-disposition to bitterness became more intense, and sought an outlet in poems that were too subjective to meet with success in an impersonal age. He sided against the so-called philosophic movement, and was at length lucky enough to enter the promised land of pension. He fell from a horse at the age of twenty-nine, and died from the shock he received. The sympathy aroused by the true ring of his personal pathos has been as a forcing-house for tales of persecution, abandonment, and misery that have gathered about the facts he has stated; and they have been crystallised once for all in Alfred de Vigny's *Stello.* Gilbert's *Ode imitée de plusieurs psaumes,* composed on his death-bed, is quoted in every collection of French poetical masterpieces, and its few lines are, indeed, worth more than all the so-called lyrical verses that were written from the middle of the seventeenth century to the last years of the eighteenth.

BUFFON was the son of a councillor at the Parlement de Dijon in Burgundy. His literary and mathematical studies were sound, and he travelled in France and Italy with the young Duke of Kingston. He began to be known in scientific circles by some translations from

Newton and by papers on scientific points. Having been made a Member of the Academy of Sciences and Director of the King's Garden, he was able to pursue his favourite study, natural history, and to publish in favourable circumstances the first three volumes of his *Histoire Naturelle.* This work, on which he was to spend forty years of his life, and to employ the help of many assistants, was never completed. Buffon is one of those men of science who are entitled by right to a place in literature. His work opens with a general description of the earth, followed by an account of minerals, of mammals, of birds, and of fishes. In 1776 Buffon published his *Epoques de la Nature,* in which a theory is given of the changes undergone by the earth in the course of the past centuries. By this book, Buffon may be considered to be the forerunner of Cuvier, and to have suggested the modern sciences of palæontology and geology. In fact, he is the first distinguished member of a class of scientific investigators, more numerous in France than anywhere else, men who combine with first-rate scientific attainments an ability to put the result of their research before the general public in language that it can understand and admire. Buffon's famous *Discours sur le Style* has nothing whatever to do with natural science unless it be to prove that, in the opinion of the writer himself, scientific attainments are insufficient in themselves to secure fame for their possessor. 'Ideas,' he says, 'are the property of all, but style the property of but a few, and those few hold the birthright to reputation. The form given to one's thoughts is alone individual, that is what belongs to the man.' This opinion is generally expressed in the aphorism, 'Le style c'est l'homme,' though Buffon did not quite put it in this shape. The great change that has now taken place in the relation of science to literature, to the advantage of the former, makes it no longer so necessary as in Buffon's time that a student of science in order to become popular should be literary.

DIDEROT was a very discursive and prolific writer. He opens up that period of French literature which immediately preceded the Revolution, and in which new political and philosophical ideas were scattered abroad with more profusion than ever. He was acquainted with the wretchedness of a life of adventure, and only escaped from dire poverty by becoming a hanger-on to those in high places who cared to encourage his views or reward his remarkable talent. He gave evidence in his very first works of the peculiarity of his mind. His pen produced the most cynical novels, while writing treatises on merit and virtue in the Plutarchian manner. He combined the moral unscrupulousness which had grown forth from deep-seated social disorders with the emotional sensibility which then forced itself upon the minds of men by a natural reaction. Diderot was an agitator in every department of philosophic thought, and in that of literary criticism as well. His *Pensées philosophiques* were condemned to be burned by the Parliament of Paris. He was shut up

in the Vincennes prison for his *Lettre sur les aveugles.*
Then began his long connection with the *Encyclopédie*,
for which he wrote articles on philosophy, on æsthetics,
and on the technical arts. The publication of this work
was twice interrupted by the Government, and the
second time Catherine of Russia offered Diderot protection at her Court. On hearing later that he was
about to sell his library under the pressure of poverty,
she bought it from him and graciously appointed him
its keeper at a fixed salary. Diderot endeavoured to
rescue French tragedy from the dry formalism into
which it had fallen, but his plays, which he called
*drames* to distinguish them from the traditional classical
models, are the work of a critic rather than that of a
man of genius. In spite of his well-meant efforts to
hold the mirror up to nature, they are clearly the work
of a philosophic writer who cannot resist the temptation of winning through them a hearing for his ideas.
Diderot was not a direct student of nature, but he
had a rare gift of reflection on the results of scientific
research, and, in his fragmentary attempts at building
up a philosophy of natural science, he comes very near
the modern ideas on evolution and transformism. His
*salons*, an account of the picture exhibitions held in
Paris, laid the basis for a new criticism of the pictorial
art. In short, Diderot has contributed original views
in most branches that appertain to the intellectual
activity of man, and his power of investing old subjects
with fresh interest bore fruit.

L'ENCYCLOPÉDIE, as suggested by its name, is a vast collection of articles on sciences, arts, and trades, for the purpose of handing down to ensuing generations all the discoveries of the past. The plan is due to Diderot, who had translated from English *Chambers' Encyclopædia*, then in its first shape. D'Alembert was entrusted with the preface to the new venture. It was started in 1746, and brought to a conclusion in 1777, after two breaks of uneven length. Writers of note were invited to contribute to it, but as the book was to bear a distinct trade mark, that of the *philosophes*, and was intended in the first place to scatter abroad their own ideas, the assistance offered by such bodies as the Jesuits and the group of Jansenistic thinkers was declined. The whole work extends to thirty-five volumes in folio. It represents explicitly the tendency of the times—a tendency which the State endeavoured in vain to curb by the material means of restraint at its disposal, and which was carried everywhere by intellectual, and, if we may say so, by spiritual agencies of the same nature as those to which socialism owes its spread nowadays. The Encyclopedists were unable for fear of imprisonment to substitute in this book their individual doctrines for the official ones placed under the guardianship of the State. But they managed to introduce their own divergent views alongside the orthodox ones at such length and with such force that their purpose was fully attained. Their philosophy is greatly derived from that of Locke; and public opinion, then divorced from the public

powers, being with them, they could not be smothered.
They encouraged no novelty in matters of literary
taste.

BERNARDIN DE ST.-PIERRE.   This author, a poet who
wrote in prose, might be called the small Rousseau.
The emotional sensibility alluded to in speaking of
Diderot had full possession of this writer, whose
opinions are, however, totally different from those of
the *philosophes*, being partly derived from Rousseau and
not out of touch with Buffon.   He was born at Le
Hâvre, studied at Caen and at Rouen, entered the
Government's engineering college, and joined the corps
of engineers.   He was doing in that capacity military
service in Germany when he was embroiled with his
chiefs by his susceptibility.   He was dismissed from
their employment.   This threw him upon the world in
search of an occupation.   Full of Utopian ideas, he
went to Russia and planned a model colony on the
shores of the Caspian Sea.   Baffled in the realisation of
this dream, he is found next in Poland, then in Saxony,
then again in France, where he set about writing an
account of the countries he had visited.   In 1768 he
lands in Ile de France (now an English colony, Mauri-
tius), having in his pocket a commission as captain of
engineers.   His stay in this island was a turning-point
in his career, for the faults in character which unfitted
him for practical life were of a kind that may be
turned to account in a literary life.   On his return he
published his *Voyage à l'Ile de France* in the shape of
letters written to a friend, and where he revealed him-

self as a gifted landscape painter with a dash of the imperishable social reformer that was in him. By that time he had formed his famous friendship with J.-J. Rousseau, with whom he held many points in common, being like him a passionate admirer of nature, leading like him a wandering and unsettled life, being unfit like him to meet successfully the struggle for existence, being like him full of whims, and burdened like him with a morbid distrust of his fellow-creatures. *Les Etudes de la Nature* brought Bernardin a step further forward in the temple of fame. In direct opposition to Voltaire and Diderot, Bernardin set about the work of bringing his contemporaries back to God and nature. Whether they answered his call or not, the fact remains that his studies of nature met with universal admiration. In the fourth volume was contained the charming story of *Paul et Virginie*, which had soon to be printed separately, and has been ever since a favourite piece of reading among young people. The *Chaumière indienne* was not written with the same guilelessness as *Paul et Virginie*. It relates the journey to India of an English scholar sent by the Royal Society of London to seek an answer to a whole budget of questions. The scholar goes to the pagoda in Benares to question the chief of the Brahmins. There is a decided irony in all that part of the book, but Bernardin returns to his romantic vein in the description of the hut and family life of the Pariah. Bernardin filled in the *Jardin du roi* the place which had been Buffon's at an earlier date.

BEAUMARCHAIS was the son of a watchmaker, and for

some time carried on that trade himself.  He studied
music in his spare hours, and by his skill in this pursuit
he succeeded in becoming the manager of the entertainments given by the daughters of Louis xv.  Being
by another side of his nature fitted for financial jobbing,
he dabbled in various affairs, and soon became rich
enough to buy letters patent of nobility.  In 1764 he
went to Madrid to rescue his sister from the hands
of a Spanish adventurer, into whose power she had
unwarily fallen.  This episode shows that he took
seriously his brotherly duties, and is related in the most
dramatic part of his Memoirs.  This incident of real
life was worked up into a play by Goethe.  A result of
Beaumarchais' dealings with bankers was litigation.
Beaumarchais, who was admirably able to gauge the
morality of the magistrates of his time, sought to
reach Councillor Goëzman by presenting his wife with
several thousand francs, a gold watch, and fifteen
sovereigns.  The matter becoming further complicated,
Beaumarchais thought he had a fine opportunity of
showing up all the bribery and corruption connected
with the successive stages of his lawsuit.  He brought
out then his *Mémoires*, in which the Parliament of Paris,
known as the Parlement Maupeou (from the name of
the Chancellor for the time), is torn to pieces with a
ruthless hand.  Once engaged upon this work of vindi-
cation, in which public opinion was ready to side with
him, though he hardly deserved more respect himself
than his victims, Beaumarchais proceeded to write his
two famous comedies: the *Barbier de Séville* and the

*Mariage de Figaro.* Like Le Sage, Beaumarchais applied to Spain for suitable representations of his own countrymen. Figaro is emblematic of the lower French middle class, with its turn for social adventure, its careless and cheerful wit, its skill and resource, the perseverance it hides under frivolous appearances, and its aptness to succeed in the struggle for existence. Figaro was all things before being a barber, a veterinary surgeon in a stud, a professional inventor of puzzles and riddles, of madrigals and of unsuccessful plays. Then, over-whelmed with debts and weary of a fruitless penman-ship, he makes lather, that he may make fun of everything, for fear of being compelled to weep. He is a master-hand at intrigue. The curiosity of the public was whetted to the highest degree by the boldness of these plays. When the author sought leave to put them on the stage, noblemen, though belonging to a class that was most bitterly shown up by Beaumarchais, supported his application. The *Barbier* was acted in Paris, and had more than a hundred nights' run. When the Revolution, the floodgates of which he had con-tributed to open, was in full flow, his old connection with the Court, and with the governing classes, brought him into danger. He sought refuge in London, and in Hamburg, and came back to die in Paris when the turmoil had quieted down.

MIRABEAU is the first political orator properly so called that we meet in the history of French literature. There had been some eloquence of that kind in the days of the Renaissance and of the Reformation, but it had completely subsided during the period of absolute kingship. Not so much because the discussion of political questions was suppressed, but rather because the suppression coincided with the general tendency in French society to separate literature and politics, and to take an interest in the former only. In the eighteenth century we see gradually a return to a healthier state of affairs, notwithstanding the efforts of the State to make the willing habit of the seventeenth century peremptory law in the eighteenth. Till the old state-craft was defeated at the outbreak of the Revolution, political eloquence flowed in indirect channels towards its goal. But when the representative assemblies of the three orders in the State, after being for a long period in abeyance, were again called together to discuss public matters, orators took possession of the field, and wielded practically the greatest power in France, till the office of the public executioner took precedence of that of the public speaker. Mirabeau was a native of Nemours. He gave his father a great deal of trouble, though it is only fair to add that his father's behaviour towards him was most unwise. Most violent means were used to curb the unruly disposition of the young man. Military discipline having failed to reach the desired end, Mirabeau was shut up for a while in the fortress of the Island of Ré. He married in 1772, fell deeply into debt, was again arbitrarily arrested, and shut up in three different places in succession. He wrote in the Vincennes

prison a memoir on the notorious *Lettres de cachet*
(warrants to arrest), which could be obtained on application to the king without recourse to the ordinary
machinery of the law, and which were often taken
advantage of to curtail individual liberty. In 1784 we
find Mirabeau in a banking establishment. At that
time he began a controversy with Beaumarchais, who
upheld against him the rights of a certain Water Company. As the opportunities of doing actual political
work increased, Mirabeau came gradually to the front,
and was elected by the Third Estate as one of its
representatives in the States General. His influence in
the assemblies of the Revolution was paramount in
matters political and economic till 1788 ; but Mirabeau
was only a liberal, though a fiery one, and abandonment of the monarchical principle was inconsistent
with his views. It is considered that he might have
checked the downward course from liberalism to
anarchy had not his death taken place in the midst of
a most critical period. His eloquence was irresistible,
and, after the lapse of more than a hundred years, the
fire, impetuosity, and earnestness characterising his
speeches are as striking as ever.

ANDRÉ CHÉNIER and his brother Joseph Chénier
were born at Constantinople. Their father was French
Consul there, and their mother a Greek. André is the
more famous of the two. After six months of military
life he left this career in disgust. He resumed in
Paris the course of his interrupted studies, and under-

took next a journey in Switzerland and Italy.  His first writings fall in those years.  A little later, being under the necessity of seeking a livelihood, he occupied a post in the French Embassy in London.  Notwithstanding his great admiration for Milton and the English Constitution he felt out of his element in England.  Like Mirabeau, his convictions were liberal. He beheld with great enthusiasm the first and heroic stage of the Revolution; but when the policy of wholesale execution was set agoing, Chénier spoke in very different tones in the articles which he was then contributing to the Paris press.  He was in hiding in the neighbourhood of Paris when some steps taken incautiously by his father, in the matter of his arrest, resulted in his being brought to trial.  He was cut off in his prime by the knife of the guillotine.  Chénier was a disciple of the Greeks, and was so much out of touch with the classical tradition inherited from the seventeenth century that he has been honoured by many as the forerunner of the romantic poets.  His pastoral and idyllic poems are imitated from Theocritus.  His subjects are those of the older and simpler Greek poets.  He speaks of the healthy enjoyment of life, of the love of country, of the reverence due to old age, of a mother's love, of the pity owed to the poor, and of the miseries of one's destiny, in tones of the truest and least rhetorical emotion.  His inspiration, vigorous and sweet at the same time, is that of a lover of the beautiful who is in warm sympathy with his fellow-creatures.  Had he lived he might have had a great influence on the course of French poetry. In point of fact, however, in addition to his being cut off in his prime, his works did not come to the light till 1820, when Madame de Staël and Chateaubriand were already directing into channels of their own the movement of reform.

MONTESQUIEU. The Eighteenth Century writers whom we have dealt with hitherto all had a great influence on the drift of their times; but their influence on posterity sinks to insignificance when compared with that of the three giants of the century: Montesquieu, Voltaire, and Jean-Jacques Rousseau. Of these three, Montesquieu was the most respected as a man, and the most weighty as a philosopher on matters politic and social, though appealing on that account to a comparatively limited circle. Voltaire was the most popular and the least grave, and Rousseau the most passionately loved and the most blindly followed to the danger of State and society. Montesquieu was a native of the Gironde and Garonne Valley, a part of France from which we have seen spring several of the most powerful leaders in intellectual concerns. Like Montaigne, he was educated in the law and connected with the Bordeaux Parliament. At the age of thirty-two he took a place among those writers for whom it was unsafe to publish their works in France. Ever since the middle of the sixteenth century some of the more independent thinkers had by necessity fallen into the habit of seeking refuge abroad, either permanently like

Saint-Evremond for instance, or for suitable lengths of time like Descartes and Voltaire. French colonies, in which men of letters of all descriptions were mixed up with the exiled Protestants, had gradually grown in Holland, in England, in Geneva, and in Prussia, forming thus with the intellectual movements in their foreign homes links of the greatest value for the liberalising of France, and putting their letterpress at the disposal of the luckier thinkers who could remain in the mother-country. Montesquieu's *Lettres persanes* were published in Amsterdam in 1721. They are a criticism of the manners and mental habits of the French people. They are written with a light, ironic touch, in which Montesquieu was not to persevere. From early manhood he was engaged in the severe study of history and political institutions. Like Montaigne again, he resigned his legal charge to travel abroad, following in this the majority of French writers, whom it is prejudice to describe as forming a close intellectual corporation, full to excess of ideas of native growth, and ignorant of foreign countries. Montesquieu stayed in Vienna, in Hungary, in Venice —where he met Lord Chesterfield, who had an important share in the shaping of his views—in Florence, Rome, Naples, Switzerland, the Netherlands, and last, but not least, in England. He dwelt in and about London for two years, and nothing that was laid open to him in this novel field of observation was lost on him. In 1731 he again like Montaigne gave himself up to a spell of quiet study in his country residence, the fruit of which was offered to the public three years later in the *Considérations sur les causes de la grandeur des Romains et de leur décadence*, a work taking up the higher historical method at the point where Machiavelli and Bossuet had left it, and carrying it on much further in the direction of what is now called sociology. The same philosophic inquiry into the reciprocal bearing of historical facts holds good in the *Esprit des lois*, printed at Geneva in 1748, after a labour of twenty-four years. In eighteen months twenty editions were absorbed by the public, as well as translations in every European language, notwithstanding that nothing could be less like a novel than this work, in which an attempt is made, amidst the greatest difficulties, to fix the laws of political development. It is a pity that beside the scholarly Montesquieu there did not arise in France a man with the gift of rhetorical expression who could have caught the ear of the people and obtained for these sound doctrines the hearing granted a little later to the violent theories of Rousseau.

VOLTAIRE presents in an accumulation the qualities that go to make the typical French writer. He has the gifts of perfect lucidity, of mischievousness, of biting satire and playful irony, of sterling good sense, of vivacity combined with coolness and self-confidence. He knows how to say in a tasteful and artistic way whatever he wishes to say, and he does it with ease and without any visible effort. It is an open question whether he had much heart. At any rate, his reason over kept watch, and no emotional impulse ever neutralised his vanity. When his personal honour, or what he mistook for his honour, was not at stake, he showed himself generous and high-minded. He was charitable and unwearying in the defence of a good cause when his personal glory along with the furtherance of such abstract principles as toleration and enlightenment could thereby be served. Versatile Voltaire, master in no field but second best in all, at once the herald and the follower of public opinion, was the most popular figure of his times, and engaged in many great controversies in which the last word has not been spoken even at the present day. He was born at Paris, and received his education from the Jesuits in the *Collège Louis le Grand*. One of his tutors, struck by his independence, declared to him that he would become a standard-bearer among the infidels. His first steps in practical life ended in misfortune. He was dismissed from the suite of the French Ambassador at the Hague; he was exiled under suspicion of having written some satirical lines against the Regent of France; he was imprisoned in the Bastille twice, the second time in the following wise. In 1722 he came into possession of independent means, and was able from that moment to carry out his wish of becoming exclusively a man of letters. He became then a favourite in the highest circles of society. Unfortunately he had a quarrel with the Duc de Rohan,[1] who instructed one

---

[1] Not to be confused with the famous Protestant leader of that name in the Thirty Years' War.

of his servants to give him a sound cudgelling.  Voltaire then challenged Rohan to a duel, but the nobleman declined to give satisfaction to the commoner and preferred to demand his imprisonment.  After spending a few weeks in captivity, Voltaire went to England.  During his stay of three years in that country, he made himself acquainted with the ideas of the English Deists.  He studied Newton, Locke, Shakespeare, and Pope.  His contributions to literature before and during this stay in England were numerous in the fields of tragedy, comedy, social satire, literary criticism, and epic verse.  But by far his most important production up to this stage is the *Lettres sur les Anglais* or *Lettres philosophiques.*  The Parliament of Paris exercised over this work its censorial rights, and condemned it as hostile to religion; but this measure was unavailing to stop the inroad of English ideas into France.  From 1734 to 1749 Voltaire took up his residence in the house of Madame du Chatelet.  He finished there his tragedy *Alzire,* in which he placed on the stage an episode of the conquest of Peru by the Spaniards.  He wrote also then the *Mort de César,* which is to some extent derived from the *Julius Cæsar* of Shakespeare.  By going to foreign parts for his tragic themes, by borrowing from Shakespeare, whom he considered on the whole to be inferior to the French playwrights, and by turning to the national history of France for dramatic subjects, Voltaire gave evidence of the straits to which the French stage had come, and shows how much he himself felt that the inherited forms of dramatic art had worn themselves threadbare. To the same period of his life belong his *Eléments de la philosophie de Newton* and his *Discours sur l'homme.* He was then enjoying the favour of the Court, and even was appointed to the office of *Historiographe du roi,* which had so often before him devolved upon fashionable men of letters. His election to the Academy was long delayed by the hostility of the clergy. It took place at last in 1746. Voltaire numbered among his numerous correspondents King Frederick the Great of Prussia, whose purpose it was to collect the largest possible number of philosophic-minded gentlemen to while away the leisures of peace with them in literary occupations, and to gain for his capital the reputation of being a centre of learning. The turn of his mind disposed him to give a preference to French philosophers of Voltaire's type. Unfortunately for him Frenchmen of that class, alternately bullied and petted, but always feared by their own Government, had developed the same defects as spoiled children do in a badly managed home. They were vain, impertinent, and quarrelsome. They expected to be fawned upon by their patrons, and to see fair play allowed to their petty resentments.

The first relations between Voltaire and Frederick were like a honeymoon. Voltaire yielded to the king's wish that he should reside at his court. He taught him the art of writing French verses, he corrected his essays for him, and received in exchange for his services plenty of money. Unfortunately the king wished to be master, and to keep in order in his own way the

troublesome set imported by him. The President of
the Academy of Sciences in Berlin was a Frenchman,
with whom Voltaire was soon engaged in a domestic
quarrel, and against whom he wrote a pamphlet of a
satirical description. Frederick, taking the law in his
own hands, had this piece of vituperation burned by
the hand of the executioner. There ensued a decided
coolness, and then hostility between him and Voltaire.
The latter asked for leave to quit the Court. As his
bad luck, or perhaps as his bad faith, would have it, he
took away some trifling property to which the king
considered he had a prior right. In consequence, Voltaire was stopped at Frankfurt on his journey back to
France, and had an opportunity, through the excessive
zeal of Frederick's agent, of adding to his knowledge of
French prisons some acquaintance with a German one.
The *Siècle de Louis Quatorze* was finished in Prussia. It
has remained authoritative mainly regarding the literature of Louis XIV.'s age, and has had a great deal to do
with the spreading abroad of the reverence in which
that reign is generally held. However, Louis XV. and
the clergy being ill disposed towards Voltaire, the
latter did not dare to take up his residence in Paris.
He doubled back from France into Switzerland, and
with the money he had made by successful literary
labours and lucky financial speculations, he was able
to buy several estates situated on the French boundary,
near the banks of the Lake of Geneva. His favourite
residence from 1760 was Ferney, a place which numbered about fifty inhabitants when he came to it, and

which he transformed into a burgh of 1200 by his
skill in fostering commerce and industry, and also by
the liberal spending of money on what could increase
the welfare of the inhabitants.   He kept up and en-
larged his correspondence all the while.   He encouraged
the *philosophes* in their work, and welcomed to his
residence the hundreds of visitors whom his ever-
growing fame brought him.   But for his increasing
sourness in matters of literary rivalry, and the scurri-
lous character of his attacks on the Church, which
could well be read as directed against every kind of
religion, these crowning years in Voltaire's long career,
during which he fought some of his noblest battles in
the cause of toleration, would command unmixed admiration.   In 1778 he was called to Paris with such
entreaty that he could hardly refuse to grant the wish
of his fellow-citizens.   He was welcomed so noisily, and
was the object of such unbounded enthusiasm, that the
old man sank from sheer exhaustion.   At the end of
three months his death terminated his triumph.   His
remains were laid in the Panthéon with those of Rousseau, who died two months later a very different death.

Rousseau and Voltaire had this in common, that they
both fell under the ban of Church and State, and they
were opposed to one another in this, that, while Voltaire was a conservative in literature, Rousseau tapped
fresh sources ; and while Voltaire was content with the
radical demolition of the doctrines on which the
monarchy was built up, Rousseau strove to set up a

positive doctrine as to what the renovation of the State should be. It is of the greatest importance in the history of literature, in the history of politics, and in the history of modern social order, that, at the moment when the effete French constitution was falling to pieces, and when French prose, as well as French poetry, was dying of inanition, having spent the impetus received at the Renaissance, a fresh impetus was given to literature and to national life from without. It would not be right to lay too much stress on the fact that Rousseau was not a Frenchman, but there is no doubt that he found in his native Republic of Geneva the pattern of the political institutions, which he submitted thereafter to a theoretical process of expansion, and which he presented to the French as a haven of refuge, with the enthusiasm of a patriot giving his nation as a model to less favoured peoples. Rousseau is generally admitted to have afforded new departures in three directions—namely, in politics, in education, and in literature. His early education was neglected. He was in the habit of sitting up at night reading novels in the company of his father, who was a watchmaker in Geneva. Father and son pored together over the lives of Plutarch, notwithstanding that these were more suited to fire the imagination of the boy than to prepare him for a dull round of daily duties. Young Rousseau escaped from Geneva when he was sixteen years old. He was received into the household of Madame de Warens. This lady had forsworn Protestantism, and she induced the young man to follow

her example.   She placed him for a while at a convent
in Turin, then in a seminary for priests in Savoy.
Rousseau began early his wandering life.   However,
from the age of twenty-two to that of twenty-nine
he lived in a close relationship to Madame de Warens,
in the course of which he studied with some regularity.
This seemed to open up for him the profession of a
teacher.   He gave himself a year's trial as a private
tutor in a family at Lyons, and failed, owing to the
excitability of his temper.   Then he went to Paris, and
from Paris to Venice, and back to Paris again.   His
intercourse with the woman known under the name
of Thérèse Levasseur began about that time, and extended over a very long period of his life.   He sent to
the Foundlings' Hospital the children she gave him,
with a hardness of heart that was rooted in his
intense selfishness, but which was not proof against
the remorse that ate the very soul out of him at a
later period.   In 1750 Rousseau had not yet written
anything, but he had developed those contradictory
features of character which, when the times are out
of joint, may be the secret of a man's power for
better or for worse.   In that year the Academy of
Dijon proposed a subject for literary competition as
follows: 'Did the restoration of sciences and of letters
corrupt morals, or did it make them purer?' Rousseau,
seemingly fascinated as by the sudden flashing up of a
light, to use his own words, wrote an essay in reply to
this question, and took up the paradoxical position that
sciences and arts, and therefore civilisation also, have

brought about the corruption that is in man. Astronomy, he says, was born from superstition, eloquence from ambition, land-surveying from land-grabbing, physics from an idle curiosity. He would destroy all that art has brought forth, and once he had uttered this opinion he kept to it consistently to the end. He maintained that all things are good till man touches them, when they are marred by his corruption. It became an affectation with him to shun the world, and he developed the tendency to misanthropy and even insanity that dwelt in him. The *Discours sur l'origine de l'inégalité parmi les hommes* which came next is a savage attack on the rights of property. Rousseau, in whom subsisted a Calvinistic trait, turned next upon theatres, theatre-goers, and playwrights in his *Lettre à d'Alembert sur les spectacles*, forgetting again in the excess of his paradoxical mood that art should be elevated and not banished. Hitherto, Rousseau had confined himself to general statements; now he was about to specialise his literary performance in three directions: the romantic, the political, and the educational. The *Nouvelle Héloïse* is such a mixture of passionateness and philosophy that minds which are neither overwrought nor overstrung have some difficulty in digesting it. Yet this novel, generally admitted to rank as the first model of the modern novel of sentiment and landscape painting, was received with the greatest applause. It is written in letters, and the author has visibly been to school with Richardson. In the *Contrat social* Rousseau exhibits the form of Government he thinks the

best, in which the Church and State are one, and enforce
upon all a faith in the Supreme Being and the immortality of the soul, while professing to put all power in
the hands of the people.   Of all Rousseau's works the
*Emile* is the only one that has been thoroughly bene-
ficial.   There is no use in dwelling on the extravagant side of Rousseau's theories on education, for he
was on the whole so well inspired that he set educators
a-thinking far and wide, and promoted a far healthier
treatment of children.   The name Emile is that of the
pupil of whom Rousseau professes to be in charge in his
book.   The famous *Profession de foi du vicaire savoyard*
appeared in one of the chapters of the *Emile*.   This bold
confession of Rousseau's personal faith brought him
into trouble with the established authorities.   It was
insufficiently orthodox for Catholics and Protestants
alike, though it contained enough positive belief to save
it from confusion with the negativeness and aridity
of a Voltaire.   The gates of Paris were closed against
the writer; the gates of his native town, Geneva,
were shut against him likewise.   He sought the protection of Frederick the Great on the lands of Neuchatel, whence he replied to his Catholic and to his
Protestant accusers.   Disturbed in his retreat by a local
outburst of indignation, he fled to the small island of
St. Pierre, which was under Bernese jurisdiction.   But
the Bernese were as intolerant as the Neuchatel folks.
Rousseau, sent again about his business, sought a last
refuge in England.   By that time the eccentricities
of his character had grown to alarming proportions.

He quarrelled with Hume, who had·received him in his country house.  In the interval the storm raised against him in France had spent itself.  He was able to accept hospitality in a small house on the lands of Ermenonville, where he spent the last months of his life.  The *Confessions* were written during the last and most troubled part of Rousseau's existence. Their accuracy may well be doubted, and at any rate the writer was not then in a state of mind that could make him a trustworthy historian of himself.

# CHAPTER VIII.

## NINETEENTH CENTURY.

### *Miscellaneous Verse.*

VIENNET (1777-1868) : Fables, épîtres.

BÉRANGER (1780-1857) : Chansons.

MILLEVOYE (1782-1816) : Elégies, poèmes épiques.

LAMARTINE (1790-1869) : *Méditations poétiques, La Mort de Socrate ; Harmonies poétiques et religieuses ; Jocelyn ; Chute d'un ange ; Recueillements poétiques.*

EMILE DESCHAMPS (1791-1871) : *Etudes françaises et étrangères.*

ANTONY DESCHAMPS (1800-1869) : A metrical translation of the *Divina Commedia* of Dante ; Satires.

CASIMIR DELAVIGNE (1793-1843) : *Les Messéniennes,* élégies.

BARTHÉLEMY (1796-1867) et MÉRY (1798-1866) ; *La Villéliade,* a mock heroic poem ; *Napoléon en Egypte,* an epic poem ; *La Némésis* (52 political satires).

ALFRED DE VIGNY (1799-1863) : *Moïse ; le Trappiste ; le Cor,* etc.

VICTOR HUGO (1802-1885) : *Odes et Ballades, Orientales, Contemplations, Feuilles d'automne, Chants du Crépuscule,* etc.

BARBIER (1805-1882) : *Les Iambes,* satires.

ALFRED DE MUSSET (1810-1857) : *Premières Poésies, Poésies Nouvelles ;* odes, stances, sonnets, épîtres, contes.

### *Dramatic Art.*

SCRIBE (1791-1861) : Comedies—*Bertrand et Raton ; La Camaraderie ; La Calomnie ; Le Verre d'eau,* etc.

CASIMIR DELAVIGNE (1793-1843) : Tragedies — *Marino Faliero ; Louis XI. ; Les Enfants d'Edouard.* Drama—*Don Juan d'Autriche.* Comedy—*L'Ecole des Vieillards.*

172

Victor Hugo (1802-1885) : Dramas—*Cromwell ; Hernani ; Lucrèce Borgia ; Ruy-Blas ; Marion Delorme ; Le Roi s'amuse ; Angelo ; Les Burgraves.*

Alexandre Dumas (1803-1870) : Dramas—*Henri III. et sa cour ; La Tour de Nesle.* Comedies—*Mlle de Belle-Isle ; Les Demoiselles de Saint-Cyr ; Un Mariage sous Louis XV.*

George Sand (1804-1876) : Comedies—*Le Marquis de Villemer ; Le Mariage de Victorine.*

Alfred de Musset (1810-1857) : Comedies—*Il ne faut jurer de rien ; On ne badine pas avec l'amour, un caprice ; Il faut qu'une porte soit ouverte ou fermée.*

Sandeau (1811-1882) : Comedies—*Mlle de la Seiglière ; Jean de Thommeray.*

Ponsard (1814-1867) : Tragedies—*Lucrèce ; Agnès de Méranie ; Charlotte Corday.* Comedy—*L'Honneur et l'Argent.*

Augier (1820-    ) : Comedies—*La Ciguë ; Philiberte ; Les Effrontés ; L'Aventurière ; Le Gendre de M. Poirier ; Le Fils de Giboyer ; Gabrielle ; Maître Guérin.*

Alexandre Dumas, Fils (1824-    ) : Dramas and comedies—*La Dame aux Camélias ; Le Demi-Monde ; Le Fils naturel ; Le Père prodigue ; Les Idées de Mme Aubray.*

## History, Memoirs.

Mme de Staël (1776-1817) : *Dix années d'exil.*

Chateaubriand (1768-1848) : *Mémoires d'outre-tombe.*

Simonde de Sismondi (1773-1842) : *Histoire des Français.*

Barante (1782-1866) : *Histoire des ducs de Bourgogne.*

Guizot (1782-1875) : *Histoire de la Révolution d'Angleterre ; Histoire générale de la civilisation en Europe ; Mémoires pour servir à l'histoire de mon temps.*

Villemain (1790-1867) : *Histoire de Cromwell.*

Augustin Thierry (1795-1856) : *Histoire de la Conquête de l'Angleterre par les Normands ; Récits des temps mérovingiens.*

Mignet (1796-1884) : *Histoire de la Révolution française ; Histoire de Marie Stuart.*

Thiers (1797-1877) : *Histoire de la Révolution française ; Histoire du Consulat et de l'Empire.*

Michelet (1798-1874) : *Histoire de France ; Histoire de la Révolution.*

Lanfrey (1828-1877) : *Histoire de Napoléon I^er.*

## *Fiction.*

XAVIER DE MAISTRE (1764-1852): *Voyage autour de ma chambre ; Le Lépreux de la Cité d'Aoste ; Les Prisonniers du Caucase ; La Jeune Sibérienne.*

MME DE STAËL (1766-1817): Novels—*Delphine ; Corinne.*

CHATEAUBRIAND (1768-1848): *Atala ; René.*

NODIER (1780-1844): *Mme de Marsan ; Jean Sbogar.*

TOEPFFER (1799-1846): *Nouvelles genevoises.*

ALFRED DE VIGNY (1799-1863): *Cinq-Mars.*

VICTOR HUGO (1802-1885): *Han d'Islande ; Bug-Jargal ; Notre-Dame de Paris ; Les Misérables.*

PROSPER MÉRIMÉE (1803-1870): *La Prise de la Redoute ; Colomba,* etc.

ALEXANDRE DUMAS (1803-1870): *Les Trois Mousquetaires ; Impressions de Voyage,* etc.

MME GEORGE SAND (1804-1876): *Mauprat ; La petite Fadette ; François le Champi ; La Mare au Diable ; Le Marquis de Villemer.*

HONORÉ DE BALZAC (1799-1850): Novels—*La Comédie humaine.*

SANDEAU (1811-1882): *Valcreuse ; Mlle de la Seiglière.*

SOUVESTRE (1806-1854): *Le Coin du feu ; Pendant la moisson.*

OCTAVE FEUILLET (1822-1891): *La Petite Comtesse ; Le Roman d'un jeune homme pauvre ; L'Histoire de Sibylle.*

ERCKMANN (1822-    ), CHATRIAN (1826-    ): *Histoire d'un conscrit de 1813 ; Waterloo ; Le Blocus ; L'Ami Fritz.*

ABOUT (1828-1885): *Tolla ; Le Roi des Montagnes ; L'Infâme ; Les Mariages de Paris ; Les Mariages de province.*

CHERBULIEZ (1832-    ): *Le Prince Vitale ; Prosper Randoce,* etc.


## *Politics, Travels, Philosophy, Critique, Letters.*

JOSEPH DE MAISTRE (1753-1821): *Soirées de Saint-Pétersbourg.*

CHATEAUBRIAND (1768-1848): *Le Génie du Christianisme ; Itinéraire de Paris à Jérusalem ; Bonaparte et les Bourbons.*

PAUL-LOUIS COURIER (1773-1825): *Pamphlets politiques et littéraires.*

LAMENNAIS (1782-1854): *Essai sur l'indifférence en matière de religion ; Paroles d'un croyant.*

VILLEMAIN (1790-1870) : *Cours de littérature française.*

VICTOR COUSIN (1792-1867): *Cours de philosophie ; Cours d'histoire de la philosophie ; Traduction de Platon ; Etudes littéraires.*

RÉMUSAT (1797-1875) : *Essais de philosophie ; Critiques littéraires.*

MICHELET (1798-1874): *L'Oiseau ; L'Insecte ; La Femme ; L'Amour ; La Mer ; La Montagne.*

TAINE (1828- ): *Les Philosophes français du 19° siècle ; Essais de critique et d'histoire ; Histoire de la littérature anglaise.*

PROSPER MÉRIMÉE (1803-1870) : *Lettres à une Inconnue.*

SAINTE-BEUVE (1804-1869) : *Tableau historique et critique de la poésie française au 16° siècle ; Causeries du Lundi, etc.*

*Etc. etc.*

CHATEAUBRIAND. The lines on which a decided renovation of French literature could proceed had begun to be laid down by J.-J. Rousseau and his disciple Bernardin de Saint-Pierre. Chateaubriand and Mme de Staël, who are the first writers of note after the period of the Revolution, and who were both compelled by circumstances to travel a great deal in foreign parts when their talent was ripening, began to write under the influence of Rousseau, adding what they could find outside of France to the inspiration they received from him. The Revolution, beginning in hopeful liberalism, advancing to a bloody anarchy, and ending in military despotism, had deeply stirred their minds. Their literary works bear the stamp of the troubled times in which they were composed. Chateaubriand was born at St. Malo, in a family of Breton noblemen. At the age of eighteen he was a soldier, but when the Revolution dispensed with the services of noblemen, and made it dangerous for them to reside in France, he left for America, and spent some months in the newly-formed United States.  He wandered about in the solitudes of the New World, and his imagination, of a decidedly sensitive and artistic kind, was greatly affected by the imposing greatness of American scenery.  He turned to account his acquaintance with the New World in the same way as Bernardin de St. Pierre had used his acquaintance with tropical scenery. Requiring a landscape in which to place the personages born from his own imaginings, and remembering Rousseau's use of the beauties of Swiss scenery, he made his *Atala* and his *Rene* move about in the solitudes of the virgin forests of America.  His first attitude towards the Revolution, for a gentleman of such noble stock, was sympathetic, but the seizure of the king made him join those *émigrés* who tried to win their way back to France by force of arms.  This attempt having resulted in failure, he fled to England, where he spent seven years in obscurity and poverty. He wrote there, in a despondent frame of mind, his first book, *L'Essai sur les révolutions*, enlarging on the mistakes and misery in which mankind is fatally entangled.  The death of his mother, and of one of his sisters, came then to make foremost in his mind another set of considerations.  He broke with any leaning he might have to the doctrines of Voltaire, and professed a return to Christian convictions.  But his mind contained more imaginative fire than spiritual force, and his return to Christianity gave more colouring to his literary work than strength or mellowness to his character.  The first fruit born of his conversion was the *Génie du Christianisme,* which was begun in England and published on his return to France. The book is mainly concerned in showing that Christianity can supply the artist and the poet with richer themes than the pagan world can ever do. While the *philosophes* had driven to an extreme the example set at the Renaissance of seeking wisdom in pagan springs, Chateaubriand, in his attempt to connect again art and poetry with religion, is very consistently brought to seek the springs of inspiration in the Middle Ages, a time in which Christian religion, to his mind, pervaded the whole of life. The novels alluded to a little above, *René* and *Atala,* had a place marked out for them as episodes in the *Génie du Christianisme.* They are samples given by Chateaubriand, showing what his new precepts could do for literature. The peculiar Christian strain in which these two short novels are written, the fiery and, to some extent, unwholesome description of psychological states over which the veil of secrecy is drawn by most people, the high colour of the style and the tinge of melancholy thrown over the whole, all going to show that the writer was in a state of mental fever, happened to correspond with the feverishness of a disturbed age.

Chateaubriand came to terms for a while with the Imperial Government, till the shooting of the Duc d'Enghien made it impossible for the Breton Royalist to co-operate with the Corsican upstart. The result was a journey to Greece, Constantinople, Asia Minor, and the Holy Land. The notes taken during this journey provided material for another book, *L'Itinéraire de Paris à Jérusalem*, which ranked high in a kind of literature well adapted to the growing curiosity and restlessness of the age : the account of travels.   In *Les Martyrs* he affords further illustration of the theory set forth in the *Génie du Christianisme* as to the comparative value to the literary artist of Christianity and paganism.   *Les Martyrs*, written in prose, with a wealth of metaphors and an intensity of description that belong properly to poetry, had something to do with the longing that arose about that time for picturesqueness and dramatic truth in history. Augustin Thierry acknowledges both Chateaubriand and Walter Scott as having pointed out to him the way in which to treat historical matter.   After the fall of Napoleon, Chateaubriand was able to take up his abode permanently in France.   He passed then from letters into politics ; he was Minister of State, Ambassador, and watched from his eminence the working of his ideas in the young generation.   After 1830, the accession of Louis-Philippe to the throne thrust him back into the shade.   He resumed then the writing of his Memoirs, to which he gave the high-sounding title of *Mémoires d'outre-tombe*, because they were to be published after his death, and would fall upon the ears of his countrymen as a voice from the grave.   We see in this the straining after effect which is the greatest blemish on Chateaubriand's work, and which, taken with the theatrical splendour and sumptuosity of his style, entitles one to doubt whether he wrote at any time in a very sincere spirit. Be this as it may, Chateaubriand is the greatest man of letters from the decline of Rousseau's star to the rise of Victor Hugo's.

MME DE STAËL, born in Paris, was the daughter of a Genevese Minister of Louis XIV., and her mother was a native of the French-speaking parts of Switzerland. She was a Protestant, and married the Swedish Ambassador at the French Court, whereby her name was changed from Necker to Staël. Her mother's drawing-room, to which she was freely admitted in girlhood, was a centre of intellectual life in which art, letters, and politics were discussed with the utmost freedom. She was prepared by her education and by the imaginative and idealistic turn of her mind to hail with delight the initial stages of the Revolution. Like Chateaubriand, she shrank from its excesses, but she never disowned her leanings to liberalism, differing from him in this, that, while they both started from Rousseau in their search after a literary renovation, she accepted and completed the task in a liberal spirit, while Chateaubriand proceeded with a sort of conservatism. She showed much daring in writing in defence of the queen Marie Antoinette, and had to fly from Paris in consequence; but she returned when order was restored, and she found herself called upon to play a part of some importance in politics. Her solid liberalism could not find favour with Bonaparte. She was exiled, sought refuge in Geneva, and went thence to Italy. In 1800 she published *De la littérature considérée dans ses rapports avec l'état moral et politique des nations*, a work showing the robust hopefulness of her temperament. Then came two novels, *Delphine* and *Corinne*, which are an indirect autobiography and record of inner life; the latter especially conveying the impression produced upon the authoress by Italian landscape and monuments. The imagination of Madame de Staël is health itself when compared with that of Chateaubriand, and tempered throughout with reason. Having taken up with unflinching earnestness the cause of liberty against Napoleon, Madame de Staël, though longing for the intellectual atmosphere of Paris, and for the company that used to meet at her own house, never fell away in the slightest from her determination; and as long as the power of Napoleon kept extending over the greater part of Continental Europe, she retreated before him from country to country. She resided for a long while at Coppet on the banks of the Lake of Geneva, where she gathered about her a large number of men, French, German, English, and Swiss, all eminent in one or another branch of literature. She travelled in Germany, and studied with a real and far-seeing interest the literature of that country, which was just reaching the height of its splendour in the hands of Goethe and Schiller. Lastly, she resided for a long while in England. Being a woman of a trained judgment, with well-balanced and keen reasoning powers, able to write in a philosophic and poetic style, she realised how much French literature would gain by being brought into unison with that of Germany and England. In her book *De l'Allemagne* she threw wide open the door already set ajar—so far as England is concerned, at any rate—by Voltaire, and carried further the emancipation of French literature from formalism. This book, written in a spirit generous to the nations trampled upon by Napoleon, was so totally at variance with Napoleon's opinion as to what the place of literature should be in his Empire that its first edition printed in Paris was destroyed by the police officers. However, Mme de Staël was able to bring the work out a little later in London. Her last work of considerable importance was *Dix années d'exil*, where her forced travels on the Continent, to the North, and to England are described. When the house of Bourbon resumed possession of the throne of France, Mme de Staël was able to return to her beloved Paris. She contracted a second marriage with a man many years younger than herself, who died a few months after her, in 1818.

1780-1857. BÉRANGER. Chateaubriand and Mme de Staël, who led their countrymen straight to the Romantic movement, which reached its height with Victor Hugo, already fully represented the literary tendencies of the Nineteenth Century. The kind of prose used in their imaginative productions brought about a second birth of lyricism, smothered since the end of the Sixteenth Century. Notwithstanding this, the mould of thought and the build of verse remained semi-classical with a

few poets, such as Béranger, who found his inspiration
in national and patriotic feelings, and in his sympathy
with the domestic life and the trials of the common
people.  He was born in Paris.  The street scenes of
the Revolution, such as the taking of the Bastille by the
people, left on his mind an indelible impression.
Having been given in a country town some work in
a printer's office, and having joined a primary school
managed according to the ideas of Rousseau, he was able
to acquire by reading a certain quantity of knowledge.
He studied attentively Molière and La Fontaine, and
took, as a pastime and as a means of entertaining his
companions when sitting round festive boards, to the
song-writing that has made him famous.  But on dis-
covering that his songs were popular, that the State
was afraid of them, and that he could draw, like La
Fontaine, into their comparatively narrow compass
every kind of poetry, he became a *chansonnier* by profession.  He was saved from poverty, which would
have been hurtful to a talent like his, by the generosity
of a member of the Bonaparte family, and later by filling a small post at the offices of the University.  His
songs came out in successive volumes, and were
generally greeted by the imposition of fines, which
his friends paid for him.  The influence of his songs on
the course of politics was considerable.  The glamour of
the Napoleonic victories was on his lyre, and he kept
alive the memory of the great warrior in the hearts of
the people, though he was in reality a friend of peace.
He was a good example of a combination of wit and

lyricism almost impossible in any other language than French, and perhaps the most original feature of French literature.

ALFRED DE VIGNY, a nobleman by birth, and a soldier at an early age, resigned his commission in 1827 that he might give himself up entirely to his literary tastes. He belonged to the inner circle of the men devoted to romanticism, and he began to be known to fame about the same time as Lamartine and Béranger, a few years before Victor Hugo. He inherited the sobriety of the *esprit français* for the want of which many romantics went altogether astray. His poetical work is not extensive, but the lyrical beauty and harmony of his lines, their sustained and contained power, the true nobility of the feelings expressed, all combine to place his poems in the very first rank. One of his most famous shorter pieces treats of the last battle of Roland in the Valley of Roncevaux. An episode of the naval battle of Aboukir was also beautifully treated by him in a patriotic strain. Vigny distinguished himself as a novelist by writing historical romances. *Cinq-Mars*, which shows Richelieu in an unfavourable light; *Stello*, in which the life stories of Chatterton, Gilbert, and André Chénier are treated in a spirit which is not quite true to history; and *Servitude et grandeur militaire*, in which military honour gives the moral element to the plot—are all beautifully written books, rich in seriousness and sincerity. A few months before Victor Hugo put his *Hernani* on the stage, Vigny brought out an *Othello* translated from Shakespeare. The success of *Chatterton*, in 1835, crowned his theatrical career.

*1810 – 1857).*
*Premières*
*Poésies,*
*Poésies*
*nouvelles;*
*odes, stances,*
*sonnets,*
*épitres, contes*

ALFRED DE MUSSET was born in Paris. He showed very early an intense dislike to any profession. Though well-born, his natural disposition was towards Bohemianism. The ambition of his youth was to become acquainted with life, to drink the cup to the dregs, and to learn everything by personal experience. He reaped the fruit of his rashness in waste of physical strength, and in the frequent misdirection of his talent. The spending of his nights in gambling and in prolonged dancing, the seeking of excitement in profligacy, and the utter carelessness with which he handled his beautiful poetic gifts, resulted in poems that are often unwholesome, though always charming. He is one of many Frenchmen blending wit and passionateness, with one side of their nature sunk in Byronism, and rising by another side to the noblest flights of spiritual life. The personage of Don Juan is a favourite one with him; but the eyes of Don Juan are sometimes turned up to heaven, and he raises from the depths of debauchery a voice with such a true ring of despair in it, that it is impossible to hear it without being touched. His first collection of poems, so far as the form is concerned, was a challenge thrown out to the defenders of classical traditions. Shortly after the publication of his second collection, from which the intention of producing a paradoxical piece of work is happily absent, and in which his finest and most spon-

*Comédies*
*"Il ne faut*
*jurer de rien*
*On ne badine*
*pas cause*
*l'amour,*
*un caprice*
*il faut qu'in*
*porte soit*
*ouverte ou*
*fermée*

taneous lyricism is to be found, he accompanied George Sand on a journey she made to Venice. The association of two such spirits, both insufficiently weighted with reason, bore evil fruit. There arose between them an estrangement, which was hotly commented upon at the time, and which brought nothing but misery to Musset. He was librarian at the Home Office under the reign of Louis Philippe. The latter part of his life is a sad picture of mental powerlessness and moral misery. He was unable to keep the respect of the public, and but few people accompanied him to his last resting-place. Alfred de Musset is a more human poet than even Victor Hugo. He writes in fewer words than the latter, and with the greatest music of soul that has, perhaps, ever been known. His *Nuits*, a series of poems, the title of which is clearly borrowed from Young's *Night Thoughts*, the opening pages of *Rolla*, the *Lettre à Lamartine*, all coming straight from the conscience and the heart, at once manly and tender, are his masterpieces.

LAMARTINE was born at Mâcon, educated at home, and received from his family its monarchical traditions. Unfit to endure the restraints of school life, he took a course of his own towards Bernardin de St. Pierre and Chateaubriand, whose manner and subjects were to his liking. Travels in Italy, at an age when a dreamy temperament is most susceptible to outer influence, produced effects on his mind similar to those made on the minds of his two favourite prose poets.

A soldier in his youth, like almost every French noble-man, he spent some years in foreign travel before 1820, when he was attached to the French Embassy at Florence. He married there a wealthy Englishwoman, who was to him a faithful and noble wife, and bore her share of the trials which the poet's unfitness for business brought upon him. In the meanwhile he had published his *Méditations poétiques*, in which there is no trace of the classical inheritance of France, except in the avoidance of eccentricities of style. These lyrical poems, bursting all at once into bloom in a field that had long presented a parched and dried-up aspect, fell upon the ears of the contemporary generation as a first satisfaction granted to the new spirit of the age. The French reading public was no longer recruited in its majority from the class of people who had applauded Racine, Voltaire, and even Beaumarchais. The hearts of the middle classes had to be won, and this could not be done by putting before them the strains that had delighted the courtiers of Louis XIV. A more human spirit, the domestic affections, the inner life of the soul, sentiments at once natural and ideal—such was the material of which the new poetry should be made in order to be read, and to fulfil its lofty mission. Even the Paris drawing-rooms, in which lingered many of the old prejudices, received with favour this poet who went back to Petrarch when he was not merely himself. After publishing *Les Nouvelles Méditations*, and *Les Harmonies poétiques*, Lamartine tried his hand at politics. Then he travelled in the East for sixteen months, and, after bringing out several other poems, he began his history of the Girondins. This exposition of the doings and fate of the moderate party among the French Revolutionists of 1789 had a practical bearing on the state of politics in the reign of Louis-Philippe. Lamartine came to power when this prince was driven from the throne in 1848, and acted then himself with great bravery the part of a Girondin. The Restoration of the Empire under Napoleon III. thrust him back into private life. He was then loaded with debt, and began to use his popularity as a means of making money. He produced a large number of books dealing with historical subjects, written in a flowing style, but without weight. He was pensioned at last, two years before his death. In the great outburst of lyrical poetry that marks the second twenty years of this century, Lamartine has struck the purest note. He was free from the passions that disturbed the peace of soul of Musset. Looking upon man and the world as the work of God, he was able to conceive them as a harmonious whole, to read everywhere the workings of the Infinite, and to confine his poetical eyesight to those realities which do not contradict one's ideal. His only misfortune was that the very harmony of his being deprived him of variety of experience, and there is not found in him that dramatic touch in the absence of which even the purest lyrical inspiration is dragged down to monotony.

VICTOR HUGO was during the first part of his long 1802-1885.

*Odes et Ballades, Orientales, Contemplations, Feuilles d'automne, Chants du Crépuscule, &c.*
*Drames. Cromwell, Hermani, Lucrèce Borgia, Ruy Blas, Marion Delorme, Le Roi s'amuse; Angelo, Les Burgraves.*
*Fiction. Han d'Islande, Bug-Jargal, Notre Dame de Paris... Les Misérables.*

life the acknowledged chief of the romantic school; and in the second half, when the wave of novelty had subsided, and when, after gaining the victory, the excitement of battle had cooled down, he became the acknowledged chief of French men of letters, a few of whom only had resisted his influence, while all agreed to honour him as their patriarch. It was said of Voltaire that, although he was second in every department of literature, he was first in none. The same judgment could be passed on Victor Hugo with the exception that in lyrics he does stand first, and as high as the French language is ever likely to admit of. Victor Hugo in his age is a still greater figure than Voltaire in the preceding age. He is also of a totally different character. While emancipating the intellect of modern society, Voltaire put forth a narrowing influence in what appertains to heart and spirit, to say nothing of his conservatism in the form of literature. Victor Hugo in contrast to him put forth a deepening, widening, and elevating influence. He set every kind of literature free from the cramping bonds of fixed criticism. He played his part—a very considerable one—in the battle for the liberties and social rights of the French people, upheld perseveringly the cause of religion and spirituality, and never came to any shabby compromise with the political powers of the day, or with any popular whim. He was born at Besançon in Franche-Comté, a province which for a long time had belonged to the Spanish Crown. It was by the merest chance that Victor Hugo's birthplace was so situated, for his father was a military officer who moved to and fro whither his duty might lead him. For all that, there is in Victor Hugo something too grand, too pompous, for a Frenchman—something that smacks of the Spaniard. His mother hailed from Vendée, a province which vowed to the aristocracy, the established Church, and the kings of the House of Bourbon a respect so deeply rooted that it rose in arms against the Revolution. The relation in which young Victor Hugo stood through his mother to the *ancien régime* became apparent in his first poetic effusions. He was in Spain with his father when nine years old, and was about to enter the Polytechnic School in Paris when, at the age of fifteen, he competed for a prize offered by the French Academy, and failed to get it, not because his poem was not the best, but because he was simple-minded enough to state his age. The *Immortels* thought it a moral offence in so good a poet that he should pretend to be so young, and they believed it their duty to punish him for a statement which on the face of it must be a lie. A little later he fell under the influence of Chateaubriand. From the very beginning of his literary career he cultivated the art of novel-writing as well as that of lyric poetry. He took to theatrical composition a little later. His work as a political satirist and as a humanitarian belongs to his maturer years, though to his death he continued to carry on composition in the most different directions simultaneously. His volumes of lyrical contents appeared in the following order. First, the *Odes et ballades*: these are akin to the ideas he had inherited from his mother. Next, the *Orientales*, the dazzling play of a splendid imagination to which sentiment and even sensation are less important than the shimmer of words. Théophile Gautier imitated this Hugoesque strain. The *Feuilles d'Automne* may be called the domestic poetry of heart and soul. The tone is homely, emotional, and pathetic. Victor Hugo passed from the Royalistic camp to liberalism about the time when he wrote these poems. In the *Chants du crépuscule* the political uncertainties of the time combined with the doubts of the poet in several spheres of thought to make up the character of the book. In the *Voix intérieures* and in the *Rayons et les Ombres* the poet keeps on the whole to the same themes. In 1841 he was elected a member of the Academy, and four years later he was made, as a reward for his liberalism, a peer of the realm by Louis-Philippe. During the Second Republic, instituted in 1848, his attention, like that of Lamartine's, was entirely taken up with politics. He sided against the party which invested Louis-Napoleon with the first dignity in the State; and his views, consistently liberal hitherto, became more and more favourable to democracy. The newly elected emperor banished him. The poet withdrew to Jersey. He never yielded an inch of his convictions to Napoleon III., and did not set foot again on French soil till after his fall in 1870. Throughout the period known as the Second Empire Victor Hugo kept pouring forth on the emperor the vials of his bitterness, in the *Châtiments* and in *Napoléon le Petit*. During the long residence in Jersey, in this forced abstinence from politics, his lyrical power grew abnormally, owing to the comparative solitude in which he lived, and to the want of the derivative channels which an active social life would have given him. The *Contemplations* belong mostly to that period. In the *Légende des siècles* the poet's gifts run into the shadowy and gigantic. The different ages of mankind are there represented in successive pictures purporting to show the ascent of man from original darkness to the ideal. In *l'Année terrible* an account is given of the battle of Sedan and the scenes in Paris during the siege. From the days of the Franco-German war to his death, Victor Hugo took up his abode again in Paris, which he loved beyond measure, and upon which he has cast no little ridicule by calling it the Ville-Lumière. As he advanced in age he played his part seriously as visible head of French literature ; and the respect due to his achievements having degenerated into flat adulation, his last productions, spoilt beforehand by the long absence of outer criticism, revealed also a growing deficiency in self-criticism. For all that, Victor Hugo in his old age was surrounded with universal love, and the thousands of Frenchmen who accompanied him to his last resting-place in 1885 were only duly honouring one of the greatest and best men of modern times.

His novels, *Notre-Dame de Paris*, *Les Misérables*, *Quatre-vingt-treize*,—the first representing a scene from the life of the common people in a mediæval frame ; the second dealing with the successful struggle of a

convict to recover his lost character: the third setting
forth an episode in the Vendean war,—are still better
known than his lyrics.  But it is as a writer of plays
that Victor Hugo achieved his greatest triumphs though
not his most lasting ones.  He set about gaining acceptance among the public for a new conception of dramatic
art, which stood in direct opposition to the classical
one.  The great battle between the rival schools of the
romanticists and classicists was fought at the acting of
Victor Hugo's play *Hernani* in 1829.  The classicists
were routed.  It was the feeling of the majority of the
audience that *Hernani* corresponded to a higher ideal
of dramatic art than the plays upheld by the classicists.
The tragic elements of *Hernani* are borrowed from
Spanish life, as had been the case two hundred years
earlier with Corneille's *Cid*.  Victor Hugo had prepared
himself for his romantic departure by a careful study
of Shakespeare.  Previously to *Hernani* he had composed on Shakespearean lines *Cromwell*, a play too un-
wieldy to be put on the stage.  After the acting of
*Hernani*, that of *Marion Delorme* became possible, and
Victor Hugo's run of success was continued in *le Roi
s'amuse*.  In his later plays, the attraction of novelty
having worn off, and freedom from formalism, which it
was his purpose to win, having been attained, the
mannerism of Victor Hugo's art was perceived by the
general public, as it had all along struck the eye of
self-possessed critics.  There was in Victor Hugo too
much imagination and not enough psychology to make
of him a first-rate playwright; but his successful

crusade instilled fresh life into the French drama, and a large number of plays by a legion of dramatists have borne witness to the fruit of his initiative.

SAINTE-BEUVE has done as much in our century to instil fresh life into literary criticism as Victor Hugo did in the field of literary production. He was born at Boulogne. His mother was an Englishwoman. He studied in his native town and then in Paris. For a time he fancied he would become a physician, but his true call was to letters, and he became a contributor to the famous newspaper called the *Globe*, whose staff was recruited from among the most talented young men of the day. He had occasion to write a criticism on Victor Hugo's *Odes et ballades*. This brought him into close association with the poet. In 1829 came out the *Poésies de Joseph Delorme*, the latter part of the title being the name under which Sainte-Beuve hid his identity. However much he might accept the position taken up by the romanticists, he was not so wedded to their habits as to be a mere reflection of Victor Hugo. If he was under the influence of any one in particular at that time, it was that of the English poets. Sainte-Beuve's success as a critic soon cast into the shade his undoubted poetical talent. No critic of literature has ever written so much or so well. He endeavoured, in his articles contributed to the *Globe*, to link the romanticists to Ronsard and the Pléiade. This might be good diplomacy, but it introduced an analogy where there is properly none, for Ronsard clearly endeavoured to set French art on a par with that of Greece and Rome, while the romanticists, cutting themselves away from Greece and Rome as from the century of Louis XIV., claimed association with the northern literatures, if with any at all. Sainte-Beuve wrote one systematic piece of literary history—his *Tableau de la poésie française.* Another lengthy piece of connected composition is his *Histoire de Port-Royal.* As for his literary criticisms, on which rests his fame, they were generally written at the rate of one paper a week contributed to the *Globe,* the *Revue de Paris,* and the *Revue des Deux Mondes.* They form at present a long series of volumes known as the *Portraits littéraires,* the *Causeries du lundi,* the *Nouveaux lundis,* and the *Portraits contemporains.* He completely revolutionised the science of criticism, simply by altering the standpoint of the critic. Literary productions were before him considered as *ouvrages d'esprit* (products of the mind). But when it became a need with modern Europe to read books written not with one's mind only but with one's whole nature, Sainte-Beuve, before judging of a literary performance, took into consideration the whole moral disposition of the writer as being of greater moment than bare literary ability.

VILLEMAIN was born in Paris, and is not wrongly looked upon as the link between the old school of criticism and the new one. Two works of his youth were crowned by the French Academy, of which he became later a member and the perpetual secretary.

He was a Professor in La Sorbonne from 1827, where he commanded success by a style of delivery which was sufficiently scholarly and yet calculated to please the general public. His most noteworthy series of lessons were collected by him in the *Tableau de la littérature française au moyen âge,* and in the *Littérature au XVIII<sup>e</sup> siècle.* Villemain followed the example set by Mme de Staël in studying the literature of other countries than France, in marking the reciprocal influence of foreign literature on the native and of the native on the foreign, and in encouraging the use of the comparative method in criticism. Spain, Italy, France, and England came more especially within his purview. In his lessons he endeavoured to act the part of an arbitrator between romanticists and classicists, calling the attention of his pupils with great impartiality to the merits and defects of either school.

PAUL LOUIS COURIER was a writer of political pamphlets, which are famous for their pointed sarcasm and the sharp crispness of the style. He was an officer of artillery, who filled his long hours of leisure with the study of Greek literature. His father held that the time given to the study of the dead languages was wasted; but to the son this kind of occupation brought the keenest pleasure. 'Are those who do not study them,' he would say, 'any the happier?' In the course of his soldiering he was taken to Italy, where he complained that the French soldiery made havoc in the public libraries; and instead of carrying out forthwith

the orders he might receive from his chiefs, he was
known at least once to delay while he was copying some
Greek treatise. In 1809, after leaving the army, he was
unfortunate enough to make a blot with ink on a manuscript which he was copying. A few words were made
thereby illegible, and there was an outcry of corresponding magnitude among scholars. Courier wrote in reply
his *Lettre à Renouard*. Then he married the daughter
of a Hellenist, and wrote his political pamphlets in the
years that followed the Restoration of the House of
Bourbon. In these papers he took to task the reactionary and ultra-conservative policy of Louis XVIII. This
put him on a par with Béranger, as a dangerous liberal
worthy of imprisonment. They were fellow-convicts in
the same prison. The last years of Courier were spent
in the country near Tours. His gamekeeper shot him.

AUGUSTIN THIERRY is the most interesting of the first-
rate historians produced by France in this century.
From as far back as the middle ages down to his times,
historical subjects had been handled inaccurately or
fancifully. He began by a criticism of the bad habits
of his predecessors. He was therefore already prepared to strike out a new path, when he was further
enlightened by reading Chateaubriand's *Martyrs* and
Walter Scott's historical romances. It became clear
to him that history should not derive its colour from
one's imagination, nor should it serve party ends or
purely literary purposes; but it should receive its
character from the men and the times it professes

to describe. In consequence, when the personalities of writers became paramount in France in imparting a fresh stamp to literary work in general, history, on the contrary, began to be told on its own merits, any purpose of the writer was withdrawn from it, and facts shone forth in their own light.

Augustin Thierry was born at Blois. In his endeavours to find in old documents the true character and real life of ancient times he lost his eyesight. His *Histoire de la conquête de l'Angleterre par les Normands* is a masterpiece in French literature. Then came the *Récits des temps mérovingiens*, in which the life of a long misunderstood period is faithfully rendered. In the preface to *Dix ans d'études historiques*, Thierry explains what labour he expended before he reached his ideal as a historian. Indeed, his Saxons and Normans, his Gallo-Romans and Franks, spring to life again in his pages in full possession of their long-lost identity, and poetical in their originality. Thierry did not allow either blindness or bad health to stand in his way, being convinced, as he said, that there is in the world something that is worth more than worldly pleasures, than fortune, than health itself —namely, devotion to science.

BARANTE attended the Ecole Polytechnique and entered the Civil Service of the State. Attention was called to him by his *Tableau de la littérature française au XVIII^e siècle*, and by the edition he gave of the most interesting *Mémoires de Mme de La Rochejaquelein*.

Like Thierry, he had power to neutralise his predisposi-
tions, and to enter into the spirit of the times he
described in the *Histoire des ducs de Bourgogne de la
maison de Valois.* He modernised the stories of
Froissart, Monstrelet, and Philippe de Commines, who
were contemporary with the period, while preserving
the simplicity and guilelessness of their style.

GUIZOT attached himself more to the philosophy of
history than to its plain pictorial rendering. He was
born at Nîmes, of Protestant parents. He received
his education in Geneva, and then became a student
of the law in Paris, and a private tutor. Some
articles on education and on literature, and also a very
remarkable preface to a new edition of Letourneur's
translation of Shakespeare, in which Guizot showed
himself endowed with a judgment in æsthetic matters
equal to that of Mme de Staël, won for him the Chair
of History in La Sorbonne. During the reigns of
Louis XVIII., Charles X., and Louis-Philippe, Guizot
had a chequered career, not only as a professor, but
also as a statesman. He was in and out of his Chair
more than once, and also in and out of office several
times. As a Minister of Public Instruction, he endowed
France with a system of primary schools on which was
reared the whole edifice of popular instruction as it
exists now. While he was Minister for Foreign Affairs,
he fell out of touch with the national feeling, and the
fall of Louis-Philippe was partly due to his unbending
home policy. His lectures gave rise to the following

works—the *Histoire de la civilisation en Europe*, and the *Histoire de la civilisation en France*. The development of modern societies viewed from their political side, and the stages in the intellectual progress of civilised man—such are the main topics written of by Guizot, in the plain style that one would naturally expect from a conscientious historian. *L'Histoire de la Révolution d'Angleterre*, treating of concrete facts rather than of abstractions, reminds one of Thierry's work. It is a lifelike rendering of a troubled period.

MICHELET is by no means so impartial a historian as the preceding ones. He had his ideas, which were of more import to him, and, as it would seem, to his contemporaries, than the mere facts of history, be they never so faithfully rendered. He was a Parisian by birth, who was educated in Paris, and who professed at La Sorbonne and at the Collège de France. A man of a militant temperament, he delivered his historical lectures with polemical intent, to arouse enthusiasm in the breast of French youth for the causes he defended. He was an adversary of the Jesuits, and, having failed to swear fidelity to Napoleon III., his Chair and his small income as a librarian were taken away from him. He wrote a History of France, a History of the French Revolution, and a short Modern History. His minor productions, such as *L'Oiseau*, *L'Insecte*, *La Mer*, *Les Jésuites*, *Le Prêtre*, *Le Peuple*, are more imaginative than practical, and show throughout an ardent polemical tendency.

Michelet may not improperly be compared to Carlyle. He was unable to disconnect the writer from the man, and to cultivate the attitude of mind of a fair observer; but the passion that carries him away is generous and active in the right service of humanity.

THIERS was, like Guizot, a native of Provence. He studied in Marseille, and was called to the Bar at the age of twenty-three. He took to politics at once, and enlisted his pen in the service of liberal ideas. His *Histoire de la Révolution française* won for him at once the widest popularity, and contributed to the downfall of Charles X. From 1830 the place of Thiers was marked in politics. Alternately in office and in opposition, the honour fell to him after the Franco-German war of being the first President of the French Republic, a post which he filled admirably amidst the greatest difficulties. In the *Histoire du Consulat et de l'Empire* Thiers gave his countrymen still more delight than in his first work. The history of this stirring period, during which the French, never stopping to take breath, wrote with the sword all over the map of Europe an epic poem in deeds, was in itself a most inspiriting topic. Thiers knew how to make the best of it, treating all the parts of such a vast and complicated subject with competent versatility, in a plain style that is never wanting in force or precision.

DUMAS.—There are two writers of that name, the father and the son. The former alone is noticed here.

He does not belong to any definite school, either as a novelist or as a playwright, and, like Scribe in light comedy, turned to financial account all the themes he could lay hold of. The newspaper press was receiving great development, and the habit of publishing, as a relief from political matter, a romance called *feuilleton* at the foot of the broad sheets was as a bait held out to the most inventive, the most rapid, and the least scrupulous caterers. Dumas was not able to fill alone his numerous contracts for a continuous supply of literature. He called to his help a large number of assistants, who may claim a large share of the sum total of the works bearing his name. His novels are books of modern romantic adventure. The most popular ones are *Le Comte de Monte-Cristo* and *Les Trois Mousquetaires.* The variety and vivacity of Dumas' imaginative power, notwithstanding the casualness with which he arrays adventure after adventure without any attempt at composition, place him among the novelists most read in our time, and among the most entertaining.

1804-1876 GEORGE SAND ranks as high in the modern literature of France as George Eliot in the modern literature of Great Britain, and there is also a certain likeness in the intellectual attitude and lives of those two women. George Sand is only a *nom de plume*, Sand being the first half of Sandeau, the name of the novelist in conjunction with whom the lady here described did some literary work. Her maiden name was Aurore Dupin, and by marriage she became Mme Dudevant. She spent the early years of her life with her grandmother at the castle of Nohant, amid surroundings well suited to develop her dreamy and fantastic native disposition. Fondness for and understanding of nature were ever characteristic of her. At thirteen she was sent to the convent of English Augustine nuns in Paris, where she passed through a crisis of religious enthusiasm. When she was allowed to return to Nohant her wildness of soul resumed undisputed sway. She read the books of the *philosophes*, those of Rousseau, those by the most noted French moralists, and devoured promiscuously every kind of literature, whether of home or foreign growth, whether of poetic or prosaic contents. Her marriage was an unhappy one. After nine years she parted from her husband, and then began to make a name for herself as a woman who owned no authority, and was a master of literature. Several of George Sand's novels deal with the marriage question—such are *Indiana*, *Valentine*, and *Jacques*. Others, written after 1840, are occupied with plans for social reform and a philosophic kind of republicanism. *Consuelo* is her most remarkable work in this line. Later, when she had got over the misconceptions of life, bred from her too highly strung imagination in matters of private conduct and of public rights, there came over her a peace and serenity which set free her purer artistic powers to write *La Mare au diable*, *François le Champi*, and *La petite Fadette*. These three are graceful masterpieces setting forth with all sweetness some touching scenes in the rural life of France. The *Marquis de*

*Villemer* is a fine piece of character painting. The enthusiast that was in George Sand is responsible for the spoiling of much of her work.

1799-1850 BALZAC was born at Tours, and began his literary career by writing a number of novels which fell quite flat. He attained to some fame only after the publication of *Le Chouan* in 1829. His father wished that he should become a lawyer, and kept him on very short commons when he took to literature, though he settled down to labours of the most strenuous kind. However, he had the misfortune to fall into debt, as the result of unlucky speculations in the book trade, and found himself in after life in very much the same position as Walter Scott when his publishers became bankrupt, or as Lamartine, who toiled year after year with a view to meeting his obligations. He would have courted, however, for the sake of popularity alone, the feverish activity which was forced upon him by a sordid cause. He fell in love with a Polish countess, and had just married her after many vicissitudes, and was laying down the burden of ceaseless work, when he died. The picture of Balzac sitting week after week and month after month in a dingy Paris lodging, absorbed in the eager composition of novels destined to the greatest fame, forms a striking episode in the long tale of the trials attending the profession of literature. Balzac is generally set down as the chief of the modern realistic school. The actual and the real were often depicted before. But what he did was to introduce strictness and close accuracy in the analysis of character as well as in the description of physical characteristics. The romantic element is utterly absent from his artistic purpose; but, as romance is part and parcel of human character, it forced itself indirectly upon Balzac, however much narrow-minded realists may decline to acknowledge it. Besides, Balzac had read Walter Scott, and himself bore testimony to the influence he received from him. Balzac, as was only natural, fell more and more under subjection to the style which gave him with the public a name for originality. He then dwelt more on the repulsive sides of life, and on physical and moral ugliness. After him, realism, conceived exclusively as the painting of vices and of horrors, took the name of naturalism. The most famous novels of Balzac are *Eugénie Grandet, Le père Goriot, Ursule Mirouët, La Peau de Chagrin, César Birotteau*, etc. Owing to their number, he classified them into categories or types under the general title *Comédie humaine*, comprising scenes from private life, scenes of military life, scenes of Parisian life, scenes of rural life, etc.

MÉRIMÉE, the son of a painter, was born in Paris, became an advocate, and received an appointment in the Civil Service of his country. His first work created quite a sensation. It was a collection of tragic and comic plays, and the two were combined in a manner that exceeded the daring of Victor Hugo. Two years later he claimed to have discovered the songs of a hitherto unknown Illyrian bard, who turned out to be himself. Then came short tales in prose, in which he showed consummate skill in giving interest to the plots, and in impressing upon the characters the stamp of truth. Instead of accumulating realistic touches as Balzac did, he set about putting the one right touch which, by itself, would show the whole man. The *Prise de la redoute,* a sketch of a few pages, and *Colomba,* a novel of a few chapters, are his masterpieces. The *Vénus d'Ille* is a story of mediæval origin. Mérimée is a realist like Balzac, but he was saved from the grossness of the latter by cultivating the Ancient Greeks.

FLAUBERT, son of a surgeon in Rouen, studied law in Paris till he was interrupted by illness. From that moment the writing of novels took up all his attention. He used to say: 'The subject of a work of art is meaningless; execution alone is important. Art should be cultivated for its own sake; an artist should be a pagan, and worship form, and nothing else.' His first imaginative composition met with the disapproval of his friends. It was the *Tentation de Saint-Antoine,* which he recast, and did not give out till 1871. In the meantime he chose for a study a family which his father had known, and after working it up for the space of three years he brought it out under the title of *Madame Bovary.* This novel outdid Balzac in point of realism, and the author was called upon to answer for the writing of it in a police-court. As, after all, it was not written in order to openly defy morals, but was simply the outcome of artistic preoccupations, Flaubert was acquitted.　He next wrote *Salammbô*, inaugurating a class of work in which he may boast of having Rider Haggard as a very inferior disciple.　The scene of *Salammbô* is laid in Africa at the end of the first Punic war, amid an uprising of the mercenary troops of Carthage.　Flaubert carried out to the utmost his precept, 'Worship the form,' applying it to himself with the greatest severity.

CONCLUSION.—We refrain from giving an account of the latest period of French literature, which has not yet attained to the dignity of being historical.

The following works are recommended:—

1. *Histoire abrégée de la littérature française,* by Charles Cottier.
2. *Leçons de littérature française,* by Petit de Julleville.
3. Saintsbury's *Primer of French Literature.*
4. Keene's *Literature of France* (Murray's University Extension Manuals).
5. Saintsbury's *Short History of French Literature.*
6. Vinet's *Histoire de la littérature française au XVIII<sup>e</sup> siècle, Poètes de Louis XIV., Moralistes,* etc.
7. Nisard's *Histoire de la littérature française.*　4 vols.
8. Paul Albert's *Littérature française.*　4 vols.

# CHAPTER IX.

## THE RELATIONS BETWEEN FRENCH AND ENGLISH LITERATURE.

ANTHONY HAMILTON is a convenient landmark whence to start on a survey of the mutual relation between the literatures of England and of France, for he appears at the dividing-point between two periods in both countries. But he offers no inducement to linger beside him, save the dryness of his wit. Rabelais before him had found his way across the Channel, as is visible in the works of Robert Burton, Sir Thomas Urquhart, Swift, Sterne, and Southey. Calvin's language and his logic had introduced their firmness and austerity. Earlier than either, French romances, tales, and allegoric compositions had restored to England, in an elaborate shape, much material derived in the obscurest mediæval times from Britain's best Gaelic strain.

In 1660, when Hamilton, after gracing the Court of Louis XIV. at Versailles, enlivened that of Charles II., English literature, nurtured in its more vital sources by Gaelic, Anglo-Saxon, Norse, and Norman blood, was, in its outer expressions, just emerging from a long spell of Italian influence. At the same time, French classical literature was touching its ripest and fullest point, and its merit, enhanced by a lull in the original productivity of Italy, Spain, Germany, and England, was about to dominate Europe for a hundred years.

Corneille, by his tragedies and his critical essays on the unities of action, time, and place; Boileau, by his 'Art Poétique,' setting up good sense as a standard of taste, and Latin rhetorics as a matter of style; Molière, by his comedy of manners, his broad comedy, and his amendment of the Italian farcical plays; Racine, by the courtliness of his art—courtly because his audience was aristocratic, his personages kings and queens, and their sentiments polite—had brought French literature so fully into touch with the centres of worldly and fashionable culture in Europe, that England for a while turned away from its rightful masters in inspiration, such as Shakespeare and Milton, and procured for its literature a whole array of French-taught patrons, such as Dryden, the Earl of Roscommon, the Earl of Mulgrave, Thomas Otway, Wycherley, Congreve, Addison, Pope, and Bolingbroke.

But while in literature, properly so called, the French were leading the English in chains behind their triumphal car, there was, in respect of social philosophy and general criticism, a steady current setting in from England to France. Such social writers as Shaftesbury, Wollaston, Collins, Tindal, and such philosophic critics as Burke, Reid, William Hogarth, Adam Smith, Hutcheson, Campbell, Addison, and Pope, appealed first to the French. There is in that list more than one name which ordinarily read Englishmen will with difficulty recognise. Yet it was on feeling some mental communion with those men that Montesquieu, Voltaire, and Rousseau, to mention the foremost only, came to Great Britain, connecting it directly with the preliminaries to the French Revolution on one hand, and, by a further action, with the reformation of French literature. A volume of *Lettres sur les Anglais et les Français* was published in 1725; and in 1731 appeared Voltaire's *Lettres sur les Anglais.* His judgments on England are crude; he writes in the vein of an overweening school-boy travelling in wonderland. He bestows full praise on what he wishes for France, namely, civil and religious liberty; but he sees Shakespeare with the eyes of Tom Thumb scanning the sleeping giant, first blankly, then knowingly, and blandly at last, when he believes he has robbed him of his boots. For Voltaire did try to walk in Shakespeare's shoes. He cut *Zaïre* out of *Othello,* and *La Mort de César* out of *Julius Cæsar.* Voltaire, however, ground Shakespeare so small in his rhetorical mill, that the *Lettres sur les Anglais* might well have passed unnoticed, had the French Government not worked strenuously to suppress them. They were condemned by the Paris Parliament, vetoed by the Pope, and burned by the hangman. This made them so popular, and gave Shakespeare such advantages, that Voltaire began to fear usurpation of his literary kingship. He turned upon his own *protégé,* and launched forth into satire against him and Otway. Voltaire's alarm knew no

O

bounds when a 'priggish youth,' of the name of Letourneur, put Shakespeare into French; and he must have
turned in his grave when Ducis, an adapter of Shakespearean plays, after years of unbroken success, was
appointed to succeed him as an Academician.   Still
Ducis had been faithful enough to the French traditions
in divesting his rendering of almost all Shakespearean
elements.   In his old age, putting in the winter months
a wreath of boxwood round the brow of 'William,'
whose bust adorned his apartment, Ducis would say
complacently: 'Behold how I honour him after the
fashion of the Greeks: they used to crown the springs
whence they drew their water.'   Thus, drop by drop,
Shakespeare trickled on to the bed of French literature
till the time of Victor Hugo.

In 1822, Guizot struck a fuller note of appreciation
in his preface to a new edition of Letourneur's translation.   He explained how literature follows in the wake
of the revolutions of the human mind (the main-line of
evolution, as recent critics would call it); how theatrical
literature rests on manners, faith, and national history,
and how in consequence it lost its force when it was
produced in Paris for a class only; how Shakespeare, in
his tragedies, is a man holding a stake in the moral life
of mankind, while in his comedies he is simply an
amused playwright.   'Man,' says Guizot, ' sees beauty
in certain combinations to which our judgment has the
key, as soon as our emotions have experienced their
effectiveness.  In the knowledge and uses of these combinations consists Shakespearean art.'   Victor Hugo's

preface to his *Cromwell* sets forth in a more personal manner a similar dramatic theory. Amid much sensible talk concerning the classical unities, and after treating of the nature of dramatic verse, local colour, and directness of expression, he builds up the doctrine that the spirit of humanity has passed through three stages. In the first, it was face to face with God and nature; in the second, men were in sight of one another when they expressed their relations in epic poetry; in the third, aware of their spiritual origin, and alive to the conflict of their double nature in its tragic and comic aspects, they held up the mirror in the Shakespearean sense to their faces, and flashed their own image upon the dramatic stage.

Victor Hugo's manifesto was the signal for an excited battle. Classicists and Romanticists, who had pressed in the lecture-room round Villemain, the professorial critic of the day, now carried their warfare into the theatres. Both bands now clamoured for victory, but Villemain preserved the attitude of an arbitrator. At one time he had, in presence of both camps, set up a comparison between Shakespeare's *Julius Cæsar* and Voltaire's *La Mort de César*. Beginning with the latter play, he touched upon its merits in their order of progression, gave a half-measure of praise, and to a breathless audience, such as exists in France alone, proceeded to read what was, he said, the capital passage. No sooner had the Classicists, thrilled by its beauty, raised triumphant shouts, than the lecturer calmly observed that these lines were imitated from Shakespeare. The shouts now came from the hitherto silent camp, whose delight increased as Villemain pointed to the wealth of life impressions crowded into Shakespeare's play by the free working of his dramatic sense.

It is noteworthy that the name of the Romantic school had, long before its rise, been hit upon by Letourneur in the course of his English studies. What an interesting story could be written of that word: designing first the language and things of ancient Rome, then applied during the middle ages to tales of adventure and sentiment, because they were so well told in Old French, the earliest Romance tongue! Letourneur has it that only two words exist in French to characterise a landscape, a scene, a spectacle, which charms the eye and detains the imagination; and they are insufficient to betoken the melancholy ideas and emotions which such a vision may arouse. The first, *romanesque*, bears along with it an uncomplimentary reflection upon the person or thing it designates; the second, *pittoresque*, only expresses the technical merits of a theme. The English word is happier and more forcible. It expresses at once the points of the physical vision and its moral effects. If a valley is picturesque, it is merely a fit subject for a picture. If it is romantic, one's spirit craves to rest there, the eye delights in its contemplation, a tender imagination peoples it with sympathetic shapes, and forgets the valley to dwell upon the ideas that are suggested by it. The fact is, that when Letourneur expressed himself with such just feeling, the intense reasonableness imparted to French literary art since Montaigne wrote in prose, and Malherbe and Boileau in verse, had not loosened its hold on literary men. Day-dreaming had no acknowledged outlet. Love of nature, patriotism, religious emotion, the inner play of sentiment and passion, were without a spokesman, save Rousseau, who was not a Frenchman. Not so in England, where Thomson, Young, and Richardson were fully engaged upon these very subjects. Letourneur introduced Young, Sterne, and Richardson to the French reading public; Thomson found a translator in St. Lambert, and a disciple in Delille.

For a time the *Night Thoughts* was the rage. Gloomy broodings and pathetic verse were in fashion. The delights of rural life were stiffly presented in pedestrian lines, cast in the classical mould. The English poets, brought into contact in France with an accumulation of original material ready for literary treatment, helped to gain recognition for themes of this kind. Aching breasts fancied the music of rushing mountain rills, and waxed eloquent over it. The voices of the winds in the pine forests were understood and caught in the chords of the lyre. To accommodate this inrush of sentiment and nature, a wing was added to the temple of French literature, and critics compelled to take cognisance of it. In fact, the emotional fires kindled by Young and Rousseau, Chateaubriand and Byron, spread to and lived in Millevoye's *Chute des Feuilles*, in Victor Hugo's *Tristesse d'Olympio*, in Lamartine's *Le Lac*, in Alfred de Musset's *Les Nuits*, in Goethe's *Werther*, in Heine, and in Leopardi.

A Scottish poetry with an inspiration more real, though less authentic, than that of Thomson, the Ossianic songs, had perhaps more influence, and found more credit, in France than anywhere else.  Its distant strain seemed to have an unmistakably Scandinavian and Gaelic ring.  Letourneur had the good fortune to translate it.  From that moment Ossian was adopted by the French nation.  As if a vision of heather glens and Highland bens had suddenly swept down from the North, an echo of the bagpipe was wafted from the shore of misty lochs; the shadow of an eagle swooped across the air; phantom Highlanders marched to the sound of the pibroch across the moors, and vanished behind spectral birch-trees.  Napoleon, surrounded by battle-smoke, paused to hear 'the voice that was no more.'  Millevoye, Lamartine, Charles Nodier, in heroic lays, lyric effusions, and dreamy love-tales, kept alive some faith in the Celtic bard.  Ninety years ago he was a hundred times more popular than Homer.  In 1773 he was a greater favourite than Shakespeare. Goethe gave him a place in *Werther*; Herder pressed him upon the German public; Cesarotti translated him into Italian; Young was outshone.  The names of Oscar, Malvina, and Trenmor became current in fiction. Then the crash came; but not till Jedediah Cleishbotham, too, had enjoyed his hour of popularity, and Walter Scott had pointed out to Augustin Thierry a new way of presenting history, and to Alfred de Vigny a new mode of working historical matter into romance. Indeed, to complete the scope of our subject, we need

not leave Scotland; for, from Walter Scott's handling
of history to history itself there is but a step. At the
end of last century, of Britain's greatest historians two
were Scots—Hume and Robertson; the third, Gibbon,
was hardly English at all.

Edinburgh was then rising to the pinnacle of its
reputation; the intellectual atmosphere was suffused
with light. The philosophic systems built by the
French out of premises laid by Locke, the social and
national histories substituted by Montesquieu and
Voltaire for chronicles, theretofore mainly military and
feudal, appealed strongly to the brilliant wits in Scotland's capital. The French spirit was so ingrained in
James' Court, that Edinburgh ministers with a turn
for history could not, without quarrelling with their
best work, have disowned their obligations to Voltaire.
When Robertson and Hume had written their works,
the rare sight was witnessed of their greater popularity
in Paris than in London. As Sainte-Beuve words it,
Paris was then the centre of the propaganda of thought
by literature and declamation. Hume, writing thence,
alluded with contempt to 'barbarian' London, with its
brawling political parties. In Paris he was fed on
ambrosia, refreshed with nectar, plied with incense,
and smothered under flowers. Little did he know what
terrible commotions were soon to shake his Elysian
hostelry. Hume was introduced to the children of the
Dauphin at Versailles. One of the boys, afterwards
the unfortunate Louis XVI., a ten-year-old child, spoke
of the Scottish philosopher's many friends and admirers

in France, and said that he himself had much profited by reading Hume's works. A younger brother (the future king, Louis XVIII.) pointed, in his turn, to the great interest with which he was looking forward to reading the same books. At last a third princely scion, who was to be Charles X., and was then four years old, lisped forth in broken fragments his compliments to the amused visitor. What a gentle Arcadia was Paris, in 1763, for the sons of kings and for men of letters!

The part[1] played by Britain in the events consequent on the Revolution was not precisely calculated to conciliate French sympathies; and the people who, as Heine says, then acted instead of writing their national epic had scant time to give to their own literature, still less to appreciate that of other nations. But it was early in this century, and while the two nations were yet at each other's throats, that the vogue of Ossian was greatest, that Madame de Staël produced her penetrating criticisms of Shakespeare, and that Chateaubriand translated *Paradise Lost*. The story 'of man's first disobedience,' however, has not permanently appealed to the imagination of a people hardly characterised by a submissiveness to the powers that be. Milton is now little read in France; he is none the less admired.

It is otherwise with Shakespeare. The translations of Letourneur, of Alfred de Vigny, of Montégut, of François Victor Hugo, the adaptations of Ducis and of

---

[1] The next four paragraphs of this chapter are due to the pen of Mr. P. Nichol.

Dumas *père*, do not nearly exhaust the list of renderings, more or less literal, of the majority of his works. The cult of England's master dramatist by the group of ' Romantics ' is well known ; equal at least to it, as nearer, and therefore coming more home to them, was the influence of the writings of Byron and Scott. Lamartine owed something, certainly not his music, to Byron, whom he admired greatly, and to whom he inscribed a *Méditation Poétique*. Hugo's *Notre Dame de Paris* is artistically purified and impassioned Scott. It was of the inspiration that came from Abbotsford that the elder Dumas drank ; the author of *Don Juan* found fit audience in the author of *Rolla*. De Musset's debt to Byron is often unfairly overcharged, but both writers give the same impression of the poet-dandy. Balzac adored Scott, whose effect on him we may trace in the occasionally tedious descriptions with which he opens most of his stories. Scott also, with Balzac himself, was one of the few men allowed to have been really great in letters by the eccentric critic Barbey d'Aurévilly. English subjects became common in the drama of this time ; witness De Vigny's *Chatterton* and the *Kean* of Dumas *père*.

We should take care, however, not to exaggerate the spell cast by English or other foreign literature on the French writers of 1830. The Romantic movement was essentially indigenous, an inevitable literary reaction. It would have gone through a similar evolution, differing only in details, had Shakespeare and Scott, still more had the philosophical playwrights of Germany, never written,

or written in Chinese.   The innovators who adopted
what they conceived to be British *sobriquets*, to spite
the classical *perruques*, were but gaily puerile Parisian
Bohemians, who, with few exceptions, knew not a word
of the English tongue : the only spirit among them who
was really 'septentrional' being the half-crazed poet
Gérard de Nerval, and his dreamy, moonlit nature held
more of Germany than of England.

With the waning of the chivalric and extravagant
graces of Romanticism, whose literary ideals, as ideals in
other regions, were precipitated to their fall when the
nation accepted the Second Empire, Scott and Byron
passed out of fashion.   But the study of English literature, contemporary and of the past, steadily increased.
Sainte-Beuve published his suggestive notices on British
authors of the eighteenth century; Taine gave to the
world his original history ; M. Emile Montégut, in the
pages of the *Revue des Deux Mondes*, began to prove his
learned appreciation of our greater and obscurer names ;
and the once most eagerly read of English story-
tellers now exercised over the French the sway which
throughout a life-time he held over the British.  Scarcely
more than in the Edinburgh or London of to-day is it
considered good taste in contemporary Paris to think
highly or to speak in praise of Dickens ; but the realistic
school of fiction in France owes to his novels none the
less a considerable and scantily acknowledged debt.
We are bound to believe M. Daudet when he asserts
that he had never seen *David Copperfield* until he had
completed his *Jack*, but there is much throughout

Daudet's writings suggestive of Dickens—often so decidedly suggestive that it cannot be the result of merely spiritual filiation. It is certain that he, like the other members of the school, is constantly indebted to certain methods inaugurated by the English novelist. The care spent on the characterisation of secondary personages, the insistence on details of individual bearing and utterance, the frequency of subject or episode painted from humble life: all these are proper to the French realists, from Flaubert downwards; and it is from Dickens they have borrowed them as much as from their acknowledged master Balzac. They have dropped, of course, the sentimentalism and the tendency to unnatural incident which some of Dickens's admirers might wish that he also had oftener discarded.

French as the Official Language of England.— Until the latter part of the reign of Edward III. all Parliamentary proceedings were conducted in French. Until the reign of Henry VI. the statutes were recorded in French or Latin. Since the reign of Henry VII. all proceedings, including statutes, have been in English, with the exception of the forms by which a bill is transmitted and the Royal assent is given or withheld. These forms are still used, and are:—1. Assent to (*a*) a *money bill* by the words, 'La reyne remercie ses bons sujets, accepte leur bénévolence, et ainsi le veult'; (*b*) an ordinary *public bill* by the words, 'La reyne le veult'; (*c*) a *private bill* by the words, 'Soit fait comme il est désiré.' 2. Refusal of assent by the words, 'La

reyne s'avisera' (last exercised in 1707). 3. Indorse-
ment (*a*) that bill is passed by the Commons, 'Soit
baillé aux seigneurs'; (*b*) that it is returned by Lords
amended, 'A ceste bille avesque des amendemens les
seigneurs sont assentus'; (*c*) that the Commons agree to
Lords' amendments, 'A ces amendemens les communes
sont assentus,' and, similarly, when a bill first passed in
Lords was sent to Commons.

As to courts of justice, it was not till 1731
(4 Geo. II. cap. 26) that an Act was passed providing
that proceedings in courts of justice should be conducted in English. From the Conquest until Edward III.,
all pleadings were written, and usually the arguments
and decisions proceeded, in Norman law French. Edward enacted (36 Edw. III. cap. 15) that cases should be
debated and judged in English, but that the records
should be kept in Latin. Accordingly, from that time
until 1731—except during Cromwell's Protectorate—
the records of the courts were kept in law Latin. But,
notwithstanding Edward's statute, Norman law French
continued to be used in the year-books or official
reports of the judges' decisions, and in the private
reports of decisions kept by the judges or counsel, afterwards published. The year-books end in the time of
Henry VIII. But the Norman law French continued to
be used in reports until Cromwell's time, though mixed
with English.

For instance, Rolle (1589-1658), one of the best
reporters, says : 'Haught semble a disallouer ceo, car il
shake son capit.' In reporting another case he has :

' Hom dit " Holt hath taken a cleaver and stricken his cook upon the head " ; et ne averr que le cook fuit mort : et pur ceo fuit adjudgé nemy bon.'

Or from *Moore's Reports* we may quote a case in 1604 at Newgate : 'Le case fuit que en home et se feme ayant longe temps vivé incontinent ensemble . . . le home dit al feme que il fuit weary de son vie et que il voiloit luymême occider : à que la feme dit que donques elle voilait aussi moryer ave lui : per que le home praya la feme que elle voilait vaer et acheter Rates-bane : et ils voilont ceo biber ensemble : le quel il fist : et el ceo mist en le drink et ils bibent ceo. Mes la feme après prist sallet oyle : per que el vomit et fuit recov' mes le home morust. Et le question fuit si ceo fuit murther en la feme. . Mountague Recorder cause l'espécial matter d'être trouvé.[1]  Quaere le résolution.'

[1] There are no orthographical accents in the original.

## CHAPTER X.

### THE OLD FRENCH LANGUAGE, ORIGIN, DIALECTS, EARLY DOCUMENTS.

OLD FRENCH can be divided into three successive periods: the Period of Formation, the Flourishing Period, and the Period of Decay.

The first is contemporaneous with the earliest middle ages, and its origin can be traced back to the conquest of Gaul by Rome. When the Roman Republic was still in existence, the *Lingua Romana* of its soldiers, merchants, and colonists came into contact with the Celtic dialects of Gaul. The campaigns of Julius Cæsar can be considered as the first link in the chain of historical events which were to bring about the formation of a French language. The *Lingua Romana* became the prevalent speech of the language-making classes of Gaul, Celtiberia, and Italy (to say nothing of its lesser homes by right of conquest), though the invasion of the Barbarians brought into play a new linguistic factor. Before the fourth century A.D., Celtic had been overpowered by its invader and driven to out-of-the-way districts; Latin, the literary dialect of Cicero, was written, but little spoken out of the governing and educated caste; it was a class-language. The *Lingua Romana* had already altered in different areas of the vast territories it had spread over. It was assuming local peculiarities which foreshadowed its breaking up into different dialects, when the Teutonic element burst upon the scenes, and acted as an ultimate dissolvent.

From that day the processes of decay, which till then might be considered as modifications within the *Lingua Romana*, assumed a regenerative character, and became the starting-point of a new language.

A Germanic tribe, the leading military and political agent in the plains of Northern Gaul, has had the honour of seeing its name affixed to the language. This Germanic title has by no means affected the language itself. Teutonic influences can be traced in goodly number in the vocabulary, in the phonetics, and in the etymology of Old French; Latin words, for instance, have been presented with meanings after the analogy of Teutonic corresponding terms. But the grammatical framework of the language, and its syntax, which developed only in the latter stage of Old French, are wholly and absolutely Latin in origin and Latin in spirit.

It is impossible, for want of documentary evidence, to say whether a period of absolute linguistic decomposition ushered in the formative period of Old French. It seems, however, reasonable to believe that at no time between 395 and 842, the date of the first Old French document history knows of, the destructive process obtained the upper hand over the constructive one. It is evident, from the way in which it spread over so many peoples and lands so distant, that the *Lingua Romana Rustica* contained a principle of exceptional vitality, which was sufficiently strong to maintain its supremacy in spite of the heavy odds arrayed against it in consequence of the breakdown of the Empire. It regulated its own decay, it absorbed what it could not reject, it upheld the high standard of linguistic efficiency which distinguishes the Indo-European races. It is also clear from the character of the first literary documents in Old French, and from the wealth and spontaneousness of its literature, that a fair amount of popular culture was extant among the classes of society in which language has its centre and whence it borrows its leverage. There was in the fresh and vivid imagination of the people an abundant supply of language-producing power. Unfettered by the weight of classical Latin, with its stereotyped forms and literature, this power preserved its elasticity, had free play, and bore fruits. Those fruits, in Gaul as elsewhere, ran into types; dialects, whose primary causes are obscure, were formed. In the valleys of the Rhône and of the Garonne, in the whole country verging towards the Mediterranean and the Bay of Biscay, from the mountains of Auvergne southwards, Early French was not French : it inclined towards the Italian and the Spanish modifications of Romance on which it bordered.

These southern dialects, known under the collective name of '*Langue d'Oc*,' fell out of the race for existence when a centre of political and military power showed itself to be placed in the Frankish portion of France, near enough for the absorption of the Mediterranean border into the circle over which it radiated. What in the *Langue d'Oc* had affinities with the *Langue d'Oïl* strengthened the northern invader by as much against its southern neighbour. Political troubles and military invasion deprived the southern speech of its national significance; it lost its literary standing and died out as a body of language. Nowadays '*Provençal*' is on the one hand a '*patois*,' on the other a study for literary antiquarians and philologists.

Its adversary, the *Langue d'Oïl*, has had a triumphant career. It has become one of the very foremost culture-languages of Europe. Geographically, to it belonged the valleys of the Saône, the Loire, the Seine, the Scheldt, and the Meuse. Scholars recognise four dialects in it. These divisions are well marked in the central middle ages. In the earlier and in the latter, from confusion in one case, from obliteration in the other, they are less distinguishable. They are more convenient in a classification than exhaustive from a philological point of view. For all round the area strictly belonging to these dialects, north of them in Belgium, and far east in Romance Switzerland, also within their respective provinces, there existed not only local forms but whole dialects that are distinguishable from any of the four leading ones.

A process of natural selection took place among the dialects of the *Langue d'Oil*. The one at the centre of political power came out victorious. It is likely that, linguistically, it was the most worthy of a supremacy which was really obtained by agencies of the political order. The other dialects were by degrees incorporated, for all the northern dialects had much in common. Their extinction was an absorption rather than a destruction. As for their literature, it died a natural death when talent ceased to use them as a channel for literary expression. By the time the conquering dialect had laid down Old French characteristics, the centralisation of literature in its hand was completely effected. Arrested in their development, the defeated dialects sank to the rank of *patois*.

The most western of the four was that of Normandy (we should say that of Neustria, for the name of Norman is a misnomer as applied to an essentially Gallo-Roman dialect). Submitted to direct Scandinavian influence by the invasion of the Norsemen, it resisted stoutly foreign contamination : so stoutly, that when the Normans invaded England they imported the language of France instead of their own, long since forgotten. That they were in reality only a numerically weak Teutonic colony in a mass of Gallic people is shown by the slight mark they have put on their adoptive speech, and by the surprising ease with which they brought, as their own, to their Saxon brethren in England, a Romanic dialect. The vowel-sounds alone of Norman French show traces of having been shaped by strange throats. And even that characteristic is not purely Norman. It is a leading feature of Old French that it developed the vowel system of Latin at the expense of its consonantal system. That development is the more striking in proportion as the locality of change becomes a more northern one, and points to the presence of Teutonic undercurrents among the influences affecting French phonetic rules. When the Norman dialect crossed the Channel with William the Conqueror's standards, it fell under Anglo-Saxon influence. It developed then into what has been called 'Anglo-Norman,' while Norman proper lost its identity in that of French.

Norman literature was great, and of a strikingly epic character. The language was Romanic, but the strain of imagination was partly of the Scandinavian type. It was cultivated both in its Continental home and at the Court of the Kings of England. Norman French differs from its fellow-dialects by some peculiarities which do not affect the material of speech, but only its outward shape. *U* takes the place of *ou*, *eu*, *oi*, and sometimes of *a*. The most frequent substitute, however, for *oi* is *ei*. This *ei*, spelt in modern French *ai*, has driven out of use the Burgundian sound *oi*, long preferred by French for the endings of verbs and for some nouns, and still noted as *oi* in the seventeenth and eighteenth centuries. This is an instance of the many reactions of the doomed dialects upon their conqueror. Besides its orthodox diphthong *ei* in three conjugations, Norman has in the imperfect of the first conjugation the sound *ou*: saying, as Littré points out, *je cuidoue* or *je cuidoe* (*je croyais* in modern French), while Old French said *je cuidoie*. Norman disliked the contact *ie* in endings, a

favourite one in Old French, and thinned it to a mere
*e.* The area occupied by this dialect and its sub-
dialects is far more extended than its name implies.
From La Rochelle on the ocean, right across the Loire
and the Seine, to the English Channel and Picardy,
with the exception of Celtic Brittany, proofs have
been found of the undisputed supremacy of Norman
French.

Its northern neighbour is the dialect of Picardy.  In
what is now Belgium, it bordered on Walloon, Flemish,
and Dutch.  On its southern side Burgundian and
Norman gave it a sufficiently definite boundary-line.
Its main dialectical features are a preference for hard
consonantal sounds and the persistence in pronunciation of the diphthong *oi.*  It uses h ud *c* and *k* rather
than soft *c* or *ch*, a guttural *g* and *ch* instead of the
sibilant *s.*  A Neo-Latin ending *icmes* in the first person plural of the imperfect was superseded by the
generic Old French contraction *ions,* or *iuns* (Norman).

The Burgundian dialect was the main dialect in the
*Langue d'Oïl*; it was so closely bound up with the
fourth dialect, the one spoken in Paris and the country
round it, that some scholars have merged them together
into one.  It touched on the east the Germanic districts of the Vosges, entered into contact in the south
with the *Langue d'Oc,* and was separated from Norman
French in the west by the dialect of Ile de France.
Out of France proper, with all due allowance for
marked local peculiarities, it occupied Romance
Switzerland and Savoy jointly with the *Langue d'Oc.*

Though French Switzerland is geographically distinct from Burgundy proper, and escaped on the whole French political influence and interference, it was in its best mediæval days well within the scope of Burgundian literary and social life.

Burgundian shows its linguistic individuality by the addition of an *i* to *a* in any part of a word and to a sounded *e*. It exchanges also nasal *n* for guttural *g*, and uses *ch* in words where Picard has hard *c* or *k*. It has a past definite of first conjugation in : *ai, ais, ait*, the diphthong *oi* in the imperfect (*oie, oies, oit*) succeeding an early Neo-Latin form in *eve, eves, evet* (Latin *abam, abas, abat*). A third person plural of past definite in *arent*, Neo-Latin also, gave way to the later form *erent*, but it was taken up again by Rabelais in the sixteenth century.

The fourth and last dialect among the leading subdivisions of the *Langue d'Oïl* was the dialect of Ile de France—that is, of Paris and the province of which Paris was the capital. It may be called Francic, by a convenient misappropriation of terms, justified by the accepted, though equally faulty, expression—Norman French. This dialect is open to the accusation of being a conception of Old French students rather than a tangible reality. Ile de France is the meeting-place of the three dialects above mentioned, rather than the cradle of an aggressive and sharply defined speech. It was a centre of assimilation and compromise, having in common with all dialects of the *Langue d'Oïl* the same substratum, and making its own the borrowings it gathered from west, north, and east. It was, so to say, neutral, and attained to excellence by the subservience of all. It can hardly be said that, either in literature or in its phonology and morphology, it has any single feature that it does not hold in common with one or other of its neighbours. The instrument of its might did not reside in its literature, or in its linguistic aptness. As said before, the reasons of its gradual spread over France were of the political order. These began to take effect in 987, when Hugh Capet, Count of Ile de France, became King of France. The gradual formation, before the year 1200, of the University of Paris gave the colouring of legitimacy to the claim of Parisian French to be paramount in letters. The work of unification was not complete in literature at the close of the middle ages, when Old French turned into Modern French. Nevertheless, so rapid was the gravitation setting towards Paris under the Capetian Kings, that the expression 'Old French' on the whole applies to the speech of Ile de France.

On looking back upon the dialects thus rapidly reviewed, one is struck by the comparative insignificance of their differences. This reveals the powerful Romance unity underlying them. It points also to the difficulties still affecting Old French studies. It is by no means easy to establish distinctions between the dialects, owing to dearth of early documents, owing to the utter confusion in the alphabetical notation of sounds in manuscripts, and owing to the action and reaction, exchanges and combinations from dialect to dialect and from century to century. Dialects and local literature are still an open question ; but where the firm foothold of science begins is in the study of the oral forms deposited in the mediæval national literature of France. The outburst of literary production coincides with what is, philologically speaking, the ' flourishing period of Old French.'

Old French was before all things a spoken language. It has the features of a language that is more spoken than written. It was formed in a happy unconsciousness of grammar, in a fortunate ignorance of the fact that each Latin form, which gave birth to a corresponding Old French form, was once part of a systematic whole, of a linguistic scheme reducible to declension, conjugation, and syntax. That is why, from a philological standpoint, it can be called a pure speech, a natural product of the phonetic influences at work in the areas where it arose—influences which have been generalised into rules and codified by philologists. That is also why, now that Old French is extinct, now that its sounds can no longer be perceived by the ear, the work of reconstituting it as spoken, from the imperfect MSS., is attended both by failures and unexpected successes. For instance, Modern French is full of blended diphthongal sounds and silent letters. A reader's first impulse is to introduce these diphthongs and silent notations into his perusal of old texts. But a closer inspection of texts and some acquaintance with the metric necessities of verse show that such diphthongs are generally two distinct vowel-sounds which have become conterminous by the loss of a Latin consonant. Also, the consonants that are noted are sounded, and many which appear in Modern French have been introduced into it by a false analogy with literary Latin, regardless of Old French precedents; for instance, the modern *b* in *absoudre* and *abstenir* is of learned introduction, the old forms being written and pronounced *asoudre* and *astenir*. The diphthong *ai*, now sounded like *è* or like *é*, consisted in the early stages of Old French of two sounds. '*Chrétien*' had three syllables, and *chapeau* also. Moreover, from our point of view, the sound and the sign appear not to correspond. For instance, the sound *eu* before an *x* is usually noted as *ex*, which is misleading to us; so are *puet*, standing for the Modern sound *peut*, and the vowel *u*, which has often in Old French spelling its Latin value, represented in Modern French by *ou*.

No uniform orthographical system was devised in the middle ages. Now that Old French studies have so much gained in popularity and trustworthiness, it will be the task of scholars to agree on a consistent orthography, if it can be done without unduly assimilating to one type the diversities in pronunciation at different times and in different places. There could be no absolute standard of right and wrong in the graphic notation of a language still engaged in the process of generalising its phonetic laws. Pronunciation varied remarkably between the ninth and sixteenth centuries.

Another stumbling-block is looseness in the construction of the Old French sentence. Like Homer, it has what we should call superfluous particles; and, on the other hand, it leaves relations often unexpressed. While we express every shade of syntax in the structure of our clauses, Old French left much to the voice, tone, and gesture; less so, however, in its later periods than in its earlier ones. Furthermore, the wealth of words in Old French is perplexing; they are much more numerous than one could expect, and their meanings are somewhat uncertain—not only subject to alterations in the course of time, but to local applications of a confusing character, to say nothing of the idiosyncrasies of the individual writer. Such a plentiful word-supply has hitherto made it impossible to publish a final dictionary of Old French; even against many of the words collected, notes of interrogation must be allowed to stand.

The flourishing period of Old French was reached when it had evolved fully its ' half-synthetic system ' in the twelfth century. A stupendous mass of literature was then brought forth. Some exposition of the half-synthetic system will be found in the grammatical part of this book. Suffice it to say at present that a workable declension (at first three declensions) with two cases, a complete conjugation, and a correct syntax gave a linguistic organisation expansive and elastic enough to meet all the wants of the age. But not only was intelligible speaking made easy: artistic composition was also provided for. For two centuries Mediæval French was the polite language of Europe, more so than Modern French is; for the Old language had no rivalry to fear from its still shapeless fellow-languages of the Roman stock. *Provençal* alone, earlier mature than French, entered the lists against it for a while.

But the half-synthetic system had no finality in itself. It stood, so to say, on the furthest outside edge of the synthetic system of language; insufficient allowance was made in it for wear and tear in the forms of language. The elements of analysis it contained took the upper hand; the synthetic machinery lost the subtle flexional distinctions on which it rested.

Then the days of Modern French began to dawn. A period of linguistic decay set in; literature, purely spontaneous and popular, unsupported by the props of an artificial school-culture, shared the fate of the language. Italian and Spanish burst forth in the literary sky of Europe, while French lost its eminence. It lost its cases, it thinned down its vowel-system, it sifted its vocabulary, it defined more closely the meaning of its words, it absorbed a great many terms directly from classical Latin; to its stores of words expressing feeling and action it added those expressive of reflection and thought; it lost or divorced in meaning its double forms derived from some Latin words of the third declension. But in two points it remained synthetic : it preserved the system of verb inflections of Old French, and its inflected personal pronouns, with a few phonetic alterations. This transformation dates from the fourteenth century. It was complete in the sixteenth. Henceforth French took a new departure, and entered upon its modern course.

There is in the Old language a main distinction to be made between the early dialects and the later literary speech. In the former, the distinction between *Langue d'Oïl* and *Langue d'Oc* is only faintly drawn. Latin is, then, a nearer analogy than Modern French; and the literary monuments, invaluable as links in the breach, are insignificant in other respects.

The very earliest written monuments are the *Cassel Glossary* and the *Glossary of Reichenau*. They both belong to the eighth century. The first is a collection of words in Romance, with their translation into High German, and arranged into chapters according to their meaning. The first chapter deals with the names of the human body and its parts, the second with domestic animals, the third with housekeeping, the fourth with clothing, the fifth with household articles, the sixth with miscellaneous words, the seventh with connected expressions. Its authorship is unknown, and the mode of its composition is disputed.

As for the *Glossary of Reichenau*, it consists of two parts. In the first we have glosses interpreting in Romance portions of the Latin text of the Vulgate. In the second we find, in alphabetical order, words taken from all departments of thought, without reference to any particular text. The author's aim was obviously to facilitate the reading of the Bible to priests who were bad scholars. But instead of giving in the *Lingua Romana* of the day the equivalent of the classical Latin words he wished to explain, he put classical suffixes to the Romance stems. This shows

with what misgivings Latinists of the eighth century
looked upon the future of the Romance dialects.   We
pick here and there glosses in which the Romance is
at once distinguishable in its pseudo-Latin garb :—

| *Latin.* | *Romance.* | *Modern French.* |
| --- | --- | --- |
| femur | coxa | cuisse |
| (in) cartallo | (in) panario | (dans le) panier |
| sarcina | bisatia | besace |
| onerati | carcati | chargés |
| rerum | causarum | (des) choses |
| pallium | drappum | drap |
| arundine | ros | roseau |
| gratia | merces | merci |
| mutuare | impruntare | emprunter |
| pruina | gelata | gelée |
| caseum | formaticum | fromage |
| galea | helmus | heaume |
| novacula | rasorium | rasoir |
| oves | berbices | brebis |
| rostrum | beccus | bec |
| sortileus | sorcerus | sorcier |
| tugurium | cavana | cabane |
| vespertiliones | calves sorices | chauves-souris |
| viscera | intralia | entrailles |
| semel | una vice | une fois |
| segetes | messes | moisson |
| reus | culpabilis | coupable |
| litus | ripa | rive |
| pueros | infantes | enfants |
| in foro | in mercato | (au) marché |
| regit | gubernat | (il) gouverne |

Next to the *Cassel Glossary*, and to that of Reichenau,
in chronological order, and far above them in order of
importance, stand the *Strasburg Oaths* of 842.

The chronicler says that on the sixteenth day before
the Calends of March, Ludwig the German and Charles
the Bald met in the town of Strassburg, and swore the

following oath, Lewis in the Romance, Charles in the German language :—

'Pro deo amur et pro christian poblo et nostro commun salvament, d'ist di in avant, in quant deus savir et podir me dunat, si salvarai eo cist meon fradre Karlo et in aiudha er in cadhuna cosa, si cum om per dreit son fradra salvar dift, in o quid il mi altresi fazet, et ab Ludher nul plaid nunqua prindrai, qui meon vol cist meon fradre Karle in damno sit.'

When the kings had thus pledged their faith to each other, the followers of each bound themselves to enforce the oath as follows :—

'Si Lodhuvigs sagrament, que son fradre Karlo jurat, conservat, et Karlus meos sendra de sue part lo franit, si io returnar non l'int pois, ne io ne neüls, cui eo returnar int pois, in nulla aiudha contra Lodhuwig nun li iv er.' .

The Oaths have reached us in genuine ninth century Romance.

We shall now imitate the author of the *Glossary of Reichenau*, and affix to the Romance stems the classical flexions :—

*Lingua Romana* :—1. 'Pro Dei amore et pro christiani popli et nostro communi salvamento, de isto die in abante, in quanto Deus sapire et podire mi donat, sic salvare habeo (salvabo) ecce istum meum fratrem Karlum, et in adjutu ero in qua una causa, sic cum homo per drictum suum fratrem salvare debet, in eo quid ille mihi alteris sic faciat, et apud Lotharium nullum placitum numquam prehendere habeo quod, mea voluntate, ecce isti meo fratri Karlo in damno sit.'

2. 'Si Ludovicus sacramentum quod suo fratri Karlo juravit, conservat, et Karlus, meus senior, de sua parte illud frangit, si ego retornare non illum inde possum, nec ego nec nullus quem ego retornare (avertere) inde possum, in nullo adjuto contra Ludovicum non illi ibi ero.'

The equivalent in Old French of the later centuries, in which the bulk of Old French literature is written, would be :—

1. 'Por deu amor et por christïen peuple et nostre commun sauvement, de cest jorn en avant, en cant dex saver et pooir me doin, si salverai jo cest mon freire Karle et en aïe serai en chascune cose, si com on par droit son freire salver deit, en ceu ke il me autresi faice, et ot Luther nul plaid onque prindrai, qui mon voil cestui mon freire en danz seit.'

2. 'Si Ludovics *le* sairement, que *a* son freire Karle juret, conservet, et Karles mis sire de seie part le fraint, se jo retoruer non l'eut pois, ne jo ne nuls ki jo retoruer ent pois, en nulle aïe cuntre Ludovic li i serai.'

In the second fragment we have introduced the definite article and the preposition *a*. The appearance of this Old French 'pastiche' could be varied almost *ad infinitum* by adopting some other of the numerous spellings of the words composing it.

It is interesting to roughly divide the words of the Oaths into three classes.

We have a few words which have not even become

accepted Old French words of the literary period. They are the dying gasp of latinity.

Then there are a few other words which have not passed from Old French into Modern French.

About a dozen words are of quite unclassical origin, being altogether from the *Lingua Romana* or from Low Latin. The larger number are of unimpeachable latinity in their stems.

In the same way we may like to see in what proportion syntheticism stands to analysis in the Oaths. The former is quite paramount. 'Case' makes itself felt in every line; suffixes are shorn off, but prepositions in their stead are wholly unrepresented; the article is not forthcoming; the subj. personal pronoun alone is freely used for emphasis.

In Modern French the Oaths read as follows:—

1. 'Pour l'amour de Dieu et pour le salut du peuple chrétien, et notre commun salut, de ce jour en avant, autant que Dieu me donne savoir et pouvoir, je sauverai mon frère Charles et en aide serai en chaque chose (ainsi qu'on doit, selon la justice, sauver son frère), à condition qu'il en fasse autant pour moi, et je ne ferai avec Lothaire aucun accord qui, par ma volonté, porte préjudice à mon frère Charles ici présent.'

2. 'Si Louis garde le serment qu'il a juré à son frère Charles, et que Charles mon maître de son côté le viole, si je ne l'en puis détourner, ni moi, ni nul que j'en puis détourner, ne lui serons en aide contre Louis.'

It is not our intention to study so closely as the Oaths the documents we still have to review in the

class which philologists call the Pre-Old French, or
Neo-Latin, or Romance class.

The two fragments we are now going to study belong
to the tenth century; we have nothing so ancient in the
*Langue d'Oïl*, whose characteristics are plainly visible
in them, whilst the language of the Oaths occupies
an undefined position antecedent to both *Langue d'Oc*
and *Langue d'Oïl*. We may therefore say that the
fragments now under consideration are written in
an archaic dialect of Old French of an intermediate
character. Latin analogy in them has not yet fully
given way to that recasting of it which we must call
French analogy; and it is from the combination of the
two that the fragments derive their interest.

The one of the fragments known as the *Chant d'Eulalie*,
or as the *Cantilène de Ste Eulalie*, is written in verse.
It is very short, consisting of no more than twenty-
nine lines. The other is less important: it is a pulpit
amplification on the prophet Jonah. It is called the
*Fragment de Valenciennes*, and presents a text broken
at almost regular intervals by whole sentences in
Latin. Both monuments are of decidedly northern
penmanship.

The substitution everywhere in the *Chant d'Eulalie*
of diphthong *ei* for *oi* shows this hymn to have been
written in the western dominions of the *Langue d'Oïl*.
It affords scope for studies of verse and of metre, as well
as of comparative grammar. There is a little more
'analysis' than in the Oaths: the indefinite article
appears once, the definite is frequent, the prepositions

*de* and *a* are used and subjective personal pronouns are freely placed before verbs. In tenses and moods Latin etymology still reigns supreme. There is yet no independent body of French analogy.

Our next fragment is in no respect more typically French than Eulalia's canticle. If anything, it is the reverse, for the Romance text is not continuous. The monkish writer breaks away into more familiar Latin at every moment, and, what is worse, gaps in the sense are not rare, and hopelessly damaged passages remain insolvable.

Of the early documents of the pre-literary period yet to be examined, two can be neglected here; the one is known under the name of *Sponsus*, the other is the *Epître de St Etienne.*

Of much greater importance are the *Passion du Christ* and the *Vie de St Léger.*

The *Passion du Christ*, the first in date of the numerous Old French amplifications on this subject, is a poem containing 516 lines. It is remarkable for a dash of Langue d'Oc or Provençal in its language, and therefore cannot be offered as a pure sample of the Langue d'Oïl in the tenth century.

Synthetic forms derived from the Latin pluperfect occur several times :—

| | | | | |
|---|---|---|---|---|
| vidra | is from viderat, | voldrat | is from voluerat |
| veggra | ,, ,, venerat, | fedre | ,, ,, fecerat |
| fura, fure | ,, ,, fuerat | agre | ,, ,, habuerat. |

These are not the only Latinisms. Such occur repeatedly in the flexions and in the interior phonetics of words. As for the metre in which this fragment of a sacred epic is written, it is the eight-syllabled line. As the poem was meant to be sung, the requirements of music helped to insure the regularity of the metre. Within each stanza the full compass of the melody was developed, and the repetition of it in every set of four lines gave to the poem the monotony appertaining to Church Lyrics.

The *Vie de St Léger*, with the mention of which we close our study of the monuments of the pre-literary period, consists of some 240 lines in the same eight-syllabled metre, divided into stanzas of six lines each. It gives an account of the life, merits, and death of St. Leodegar, whose martyrdom appealed to the devotional feeling of ecclesiastic poets. But it does not appear that he was a privileged object of their respect; for, says the unknown romancer, 'as we have to praise the Lord God and to do honour to his saints, we sing of the saints who for his sake underwent heavy trials, and the time has come for us to sing of St. Leodegar.'

The fragment that has reached us is therefore a single portrait from an otherwise lost gallery. It stands chronologically too near the *Passion du Christ* to mark a distinct step in the development of the French language.[1]

---

[1] For detailed information on the Old French language see *An Introduction to Old French*, by F. F. Roget (Williams and Norgate).

For the phonetics of Old French and its grammatical forms see *Grammatik des Altfranzösischen*, by Dr. Eduard Schwan.

Mr. Gaston Paris has as yet published only the first volume of his proposed *Manuel d'ancien français*. The second, third, and fourth volumes are to deal with the language and to contain, with a lexicon, fragments of the literature.

# CHAPTER XI.

## THE LINGUA ROMANA IN GAUL AT THE TIME OF THE FRANKISH INVASION.[1]

It can be safely said that after the first Punic war
(241 B.C.) unity of speech was broken in the Latin language. The Archaic Latin, alone in use down to that
time, divided itself into two branches—the one, the literary language written and spoken by the higher classes
and which came under a strict Greek schooling ; the
other, the speech of the masses, which was a direct
development of Archaic Latin, and which followed
courses diverging more and more from the classical Latin
known to us, as the centuries sped by. This popular
speech was, above all things, a living and changing one.
Yet its evolution obeyed certain fixed general laws,
which can be traced in almost all parts of the Roman
Empire, and which formed the common ground for the
evolution of the modern languages of the Roman type.
When the information we can get from different sources
about the differences distinguishing the Lingua Romana
from the classical tongue is put together, the following
picture can be drawn of it at the time when the inva-

[1] The authority adhered to most closely in writing this chapter is
*Grammatik des Altfranzösischen*, by Dr. Eduard Schwan.

sion of the Teutonic tribes, and more especially of the Franks, determined its further development into Old French and thence into Modern French.

1. The Lingua Romana did not divide its vowel sounds into long ones and short ones, as classical Latin came to do under the influence of Greek prosody. In popular verse the absolute quantity of the vowels was not taken into account, but only their position before one or two consonants as the case might be, and their relation to the primary and secondary tonic accents in connected utterance. The consequence of this was a modification in rhythm which led to the introduction of rhyming measures, and which resulted in the building up of a prosody in French, in which the length of the vowels goes for nothing, and in which the tonic accent plays an important part in securing the harmony of the line.

2. The failure of the Lingua Romana to distinguish absolutely between long and short vowel sounds was a consequence of the comparatively weak intonation of these sounds. A larger number of monophthongs and diphthongs belongs to the literary Latin in which Horace and Virgil wrote than to the dialect of the people. For instance, the classical words, *coepa, poena, mittere, fidem, firmum, bibere, pilum, in,* were all pronounced almost alike in Romance, so far as the vowel sounds of the first syllable are concerned, this sound being approximately that of *é* in modern French.

3. The vowel bearing the tonic accent, when it stood immediately before *i, o, u,* was fused with it into a

diphthong. *Cŭi, fŭi, dĕu, mĕu, dŭŏ* stood for the classical forms *cu-i, fu-i, de-um, me-um, du-o.* The proximity of an accented vowel to an *i* might result from the dropping out of the consonant between the two vowels. To classical Latin, *ama'vi,*[1] would correspond *ama'-i,* and later *amāi',* the late Romance and early French for what is now *j'aimai.*

4. Like vowels clashing in the body of a word were drawn together into one, as in *prendre* from classical *prehe'ndere*; such vowels became long by position without any reference to the metrical value that would have been theirs in a classical line, but simply as a working of the consonantal sounds between which they were set.

5. *i* within a word dropped out before an *e* accented in popular Latin ; but, if any other vowel than *i* preceded the accented *e*, the *e* fell out, so that on the one side, the Romance accusative *pare'te* came to stand for *parie'te* (cl. *pari'etem*) ; while on the other side Romance *fŭĕ'sti* instead of classical *fŭi'sti* (in which the accent is on the *i* and in which the *u* forms a sound of its own) became *fu'sti.*[2]

6. The Latin law of accent is well known. Words whose last syllable but one is long have the accent on that syllable; while words whose last syllable but one is short have the accent on the third syllable from the

---

[1] The sign ' after a vowel indicates the tonic accent.

[2] There is the same shifting of the accent in

$$\begin{Bmatrix} locave'runt, \\ laudave'runt, \end{Bmatrix} \text{Rom.} \quad \begin{Bmatrix} lo(c)a'erunt \\ lau(d)a'erunt \end{Bmatrix} \text{Fr.} \quad louèrent.$$

end. In words belonging to this last class, the short vowel following immediately the accented syllable was thrown out. In Romance, *o'clu* stood in the accusative instead of the classical *o'ŏlum*.

7. The *i* or the *e* standing immediately before another vowel, either *o, u,* or *a,* lost its value as a vowel and had a consonantal *j* sound, thereby cutting a syllable out of the word. Three-syllabled *facio* became two-syllabled *fakjo*. This substitution of the sounds *kj* for the sounds *ki* reacted upon the intonation of the preceding vowel *a*.

8. When the *i* thus replaced by *j* bore the tonic accent, this was perforce thrown back on the preceding syllable. For instance, the classical Latin *trifo'lium* became in French *trèfle* with the tonic accent on the first syllable by the working of that law.

9. But if the *j* substituted for *i* was followed by a suffix, such as the diminutive suffix *-ŏlus*, the accent instead of retreating advanced to the next syllable. Classical *fili'olum* corresponds thereby to French *filleû'l*. Romance intermediate forms : *tre'flju, filjo'lu.*

10. The *u* standing immediately before a vowel took the sound *v*, classical *vi'dua* is in French *veuve* through the intermediate Romance *ve'dva*; but the *v* drops out when a group of consonants difficult to pronounce would result from its maintenance. When the *u* changed to *v* bore the accent, this was thrown back to the preceding syllable. Classical *consu'ere* is in French *coudre* through the intermediate Romance *co'svere.*

11. On the whole the tonic accent stood on the same

syllable as in literary Latin; but short vowels followed by such consonantal groups as *gr, dr, br* always bore the accent in Romance, so that French *entié'r* came to be accented differently from classical Latin *i'ntĕgrum*.

12. In the third person plural of the perfect in some primary verbs, analogy with so-called secondary verbs brought about the throwing back of the accent on the stem instead of its falling on the long penultimate as in classical Latin. In that way French *fu'rent* does not correspond to classical *fue'runt* because the Romance form was *fo'runt*.

13. *h* counted for little or nothing. Romance *onorc* is the classical *honorem*.

14. Final *m* was deadened, as visible already in classical metric. Rom. *a'nma* for classical *a'nimam*. Only monosyllabic words kept final *m*. French *mon, ton, son* are related to classical *meum, tuum, suum*, through Rom. *mem, tvom, svom*. Final *s* and final *t* were pronounced.

15. *n* was dropped before *s*, and the preceding vowel, already long by position, remained so in compensation for the disappearance of the *n*. French *pesé'r*, from classical *pēnsa're*, through Rom. *pēsa're*.

16. *k* and *kr* were liable to be corrupted into *g* and *gr*; while *b* and *v* were interchangeable. Cf. French *gonfler* with classical *conflare*, and French *brebis* with classical *vervecem*.

17. The placing, with a view to ease in pronunciation, of an *i* or *e* before an initial *s*, followed by a consonant, was early practised in the Lingua Romana. *Espa'ta*, French *épée*, stood for classical *spa'tham*.

18. Romance preserved only two out of the six cases of literary Latin, namely, the nominative or case of the subject, and the accusative or case of the object. The relations expressed by the genitive, dative, and ablative were given effect to by prepositions. The preposition *de* took the place of the genitive suffix and the preposition *ad* took the place of the dative suffix. This was brought about by the gradual wearing down of the distinct suffixes till they became undistinguishable, and also by a preference given to analytical modes of expression over synthetical.

19. The number of declensions was reduced from five to three, corresponding on the whole to the first, second, and third classical declensions. The words belonging to the fourth and fifth were absorbed into the first, second, and third.

20. All Romance languages have the definite article, and the indefinite article. This shows that *ille* and *unus* were very early taken away from their original function, which the former could no longer fill without the prefixing of *ecce*.

21. The Romance dispensed almost altogether with the neuter gender of classical Latin. Some neuter nouns, by the working of the nearest analogy became masculine, and others feminine.

22. The comparative and the superlative in adjectives and adverbs were no longer expressed by suffixes, but with the assistance of intensive adverbs, such as *plus*. There were a few exceptions.

23. The particle *ecce* was placed before the demon-

strative pronouns of classical Latin to restore their wasted demonstrative force.

24. The synthetic passive voice was not used. The past participle of notional verbs, with *esse* reduced to the function of an auxiliary, was used instead. Deponent verbs were assimilated to active verbs.

25. The present, the perfect, the imperfect, and the pluperfect were the only synthetic tenses in use. Instead of the future stood the infinitive of the verb, with *habere* as an auxiliary.

26. The supine, the participle future, the perfect and imperfect of the subjunctive all disappeared.

27. The general framework of the four conjugations was kept, but several verbs passed from one conjugation into another. For instance, cl. *ca'dĕre* was in Romance *cadĕ're*; hence Old French, *cheo'ir* with the accent on the last syllable; cl. *ridĕ're* was in Romance *ri'dĕre*, hence Fr. *ri're*, with the accent on the first syllable; cl. *reci'pere*, became *rekepe're*, hence *recevoir*.

28. In composition, words preserved the accent on the root instead of throwing it back on the preposition, as in classical Latin. In consequence, the root syllable preserved its full original sound. There were, however, many exceptions to this general practice.

29. The suffixes in use in literary Latin were replaced by others closely related: *-ērius* stood for classical *-ārius*; *-cŭlus* stood for cl. *-tŭlus*; *-ūminem* for classical *-ūdinem*; and *-ūta* for *-ūca*.

30. Monosyllabic classical words, and generally those which are short, and in which the stem is very

prominent, were often lengthened by the addition of a diminutive suffix. For instance, Fr. *solei'l* is traced back to classical *sol* through Rom. *sole'clu* (for *soli'culum*). In the same way, instead of the original root verbs, fresh ones were formed from derivatives. French *aiguise'r* is connected with cl. *acu'ere* through Rom. *acutia're* (from *acu'tus*).

31. The Romance was not content with developing the archaic stock of words which it held in common with the classical dialect. It coined words of its own and it borrowed words from Greek, Celtic, and Germanic sources.

32. The secondary accent of Archaic Latin was preserved. Its place depended upon that of the principal or primary accent. It stood on the syllable immediately preceding the principal accent, when that syllable was long, and the first in the word, as in *cā'nt'are*. It stood on the syllable next but one to the principal accent, counting backwards, when that syllable was loṅg, as in *benedī'ctio'ne*. It stood on the syllable next but two to the principal accent when the syllable next but one was short, as in *do'mĭnice'lla*. Modern French, too, has primary and secondary accents.

# CHAPTER XII.[1]

## HISTORICAL GRAMMAR, THE NOUN, ETC.

THE ALPHABET.—The letter *h* is not sounded in modern French. The so-called aspirate *h* has no aspiration; this name meaning now that the last consonant of the preceding word is not to be joined in pronunciation on to the vowel following the *h*, and that an *e* mute preceding this *h* is never elided. The aspiration existed in words beginning with *h* derived from Germanic dialects; but in the course of time the aspiration was lost.

The letter *w* does not properly belong to the French alphabet. It was replaced by *gu* and hard *g* at an early date in the words beginning with *w* that were borrowed from Germanic sources. At present it appears only in a few words borrowed quite lately from foreign languages, such as *wagon*, from English *waggon* (cf. German *wagen*).

ACCENTS.—The use of accents as orthographic signs has not been determined by the history of the language;

---

[1] In this chapter and the following ones, it is assumed that the reader has made himself acquainted with the contents of Eugène's *Comparative French Grammar* (Williams and Norgate).

the fixed rules given on the subject turn on usage, and they are revised from time to time by the French Academy. The accents were first written after the discovery of printing, and the signs then introduced were taken from Greek; yet there is no analogy between the French orthographic accents here alluded to and the Greek ones which supplied them.

SOUNDS.—The double *-ll* with the double liquid sound known as *l mouillé* is generally losing its full pronunciation. It is now pronounced like *y* between two vowels, but this departure from the practice historically established of sounding the double *-ll* is rightly blamed by Littré.

The ARTICLE.—Classical Latin had no article; for the sake of clearness in speech it became customary towards the end of the Roman Empire to add to substantives the demonstrative adjective *ille* in the places in which *le, la, les* are now used in French. *Illum* became *illom* in Romance, and later *illo*, from which arose the Old French *lo*. A softening into *le* took place in the eleventh century. As for the plural *les* it is derived from Old French *los* leading back to classical Latin *illos*. The contractions *du* and *au* were, in the Middle Ages, *del* and *al*, the *l* being changed into *u* according to a well-known phonetic rule. In *des* contracted from *de les*, the *l* became mute. In *aux*, from *à les*, the *u* stands for the primitive *l*, while the *x* instead of the primitive *s* is quite arbitrary. *Es*, contracted from *en les*, is still found only in some standing phrases (*bachelier-ès-lettres*) and geographical names.

When the Latin preposition *de* had replaced in Romance the flexion of the genitive, the partitive use of the genitive article suggested itself quite naturally. As it was classical to say *unus de libris*, Romance came to say *habeo de illis libris* in which *de illis* corresponds to the English 'some' and to the modern French *des*.

The SUBSTANTIVE.—In the Romance the prepositions *de* and *ad* were substituted in the genitive and in the dative for the flexions of classical Latin. As it was classical to say *unus de illis* and *scribo ad patrem*, there is nothing surprising in the increase of these prepositional phrases. Old French had at first three declensions with two cases to each, as follows :—

SINGULAR.

| | | | |
|---|---|---|---|
| *Nominative*—Ro'sa-rose, | mu'rus-murs, | pa'stor-pastre. |
| *Accusative* —Ro'sam-rose, | mu'rum-mur, | pasto'rem-pasteur. |

PLURAL.

| | | | |
|---|---|---|---|
| *Nominative*—Ro'sae-rose, | mu'ri-mur, | pasto'res-pasteurs. |
| *Accusative* —Ro'sas-roses, | mu'ros-murs, | pasto'res-pasteurs. |

Accordingly Old French said in the nominative, *la rose est belle, le murs est haut, le pastre est venu*; and in the accusative, *j'ai vu la rose, le mur, le pasteur*. In the twelfth century, the nominatives singular in the three declensions were unified and the distinguishing *s* received from the nominative singular of the second Latin declension was applied to all three; while the absence of *s* became the distinguishing sign of the accusative singular, or objective case. In the fourteenth century this last distinction between the nominative and the accusative disappeared, and the objective form without the *s* was applied throughout the singular.

As for the plural, in which the *s*, in analogy to the accusative plural of the second Latin declension, was the mark of the objective case, the *s* was in due course applied throughout; so it came to be that the absence of *s* is the sign of the singular number in modern French (except in those words where a final *s* results from other causes), while the presence of *s* is the sign of the plural number. The form of French nouns is thus shown to have been determined by the corresponding accusative noun-forms in Latin both in the singular and in the plural. There are, however, a few instances of modern French words derived from Latin nominatives. As for the Old French nominative *pastre*, accusative *pasteur*, the difference in form and accentuation between the two cases was strong enough to hand them both down to the modern language, in which a somewhat different meaning attaches to each. Modern *pâtre* is a keeper of sheep, and *pasteur* a keeper of souls. All the parts of speech liable to declension in Latin underwent, in the course of their history, a treatment analogous to the one we have just described as applying to substantives.

The PLURAL.—The use of *s* as the sign of the plural number has been accounted for in the preceding paragraph. In nouns ending in *-nt* in the singular, it was, till the days of our grandmothers, habitual to suppress the *t* of the singular before the plural *s*. This practice is preserved in the *Journal des Débats*, and in the *Revue des Deux Mondes*. Substantives ending in *s*, *x*, *z*, have no flexional *s* in the plural, because the sibilant ending the singular would be unnecessarily doubled by such an addition. The presence of *s, x, z,* in the plural of nouns was at first often only an arbitrary practice, which is now enforced by the tyranny of usage. There is no reason why nouns ending in *-au* and *-eu* should receive an *x* rather than an *s*. In the Middle Ages, *s, x,* and *z,* were interchangeable signs, and used quite promiscuously. Were modern grammarians wise, they would not insist on the affixing of *x* either to nouns ending in *-au* and *-eu* or to the seven substantives in *-ou* which vex the modern schoolboy. As for the change from *-al* into *-aux*, *-al* became regularly *-als* in the earlier Middle Ages. There was no such thing as *chevaux*, but *chevals*, with every letter sounded, was the rule. Later, *-al* became generally *-au* before a consonant; *chevals* was then pronounced and written *chevaus*, till the *x* was arbitrarily substituted for *s*; when the sibilant sound that could be represented by either became mute. The change of *-ail* into *-aux* in some seven words is by analogy with the preceding.

Some substantives ending in *l* in the singular

wavered between the two plural forms, the older one, in which the *l* was preserved and the newer one, in which *l* became *u*. Both forms existing concurrently in the modern language had but one and the same meaning in the plural till grammarians allotted to each a certain fixed portion of their joint general acceptation. They laid down, for instance, that *les aïeux* should mean the ancestors only, and *les aïeuls* the grandfathers.

GENDER.—The words *amour*, *orgue*, and *délice* are given in modern grammars as being masculine in the singular and feminine in the plural. This is only another instance of arbitrariness receiving the sanction of usage. In Old French, Latin substantives ending in *-or* became almost all feminine when they denoted abstract ideas. The only exceptions now are *honneur*, *amour*, and *labeur*, which are masculine. Yet in the Middle Ages the two former of these were feminine also. Hence the handing down in the case of *amour* of a certain number of phrases in which it is feminine. These are recognised by modern grammarians as correct only in the plural.

*Orgue* is from the Latin *organum*, a neuter early assimilated to the feminine nouns in Old French. In the 16th century, Latinising grammarians thought that by transferring it to the masculine gender they would bring it nearer to the original neuter. Hence an opposition arose between the feminine gender established in popular use and the masculine fathered upon the word by scholars. A compromise was struck by framing the rule that is now binding.

The 16th century Latinists acted similarly regarding *délice*. They knew that this noun, a feminine plural in ordinary Latin, possessed a rarer singular form which was neuter. They at once decided that the French singular should follow the rare Latin singular and be masculine.

In the two genders of *gens* we have a conflict between the etymological meaning of that word, which is feminine, being the same as that of Latin *gens, gentis,* a family, a nation ; while the idea that has come to underlie the word in French is that of men, of male attendants. It remained feminine, in some very current phrases in which the adjective stood before the noun. This peculiarity was taken advantage of to word the extraordinary rule that adjectives preceding *gens* should be put in the feminine and those following in the masculine.

The same process of gradually diverging from the original meaning was seen in *personne* and in *chose* when used in a more general sense than was allowed to them in Latin. As indefinite pronouns, they could no longer be said to represent the primitive feminine idea which was theirs in Latin, and they were used in the masculine, in keeping with the new meaning given to them. *Enfant*, from Latin *infant-*, with the same ending in the masculine and in the feminine, is a noun which has resisted the adjunction of final *e*, when it is used to express a female child.

The double genders of *œuvre, couple, foudre* are accounted for by similar historical processes. For instance, in *foudre* the feminine arises from the fact that in Romance the neuter plural *fulgura* was mistaken for a feminine singular.

FEMININE OF SUBSTANTIVES.—The current rules for the formation of the feminine of substantives were produced by a historical development similar to that of adjectives. Latin etymology is the starting-point. Phonetic changes take place. Some of the suffixes inherited from Latin are replaced by French ones; some nouns are driven by the force of analogy from the class to which they historically belong into another; and then usage, as fixed by grammarians, decides without appeal.

The ending *-esse* in such words as *abbé*, feminine *abbesse*, etc., came from the Latin suffix *-issa*, which appeared in words borrowed from the Greek, and was also added to words of Latin origin. The nouns in which *-eur* becomes *-eresse* show a weakening of the last syllable of the masculine by the transference of the tonic accent to the next syllable in the feminine. In *ambassadrice*, from *ambassadeur*, the ending *-rice* is fastened on to the *d* in analogy with nouns ending in Latin in *-tor*, French *-teur*, feminine *-trix*, French *-trice*. These feminine endings are not of popular formation. They were deliberately affixed by scholars to words which did not come to them from the people, but for which they obtained admittance into the current language. In the same way *cantatrice* copies Latin *cantatrix*. *Impératrice* copies Latin *imperatrix*.

The people said *chanteuse* and *emperesse*, the latter of which is still found in English.

The feminine of *compagnon* is usually given as *compagne*. In point of fact the latter word stands on a par with *compains* as found in the *Chanson de Roland*; *compagnon* is a dimiuutive which has superseded it. In the same manner *mulet* stands now as a masculine to *mule*, the original masculine form *mul* having gone out of use. Such nouns as *gouverneur* aud *serviteur* have no feminines of their own in the modern language. Their so called feminines *gouvernante* and *servante* are derived from the present participle of the verbs *gouverner* and *servir*. The historical feminine of the former word survives in the English *governess*. While *brebis* is from the Latin *vervecem*, the corresponding masculine *bélier* is from the same root as the English bell. The full phrase was *le mouton bélier*, that is, the sheep which had the bell, the leader of the flock. *Le lièvre* (the hare), and its feminine *la hase* are similarly derived from different linguistic families. The first is from Latin *leporem*, and the secoud from the Teutonic root which gives *hase* to modern German. The origin of *guenon*, the feminine of *singe*, is unknown. In *la tante* the blunder has been committed of gluing on to the word the singular of the possessive adjective. *Tante* was originally for the Latin *tua amita*. The English has the correct form in *aunt*.

THE FEMININE OF ADJECTIVES.—Adjectives ending in *e* mute in the masculine do not add a flexional *e* in the feminine for the same reason that nouns ending in *s* in the singular do not add a second *s* in the plural. The fact that most of these adjectives had no feminine ending of their own in Latin would not have prevented their taking the flexional *e* by analogy with the much greater number which do so, if the etymological masculine had ended in any other vowel than *e*. The accent grave in such feminines as *légère* indicates to the eye that this vowel receives an open sound so as to enable the voice to pass on to the pronunciation of the flexional *e* mute. The sign of diæresis in such feminines as *aiguë*, and the *u* after *g* in such feminines as *longue*, are merely orthographic signs showing that the etymological pronunciation is preserved. *Aiguë* represents the three-syllabled Latin *acu'tam*, and *longue* corresponds to *lo'ngam*. Adjectives which double the final consonant before the suffix *e*, like those using an accent grave in the same position, do so to mark the full pronunciation of the final consonant of the masculine, caused by the necessity of passing on in pronunciation to the final *e*, while maintaining the tonic accent on the same syllable as in the masculine. The doubling of the consonant usually takes place after short vowels. In adjectives ending in *x*, the *x* is an arbitrary substitution for *s*. *Favori* is from the Italian *favorito*, which accounts for the *t* of its feminine. The *c* preserved in the feminine *grecque* shows the lengthening of the vowel *e*, which alone distinguishes in sound the feminine of that word from its masculine.

. Adjectives ending in *-eur* are known to form their

feminine in four different ways. Those adding *e*, and derived from Latin adjectives in which there was no specific feminine ending, took *e* by analogy with the ordinary French practice. Those feminines ending in *-euse*, an ending in which the final *r* of the masculine disappears, owe the loss of the *r* to the practice in some parts of France of not pronouncing it at all at the end of words. *Flatteuse* leads back to the provincial pronunciation *flatteu* instead of *flatteur*. The ending *-osus*, fem. *-osa*, offers the nearest Latin analogy. We have already spoken, with reference to the feminine in nouns, of the feminine ending *-trice* of learned formation. As for the ending *-eresse* also already alluded to, it was very generally prevalent in the Middle Ages, though it is not frequent in the modern language. The *-esse* represents the Latin suffix *-issa*, while the *-er-* before it is the weakened *-eur* of the masculine.

The five adjectives *beau, fou, mou, nouveau, vieux* are usually given as having three terminations. As a matter of fact, the forms just given are merely younger ones, while those with the final *l* reproduce the *l* that terminated their respective Latin stems. There was a marked tendency in Old French to replace the first of several consonants by a vowel; even though some of them did belong to the next word. For instance in *un bel cheval*, the *l* was softened down to a *u* by a back influence of the consonantal sound *ch*. The same process gave rise to the forms *fou, mou, nouveau, vieux*. This last adjective being from the Latin Accusative *vetulum*, a diminutive substituted for the classical *vet-*

*erem*, the final *x* is shown to be spurious. When once
it was there it could not but be pronounced like soft *s*
before words beginning with a vowel or a so-called
*h* mute; hence the liberty to say *un vieux ami* for the
more correct *un vieil ami*. It is usual to say that, in
this class of adjectives, the *l* is allowed to stand before
the vowel for reasons of euphony. History warrants no
such explanation. The *l* was preserved simply because it
was pronounced when standing before a vowel or an *h*
mute, and could not possibly be dropped on that account.
The same phenomenon appears in such verb forms as
*aime-t-il* in which the *t* has nothing to do with euphony
but fills the same purpose as in the Latin *amat ille*.

The most frequent gender-flexions in Latin were those
which we find in *bonus, bona, bonum*. In Romance the
neuter and the masculine coincided phonetically, and
both have lost their flexions in Modern French. As for
the *a* of the Latin feminine, it is represented by the
flexional French *e*. At first Latin adjectives like *grandis*,
neuter *grande*, which have no flexion of their own in
the feminine, imparted this peculiarity to the French.
It was then correct to say *un homme grand, une femme
grand*, since there would have been in Latin *grandis* in
both phrases. In course of time, however, an assimilation took place to the more general practice of putting
an *e*, too late nevertheless to correct such well-established
phrases as *la grand rue, la grand ville;* so grammarians,
unmindful of the fashion in which these phrases which
they felt to be in harmony with the *génie de la langue*,
as the French call it, had come about, decided to mark

by an apostrophe that the *e* had fallen out, leading to a complete misunderstanding of what had taken place.

PLURAL OF ADJECTIVES.—As we have seen with nouns, the plural in adjectives was fixed by a historical development on which the rules of grammarians, often sanctioning wrongful usage, have engrafted themselves. For instance, *bleu* takes an *s* while *hébreu* takes an *x*. The change of final *l* into *u* in the plural has remained in such an unsettled condition that some adjectives ending in *-al* are never used in the plural at all, so as to avoid the embarrassment of choosing between *-als* and *-aux*. The plural of *tout*, namely *tous*, in which the *s* is pronounced when that adjective stands as a pronoun at the end of a sentence, or emphatically within a sentence, drops the *t* in analogy with the old spelling *enfans*, for modern *enfants*.

COMPARATIVE AND SUPERLATIVE.—The analytic comparatives in Latin were formed with the assistance of *magis*. This adverb having been transferred to another grammatical function in French (cf. *mais*), the office of forming the comparative and superlative devolved upon *plus*. For the bulk of the comparatives and superlatives formed in Latin by suffixes the analytical formation with *plus* was substituted. But those adjectives which were in most frequent use resisted the analytical tendency. In the modern language these are reduced to three, *bon, mauvais* and *petit*. A few synthetic superlatives of learned formation must be added to these, such as *richissime, rarissime* ; but these, considered historically, are blunders. If the people had handled them they would be *richime, rarime.*

NUMERALS.—For naught the French say *zéro,* a word of Arabic origin. The discredit into which the forms *septante, huitante, nonante* have fallen is accounted for by the practice of counting by twenties. *Quatre-vingts* stands in a line with the now extinct *cinq-vingts, six-vingts. Vingt* having stood as a unit of quantity, the practice of giving it a plural like every other noun is historically justified, and also the apparently paradoxical rule, that the *s* is not to be put if another numeral follows, for *vingt* may then no longer be considered as a noun. In the case of *cent* the habit of putting an *s* in such phrases as *deux cents, trois cents,* is justified by the Latin *ducentos, trecentas,* etc. The numerals from seventeen to nineteen are formed in the same manner as in the Lingua Romana where *decem septem, decem octo, decem novem* were in use. The rule as to spelling *mil* in dates of the Christian Era is absurd. History knows of the spelling *mil* as derived from Latin *mille* and of the spelling *mille* as derived from the Latin *millia.* The first is therefore a *bona fide* singular and the second a *bona fide* plural. It should be *mil soldats* and *deux mille soldats,* if *mil* were worth preserving at all.

The ending of the ordinal numerals *-ième* represents Latin *-esimus* through Old French *-iesme.* But Latin did not form all its ordinals in that way; from '1st' to '10th' Old French followed the corresponding Latin forms. But specific meanings and uses were gradually assigned to these older forms and fresh ones were coined for ordinary use ending in *-ième*, like *troisième*, etc.

PERSONAL PRONOUNS.—These are, in modern grammars, divided into disjunctive and conjunctive; and still more recently into emphatic and unemphatic. These names show an effort at classifying the personal pronouns according to their history. But other pronouns than the personal ones have a double set of forms, and neither of the distinctions adopted covers the ground it is intended that it should. To make matters worse, the two sets of forms which it is advisable to impress separately on the mind of the learner are not always phonetically distinct. The subject forms of the personal pronouns were very seldom used in Latin, and comparatively little used in the earlier periods of French. As for the third person, Latin had no complete pronoun, and the demonstrative pronoun *ille* had to be drawn upon to supply this vacancy. In close connection with the verb when used as either subject or object, personal pronouns come very near preserving the cases whereby their relation to the verb was marked in Latin. *Je le lui donne* represents very accurately *ego illud* (or *illum*) *illi dono*, allowing for the transitional forms of Romance. *Il me parle* and *il me voit* represent in the same way the synthetic phrases *ille mihi parabulat* (Romance of Greek origin instead of the classical *loquitur*), and *ille me videt*. For phonetic reasons, *mihi* and *me* both became *me*; *tibi* and *te* both became *te*; *sibi* and *se* became *se*; but, also through the working of phonetic causes, in the demonstrative pronoun of the third person the direct and indirect object forms are distinct, *le* standing for *illum*, *lui* for *illi* (Rom. *ellui*, and *ellei*); plural *les* standing for *illos* and *illas* as direct object, and *leur* for *illorum* as indirect object. That the genitive form of the Latin should have been preferred to the dative form, in expressing the indirect object of a verb, illustrates a tendency that marks deeply the whole development into French,—that of preserving the bulkier forms rather than the shorter ones. The preceding remarks all apply to those forms of the pronoun called conjunctive or unemphatic.

In the disjunctive or emphatic forms there is no remnant of Latin synthesis or of case flexions. Here the Latin pronominal forms, under the stress of emphatic accent, passed into the analogical forms *moi*, *toi, soi*; *lui*, fem. *elle*; *nous, vous*; *eux*, fem. *elles*. The use of these with prepositions is absolutely parallel to that of ordinary French nouns. As said before, the strong disjunctive forms and the weak conjunctive ones are not always phonetically distinct. Some of them, through the ordinary working of phonetical rules, could not but come to be pronounced alike. For others, the strong form superseded the weak form in the office belonging properly to the latter (cf. the imperative *donne-le-moi* with the negative *ne me le donne pas*). For all those reasons it might be better to give up the appellations in use, and, taking one's stand on a broad law in language, to divide the French pronouns into synthetic forms and analytical forms. We shall now give a table of both sets of forms, in the successive shapes they have passed through :—

FORMS OF SYNTHETIC ANALOGY.

| | | | Mod. French. | Old French. | Romance. | Latin. |
|---|---|---|---|---|---|---|
| *Sing.* | Subj., | . . | je | jo | ĕŏ | ego |
| ,, | Obj., | . . | me | me | me | me & mihi. |
| *Plu.* | Subj., | . . | nous | nos | nos | nos |
| ,, | Obj., | . . | nous | nos | nos | nos & nobis. |
| *Sing.* | Snbj., | . . | tu | tu | tu | tu |
| ,, | Obj., | . . | te | te | te | te & tibi. |
| *Plu.* | Subj., | . . | vous | vos | vos | vos |
| ,, | Obj., | . . | vous | vos | vos | vos & vobis. |
| *Sing.* | Snbj., | . . | — | — | — | |
| ,, | Obj., | . . | se | se | se | se & sibi |
| *Plu.* | Subj., | . . | — | — | — | — |
| ,, | Obj., | . . | se | se | se | se & sibi |
| *Sing.* | Sub., | . | il | il | e'lle | ille |
| ,, | Dir. Obj., | . | le | le | ĕllŏ | illum |
| ,, | Indir. Obj., | . | (lui) | li | ĕllĭ | illi |
| *Plu.* | Subj. | . . | ils | il | | illi |
| ,, | Dir. Obj., | . | les | los | ĕllŏs | illos |
| ,, | Indir. Obj., | . | leur | lor | ĕllŏrŭ | illis (illo'rum) |

In the pronoun of the third person the feminine forms coincide with the masculine forms except in the sing. dir. obj., where *la* resulted from Rom. *ella*, Lat. *illam*, and in the nominatives *elle*, *elles*, Rom. *ella*, *ella(s)*. *Lui* is not derived from Old Fr. *li*, but from the strong Romance form *illui*.

FORMS OF ANALYTIC ANALOGY.—These arose on the whole from the same Romance and Latin forms as the preceding set. The case flexions of Latin being supplanted by prepositions, the Latin and Romance endings had little to do with the shape of these pronouns. As they stood in places in which they were emphatically accented, it was the accent that determined the principle of their phonetics, and their form remains the same in whatever relation they may stand to the verb.

| | | | | |
|---|---|---|---|---|
| *moi* | is | from | emphatic | *me* |
| *nous* | ,, | ,, | ,, | *nos* |
| *toi* | ,, | ,, | ,, | *te* |
| *vous* | ,, | ,, | ,, | *vos* |
| *soi* | ,, | ,, | ,, | *se* |
| *lui* | ,, | ,, | ,, | *ellui* |
| *eux* | ,, | ,, | ,, | *ellos* |
| *elle* | ,, | ,, | ,, | *ella* |
| *elles* | ,, | ,, | ., | *ellas* |

The original forms here given are obviously the Romance ones.

The forms of the third person present the peculiarity that, according to their place in a Romance sentence, one of the two syllables of *ille* was slurred over. When the accent fell on the last syllable the vowel of the first syllable (*e* in the Romance, and *i* in the Latin) fell out. If the accent fell on the first syllable it was the second syllable that shrank to nothing. The dropping of the first syllable was quite systematic in *ille* used as an article.

Modern French *ils* is not from Latin *illi*; it rests on a transfer of old French *ils* (from *illos*) into the place of the etymological plural *il*.

The so-called pronominal adverbs *en* and *y* are from Latin *inde* and *ibi*. The *y* is a mere substitute for *i*. These supply, in the synthetic set of pronouns, the place of the distinct genitive and dative cases which have died out. Their use with reference to persons is only limited, because their pronominal character has not been fully developed.

The Latin neuter forms accented *i'llud* and *illu'd* have left traces in Modern French. Indeed, their disappearance was impossible, since the language had ideas to express which are inconsistent with the use of definitely masculine or feminine pronouns. In *il est difficile d'être heureux, il* stands plainly for *i'llud*, and if the reply to the preceding remark is *je le sais, le* is just as plainly for *illu'd*.

The use of *tu* instead of the more formal *vous* (cf. Eng. *you* v. *thou*) has been greatly extended since the French Revolution, when it was widely used in keeping with the professions of 'equality and fraternity' made in those times.

The unemphatic forms of pronouns being grammatical only in immediate connection with a verb (with but a few exceptions) the emphatic form has to be used conjointly with it, when, for oratorical purposes, it is necessary that special stress should be laid on the person. Hence such phrases as *moi je le ferai* or *je le ferai moi-même*, etc.

Possessives.—These are either adjectives or pronouns. In the adjective proper, the Old French forms for the subject singular, *mes, tes, ses*, from Latin *meus, tuus, suus*, disappeared and the objective forms *mon, ton, son* took their place. The same thing occurred in the plural, where *mes, tes, ses*[1] have superseded the Mediæval nominatives *mei, tui, sui*. *Votre* is from *vostrum*, an archaic Latin form preferred by Romance to the classical *vestrum*. *Leur* is from *illorum* and takes an *s* as if it represented an ordinary Latin accusative instead of being a heavily inflected genitive case. As for the practice of using *mon, ton, son*, instead of *ma, ta, sa*, before a feminine noun beginning with a vowel or silent *h*, it was introduced as late as the 14th century; Old French elided very properly the vowel in *ma, ta, sa*, saying *m'épée*, etc. *M'amie* represents alone in the modern language the older state of affairs. But even here the elision was so well forgotten that the spelling *ma mie* crept in, giving birth thereby to the term of endearment *mie*, as found in *ta mie*, 'thy sweetheart,' still forthcoming in popular songs.

The pronominal forms have the same origin as the adjectival ones. As they bore an accentual stress, they grew mostly into fuller forms (cf. Eng. my book, in which *my* may be pronounced with a short *e* sound, and this book is mine). At first *mien, tien, sien* were simply alternative forms to *mon, ton, son*, and their pronominal value was distinctly marked only after the definite article was placed before them. In *le nôtre* and *le vôtre* the fullness and length of the vowel is indicative of the pronominal stress, and not a consequence of the dropping out of the *s* for which the circumflex stands. In

[1] Latin *meos, tuos, suos*.

the adjectival forms *notre* and *votre* the *o* is short, and the dropping of *s* is without a sign.

DEMONSTRATIVES.—We have to distinguish here again between primitive emphatic and primitive unemphatic forms, the first leading to the pronoun *celui* and the second producing the adjective *ce*, from different Latin demonstrative stems, which both received in Romance the prefix *ecce*.

The Latin *eccistum* and *eccisti* were in Romance *ekkestu* and *ekkestui*. The former in the eleventh century had become *icest* and the latter *icestui.* · A little later, *cest*, the direct object form proper, stood for both nominative and accusative, while the other form, evolved from the Romance dative, died out. *Cest* became *cet*, and as the *t* was not sounded when a consonant or an aspirate *h* followed, it ceased to be written in such connections. Modern grammars often reason as if *ce* was the original form and the *t* put to it before vowels as a euphonic addition, but exactly the reverse process took place. The Romance *ekkeste* had emphatic forms as well as non-emphatic forms, but the former have given rise to no pronoun in the modern language. The non-emphatic forms are alone represented in modern *ce*.

The Romance *ekkelle* (Lat. *ecce ille*) has failed to hand down its non-emphatic forms. The Mediæval *icil*, fem. *icelle*, with the ind. obj. form *icelui*, is dead to ordinary use, though still occurring in legal phraseology and in some popular archaic phrases. Modern *celui* may be looked upon as a stem in which there is no longer an appreciable connection with *icclui*, and in which the old opposition to *iste* is so lost sight of that the adverbial particles *ci* and *là* are added to it to express the differences tween 'nearer' and 'further,' totally obliterated in *ce*, *celui* as they now stand. In this way *celui-ci* has now the function of Romance *ekkcsti*, and *celui-là* the function of *ekkelle*, in the places where these forms stood pronominally in contradistinction. *Ecce iste est meus liber* becomes in French *celui-ci cst mon livre; ecce ille est meus liber, celui-là est mon livre.* In their adjectival connection *ecce iste liber* and *ecce ille liber* are represented by *ce livre-ci*, and *ce livre-là.*

The neutral pronoun *ce* should not be confused with the masculine adjective *ce.* The former represents the Latin *ecce hoc*, which passed through forms *iko, ikjo iczo*, spelt *iço*, then *ço*, and finally modern *ce.* It is used pronominally in demonstrative reference to things or ideas which stand in the mind definitely as nouns, but which cannot come under a masculine or a feminine category.

RELATIVES.—The relative *lequel* is used both as an adjective and as a pronoun. Its adjectival use is a logical outcome of such a connection as *quales homincs*, known to classical Latin.

The primitive Latin relative *qui, quae, quod* has a progeny of Modern French forms which are only used pronominally. The previous use in Latin of the relative pronoun after prepositions here also laid the basis for a distinction between emphatic and unemphatic forms, while the extreme likeness of dative *cui* to nominative *qui* prepared the way for much confusion.

In sentences like *vir quem video* the stress lay naturally on *vir*, while in *id de quo loquor* and in *vir de quo loquor* the absence of any stress on the preposition *de* threw a stress on *quo*, bringing about in French the emphatic forms *ce de quoi je parle* and *l'homme de qui je parle*. The form *qui* stands in the subjective for masculine, feminine, and neuter, and after prepositions for masculine and feminine only. The form *que* stands in the direct object for masculine, feminine, and neuter; the form *quoi* stands after prepositions for neuter only, and the Latin dative has left no trace in the modern language, neither has the genitive. As a substitute for the latter there stepped in *dont* (from *de unde*) filling here a function similar to *en* in the scheme of personal pronouns. *Dont* may be used instead of *de qui* in reference to persons. It must be used in reference to things, and after the neutral pronoun *ce* it may replace *de quoi*. Its two parts were once separable, as is evident in the older spelling *d'ont*.

INDEFINITES.—Among these *autrui* is derived from an old Romance emphatic dative, *alterui*. It has long ceased to call up to the mind its primitive case relation. *On* from *hominem*, *rien* from *rem*, and *personne* from *personam* have all lost the definite noun-sense they had in Latin, and have gradually become so vague and abstract that, in the case of the two latter, their original feminine gender is no longer compatible with their office. They are really neutral in meaning, and in the absence of a neuter they have passed to the masculine gender as indefinite pronouns. As for *on*, which was originally masculine, it goes the length of being connected with a feminine in the predicate (cf. *on est vieille* with *on est vieux*).[1]

---

[1] The grammatical rules commented upon in this chapter from the historical point of view are contained in Eugène's *Comparative French Grammar*, from § 1 to § 71. Our remarks should be read in conjunction with them.

# CHAPTER XIII.



Moods.—These are the same as in Latin, except the so-called conditional mood, which is an invention of French grammarians. Its name is derived from its appearing in principal clauses subjected to a condition expressed with *si* in an associated dependent clause, but its origin is not to be sought in that direction at all.

Latin had a future present and a future perfect, which it used in principal clauses without restriction, and in dependent clauses containing a direct temporal statement (ex.: cum Romam *venero*, ad te *scribam* quod *perspexero*). French can translate such sentences literally (quand je *serai venu* à Rome, je *t'écrirai* ce que *j'aurai vu*).

When one or a series of such direct temporal statements (indicative mood) was subordinated to the belief, hope, or feeling of a person expressing his mind in a main clause, Latin had recourse to the construction known as the *accusativus cum infinitivo*. By means of the present, perfect, and future tense-forms of the infinitive, or by periphrases of a similar nature, it could adhere strictly to the rules on the sequence of tenses (ex.: dico me ad te scripturum esse; dico me ad te scripsisse,

credebam eum scripturum esse, etc.).   The elasticity of
the 'infinitive' formation of dependent clauses admitted
of such constructions receiving great development.

But when these constructions with the infinitive were
greatly superseded in Romance by a construction
with *quod* and a finite verb-form (saying instead of *spero
Petrum me amaturum esse, spero quod Petrus me amare
habet*), the want was felt of new indicative tense-forms
to express from the stand-point of a person in the
past the relation which in classical Latin was expressed
by the *accusativus cum infinitivo*: thence came the
further Romance formation, *sperabam quod Petrus me
amare habebat*, leading to the French, *j'espérais que
Pierre m'aimerait.*

The function of the subjunctive in conditional clauses
and in principal clauses connected therewith having
become uncertain through the growth of confusion in
flexions, the indicative mood, with the new indirect
future present and future perfect, took the place of the
subjunctive where it failed.   Then grammarians, looking
at the historical process, not from the beginning, but
from the end, invented the conditional mood.

TENSES.—French has in the indicative mood preserved the synthetic present, imperfect, and perfect of
Latin (giving to the last the name of past definite
or preterite).   It has introduced a new analytical
tense, the past indefinite, for which there is no
equivalent in Latin.   It has lost the synthetic Latin
pluperfect and supplied it by an analytical formation.

It has introduced the past anterior, an analytical tense all its own. The future present and future perfect were preserved in a renovated synthetic shape due to Romance. The imperative was preserved, though somewhat reshaped, in analogy with the French present of the indicative. In the subjunctive the French present corresponds to the Latin present; the French imperfect is derived from the Latin pluperfect, while the French perfect and pluperfect are analytical, the first of the corresponding synthetic Latin tenses being lost, and the second having been diverted. The two tenses of the conditional have been mentioned in the preceding paragraph. The Latin perfect infinitive has been supplanted by an analytical formation. The gerund has practically died out except after the preposition *en*; the supine has disappeared. The present participle remains and so does the past ·participle, but the future participle is no more. In the passive the tenses are all analytical.

CONJUGATIONS.—Grammarians distinguish on one hand four regular conjugations, and on the other a more or less classified mass of so-called irregular verbs. But history knows nothing of either regular or irregular conjugations. It can only recognise that the majority of French verbs belong to four types while a minority belongs to many types. The most important and most used verbs of the language are those which failed most signally to conform to a type, because being most frequently used, their individual character was little exposed to the inroads of analogy and preserved itself through the centuries.

To the first conjugation ending in *-er* belongs the group having in Latin *-a're* in the infinitive present. To these were added from the fifteenth century by scholars, who were misled by outward appearances, some verbs ending in Latin in *-ĕre*, such as *prohiber* from *prohibe're*. Had natural analogy instead of artificial imitation been brought to bear upon such verbs they would have received the ending *-oir* and have been added to the third conjugation.

To the second conjugation belong verbs ending in Latin in *-īre*; only those were considered regular by grammarians which in some persons and tenses inserted in the Latin the inchoative particle *-sc-* between the stem and the flexion.

The third conjugation ending in *-oir* contains the verbs which ended in *-ēre* in Latin or in Romance. It contains only seventeen verbs, and corresponds to the second conjugation in Latin.

The fourth conjugation ends in *-re*, embodying the ending *-ĕre* of the Latin third. It contains fifty verbs.

AUXILIARY VERB AVOIR—We give some of the simple tenses in Old French showing their Romance derivation.

| *M. Fr.*, avoir. | *Old French*, aveir. | *Romance*, abe're. |
|---|---|---|
| *Old Fr. Pres. Ind.* ai (a'bjo) | *Pres. Subj.* aie (a'bja) | |
| as (a'bus) | aies (a'bjas) | |
| a (t) (a'bet) | aiet-ait (a'bjat) | |
| avons (ab-') | aiens-aions (abja'mus) | |
| avez (ab-') | aiez (abja'tis) | |
| ont (a'b-) | aient (a'bjant). | |

*Old Fr. Imp. Ind.*  aveie-avoie (abe'a)
                      aveies-avoies (abe'as)
                      aveit-avoit (abe'at)
                      aviiens (abea'mus)
                      aviiez (abea'tis)
                      aveient-avoient (abe'ant).

| *Pret Ind.* | | *Perf. Subj.* | |
|---|---|---|---|
| oi (a'bvi) | | ĕusse (abue'sse) | |
| eus (abue'sti) | | ĕusses | |
| ot-eut (a'bvit) | | ĕust | |
| eumes (abue'mus) | | ĕussiens | |
| eustes (abue'stis) | | ĕussiez | |
| orent-eūrent (a'bverunt) | | ĕussent | |

| *Fut. Ind.* | | *Pres. Cond.* | |
|---|---|---|---|
| avrai (a'ber a'bjo) | | avreie-avroie | |
| avras | | avreies-avroies | |
| avra | | avreit-avroit | |
| avrons | | avriiens-avriions | |
| avrez | | avriiez | |
| avront | | avreient-avroient | |

*Imperative,* aie-aies (abjas)     *Pres. Part.*   aiant (abjante)

*Past. Part.* ĕu(t) (abu'tu), fem. ĕu(d)e.

The classical Latin and Modern French may in each set of forms be supplied by the reader.

Before becoming an auxiliary, *avoir* was a notional verb; hence two sets of forms in principle, that in which it bore its own accent as a notional verb, and that in which it had no accent of its own as an auxiliary verb. However, in the history of the verb, the distinct phonetics can hardly be traced in each form. . They were very frequently confused.

The forms *avons, avez, ont,* are not purely etymological.

AUXILIARY VERB ÊTRE.—We give some of the simple tenses in Old French showing their Romance derivation.

*Modern French,* être.    *Old French,* estre.    *Rom.,* e'ssere.

*Old Fr. Pres. Ind.* sui (som)  *Pres. Subj.* seie-soie (sea)
      es (es)       seies-soies (seas)
      est (est)       seit-soit (seat)
      sommes (somns)   seiens-soiens-soions
                (seamus)
      estes (estis)     seiez-soiez (seatis)
      sont (sont).      seient-soient (seant).

This verb had two imperfects in Old French. The older one, derived from Latin *eram*, disappeared very early on account of its confusing likeness to the future *ero*. Another imperfect was coined in its place from the Latin stem *stab-* as forthcoming in *stabam*, the imperfect of *stare*. It is likely that the analogy presented by such verb forms as *mettait* had something to do with determining *était*, just as *sont* (*font, vont*) may have affected *ont*, in the verb *avoir*.

## IMPERFECT INDICATIVE.

| *Older Form.* | *Newer Form.* |
|---|---|
| ere (era) | esteie-estoie |
| eres (eras) | esteies-estoies |
| ere (t) (erat) | esteit-estoit |
| —— | estiiens |
| —— | estïez |
| erent (erant). | esteient-estoient. |

*Pret. Ind.* fui- fus (fui)  *Perf. Subj.* fusse (fosse)
      fus (fosti)       fusses (fosses)
      fut-fu (fo'it)     fust (fosset)
      fumes (fo'imus)   fussiens
      fustes (fostis)    fussiez
      furent (forunt)   fussent (fossent.)

In the future we have the same phenomenon as in the imperfect. There existed an older form from Latin *ero* which shared the fate of the imperfect from *eram*. Instead of it, a new future was formed from the infinitive *e'ssere* in the ordinary Romance manner.

## FUTURE INDICATIVE.

| *Older Form.* | *Newer Form.* |
|---|---|
| ier (ero) | serai ( [e's] sere a'bjo) |
| iers (eris) | seras |
| iert (erit) | sera |
| iermes (e'rimus) | serons |
| —— | serez |
| ierent (erunt). | seront. |

Pres. Cond. seroie. Imperat. sois. Pres. Part. estant. Past. Part. estet.

It is doubtful whether the present participle was formed from *estre* by analogy with *mettant* from *mettre*, or whether the Latin *stantem* should be gone back to. Be this as it may, there is no doubt that the past participle *estet* is from Latin *status*. As for the Romance infinitive *e'ssere*, it offers an analogy with the elongated forms *po'tere*, *offe'rere*, etc., substituted in Romance for the Classical *posse*, *ófferre*.

The circumflex on the preterite forms *nous fûmes*, *vous fûtes* is a blunder against phonetics committed by the sixteenth century grammarians. There was no *s* in *fuimus*, and the only excuse for the circumflex is that it may mark the length of *u*, but there are many long *u*s which dispense with this sign.

AIMER, ORDINARY PARADIGM OF THE FIRST CONJUGATION.—The best historical division of French verbs is into primary and secondary verbs. The latter are distinguished from the former by a uniform feature: they had in the Romance perfect the tonic accent on the last syllable but one. Originally all secondary verbs formed their perfect by means of the suffix *-vi*. But in the

Lingua Romana this suffix already failed to appear in
its primitive purity, because the forms in use in classical
Latin, and which were contracted by the poets, found
their way into popular Latin also. A comparison of the
different Romance languages leads back to the three
following types, as characterising the perfect in secondary verbs. The perfect in Latin is in French the
preterite or past definite.

**FUNDAMENTAL ROMANCE FORMS.**

| | | |
|---|---|---|
| canta'ï | rende'ï (rende'di) | parti'ï |
| canta'sti | rende'sti | parti'sti |
| canta'vit | rende'it | parti'vit |
| canta'mmus | rende'mus | parti'mmus |
| canta'stis | rende'stis | parti'stis |
| canta'runt[1] | rende'runt | parti'runt |

**CLASSICAL LATIN FORMS.**

| | | |
|---|---|---|
| canta'vi | re'ddidi | parti'vi |
| cantavi'sti | reddidi'sti | partivi'sti |
| canta'vit | re'ddidit | parti'vit |
| canta'vimus | reddi'dimus | parti'vimus |
| cantavi'stis | reddidi'stis | partivi'stis |
| cantave'runt | reddide'runt | partive'runt |

The gap yawning between the classical forms and the
Modern French forms is easily accounted for by the
general phonetic laws affecting the transition from
Latin into French.

**MODERN FRENCH FORMS.**

| | | |
|---|---|---|
| chantâï' | rendi's | parti's |
| chantas | rendis | partis |
| chanta | rendit | partit |
| chantâmes | rendîmes | partimes |
| chantâtes | rendîtes | partîtes |
| chantèrent | rendirent | partirent |

In the preterite of the first class, here represented by

---

[1] See No. 12, p. 247, and note 2, p. 245.

the Romance *canta'ï*, *v* disappeared throughout because it stood between two vowels immediately after the accented syllable. The *-ti* of the second person was dropped, as is usual with those suffixes following the accented syllable which could not be incorporated with it. In the first person of the plural, the *i* of *canta'vĭmus*, being a short *i* between two consonants after the accented syllable, could not survive. In the second person plural the full primitive suffix *-stis* brought into proximity with the accented vowel *a*, through the disappearance of the intermediate *v*, shrunk to its present reduction *-tes*. In the third person plural the accent was thrown back to the *a* as the result of the falling out of *v* (see p. 245, No. 5).

In the preterite of the second class, here represented by the Romance *rendeï*, the original suffix *-vi* lost its place to a re-duplication introduced at a very early date in analogy with the perfect *dĕdi* of the primitive Latin verb *dare*. The tonic accent fell on the penultimate, again in analogy with the accentuation of *de'di* from *dăre*, root *da-* or *ded-*. Though in this class the termination *-evi* is not represented, the termination *-edi* (with accent on the *e*) is similarly constituted and obeyed the same phonetic laws. The *d* dropped out like the *v* for the same cause; the tonic accent exerted the same influence on the suffixes, and was thrown back one place in the third person plural for the same cause. As for the *s* which appears in Modern French at the end of the first person singular, it is an etymological blunder.

In the preterite of the third class, here represented by the Romance *parti'i*, the primitive termination *-i'vi* presents a close approximation to the *-a'vi* of the first, and there is nothing further to remark.

There is in the ordinary French grammars no trace of this division, rooted in history, of French verbs into primary and secondary verbs, but there appears a totally arbitrary division into regular and irregular verbs. Modern verbs might fitly be classed into three conjugations, using as a basis the three types of preterite sketched above, and leaving out for further classification what in the present four regular conjugations cannot be made to fit into the plan suggested. Unfortunately, it is too late to mend French grammars in that way.

Returning, therefore, to the time-honoured but unhistorical division into four conjugations according to the ending of the infinitive, we have still some fault to find with the paradigm *aimer*, which is the traditional one in the first conjugation; for it presents in its stem a development which it has in common with many so-called irregular verbs. In the Latin conjugation of *amo* the tonic accent did not rest permanently on the same syllable, as is made clear by the comparison of *a'mo* with *ama'vi*, and with *ama'mus*. The tonic accent passed from the root syllable to the one or the other of the ensuing terminational syllables, according to the varying length of the whole word. The same thing occurred in some nouns, where we have seen the differently accented Latin forms give rise to different French words, as *pâtre* from *pa'stor*, in contrast to *pasteur* from *pasto'rem*. In keeping with the general law that the accented vowel was strengthened or lengthened by the effect of the stress laid on it, Latin *a'mo* was in Old French *aim*, but *ama'mus* became *amons*. This alternate thickness and purity of the root vowel, caused by the shifting of the accent, remained characteristic of many so-called irregular verbs, as is seen by comparing *je sais* with *nous savons, je peux* with *nous pouvons*. It has now disappeared from the verb *aimer*, the forms with the pure vowel having been assimilated to those with the thickened intonation. Yet this should have sufficed to preclude grammarians from setting up *aimer* as the pattern of regularity. Therefore, we shall adopt as a paradigm the verb *chanter*, in which the *a* is so hemmed in between consonants that the mobility of the accent did not affect it.

As the simple tenses of verbs belonging to the first class (preterite in *-avi*) have had a great influence in shaping the terminations affixed to other verbs, we shall now give them in their historical sequence.

## PRESENT.

| INDICATIVE. | | SUBJUNCTIVE. | |
|---|---|---|---|
| *Rom.* | *Old Fr.* | *Rom.* | *Old Fr.* |
| ca'nto | chant | ca'nte | chant |
| ca'ntas | chantas | ca'ntes | chanz |
| ca'ntat | chante(t) | ca'ntet | chant |
| cant . . . | chantons | cant . . . | chantiens |
| canta'tis | chantez | cant . - . | chantiez |
| cantant | chantent | cant . . - | chantent |

The *e*, which in Modern French ends the first person

singular, was first introduced in the fifteenth century.
The *e*, which in the modern subjunctive appears in the
three persons of the singular, dates also from that time.
The forms for which no Romance suffix is given were
subjected to analogical influence by the corresponding
forms of the verb *avoir*.

## IMPERFECT.

The present terminations of this tense are not
directly descended from corresponding Romance forms.
In Old French the etymological forms succumbed
before the eleventh century to the attraction put forth
by the already fully evolved imperfect of *avoir*. The *s*
of the first person in Modern French is a blunder. It
is generally interpreted as differentiating the imperfect
from the preterite. Unfortunately for this theory it
is not pronounced. The real distinction is that in
the imperfect the *ai* has an open sound, while in the
preterite it has a closed sound (cf. è and é). The same
difference in the pronunciation of *ai* distinguishes in
the first person the future from the conditional.

## PRETERITE.

| INDICATIVE. | | SUBJUNCTIVE. | |
|---|---|---|---|
| *Rom.* | *Old Fr.* | *Rom.* | *Old Fr.* |
| canta'ï | chantai | canta'ssem | chantasse |
| canta'sti | chantas | canta'sses | chantasses |
| canta'vit | chanta(t) | canta'sset | chantast |
| canta'vimus | chantames | cantass- . . . | chantassiens |
| canta'stis | chantastes | cantass- . . . | chantassiez |
| canta'runt | chantereut | canta'ssent | chantassent |

### FUTURE.

| DIRECT (Ind.). | | INDIRECT (Cond.). | |
| --- | --- | --- | --- |
| *Rom.* | *Old Fr.* | *Rom.* | *Old Fr.* |
| ca'ntar a'bjo | chanterai | ca'ntar abe'a | chanteroie |

| IMPERATIVE. | | INFINITIVE. | |
| --- | --- | --- | --- |
| ca'nta | chante | canta're | chanter |

| PART. PRES. | | PART. PERF. | |
| --- | --- | --- | --- |
| canta'nte | chantant | canta'tu | chantet |

In the imperative the second person singular alone
comes directly from the corresponding Romance form.
The other forms are borrowed from the French indicative
or subjunctive.

THE WORKING OF ANALOGY IN VERBS.—The verbs
*être* and *avoir* are those most frequently used in current
speech ; and by far the greater number of other verbs
belong to the first conjugation. In consequence the
terminations of *être* and *avoir*, as well as those of such
verbs as *chanter* and *aimer*, forced themselves by the
working of analogy on other verbs, and disturbed their
phonetical development.

1. The first person plural in the indicative present
ends in all verbs in -*ons* with the exception of *sommes*
from *être*. It may be taken that *sommes* has forced its
accented *o* throughout the different conjugations and
ousted the sound combinations which should have
resulted from such different Latin vowels as long *a*, long
*e*, short *i* and long *i*.

For classical *amāmus, debēmus, legĭmus, vestīmus,*
French puts uniformly *aimons, devons, lisons, vêtons*.

In all verbs the second person plural present indicative

ends in *-ez* and the third in *-ent*.  The only instances of a preserved correspondence with the Latin are the forms *faites*, and *dites* (also *redites*, *refaites*, etc.).  The analogy of the second person plural is with the corresponding form of *chanter*, and, in the case of the third person, with the Latin ending *-ant* characteristic of the first Latin conjugation.

2. In the present and the imperfect of the subjunctive of all conjugations, the endings *-ions* and *-iez* in the first and second persons of the plural are due to the analogical force put forth by the corresponding persons of *avoir*, and in the case of *-ions* the influence of the *-ons* of the present indicative has also made itself felt analogically.   (Cf. Old French *chantiens*.)

3. In all conjugations the imperfect has the same termination.  Analogy with the corresponding forms of *avoir* has led to this uniformity.

4. In all verbs the present participle was formed in analogy to Romance *cantante*, French *chantant*, the *-ent-* and *-ient-* of Latin (cf. *monentem*, *audientem*) being altogether superseded.

FINIR, ORDINARY PARADIGM OF THE SECOND CONJUGATION.—Grammarians restrict the regular second conjugation to those verbs ending in the infinitive in *-ir* which in certain persons and tenses introduce *-ss-* between the stem ending in *i* and the flexion.  When this *-ss-* is viewed etymologically it appears to be the Latin inchoative particle *-sc-* (Greek σκ).  This particle, however, had completely lost its meaning when it came

into general use in the Lingua Romana, and its general
introduction is only another instance of the tendency to
lengthen verb and noun forms which appears to have
been a necessity with Romance. It points to such formations as *fini'skimus* for classical *finīmus*, French
*finiss-ons*, and *appare'skimus* for classical *apparēmus*,
French *apparaiss-ons*.

Since the office of the -*ss*- is restricted to strengthening the verb form in which it stands, it is better to put
together the verbs that have it as strong verbs of
the second conjugation, and to call those which do not
have it (generally dubbed irregular verbs) the weak
verbs of the second conjugation. Therefore *finir* cannot
be taken as representing the second conjugation viewed
historically but only as being characteristic of its strong
verbs.

### PRESENT.

| INDICATIVE. | | SUBJUNCTIVE. | |
|---|---|---|---|
| *Rom.* | *Mod. Fr.* | *Rom.* | *Mod. Fr.* |
| fini'sco | finis | fini'sca | finisse |
| fini'skis | finis | fini'scas | finisses |
| fini'skit | finit | fini'scat | finisse |
| fini'sk- | finissons | fini'sc- | finissions |
| fini'sk- | finissez | fini'sc- | finissiez |
| fini'scunt | finissent | fini'scant | finissent |

### IMPERFECT.

| INDICATIVE. | | SUBJUNCTIVE. | |
|---|---|---|---|
| *Rom.* | *Mod. Fr.* | *Rom.* | *Mod. Fr.* |
| finiske'ba | finissais | finii'ssem | finisse |
| etc. | etc. | etc. | etc. |

The *s* which the Modern French has at the end of the
first person, has crept in from the second person at the
instigation of grammarians, whose labours in the cause

of artificial uniformity seem to be ever ready to go counter to natural analogy and etymology.

**PRESENT PARTICIPLE.**

*Rom.* finisca'nte.      *Mod. Fr.* finissant.

The *k* sound was throughout assimilated to the sibilant *s*. The above are the only persons and tenses in which the strengthening particle *-ss-* was inserted.

RECEVOIR, ORDINARY PARADIGM OF THE THIRD CONJUGATION.—This verb, with the verbs conjugated like it, has less than any other so-called regular verb the right to appear in a scheme of regular conjugations. Some excuse can be pleaded for putting together the verbs ending in *-er*, for they are all secondary verbs of the first class (this class being characterised by the ending *-avi* of the Latin perfect). The putting together of the verbs ending in *-ir* is not without some excuse too, since the *-ss-* nowhere affects the whole conjugation of any verb in this class, and since they belong largely to one and the same class (ending *-ivi*) of secondary verbs.

But the verbs ending in *-oir* are primary verbs. They are derived from the second and third Latin conjugations, in which the perfect is in principle formed in three different ways—namely, in *-i*, in *-si*, or in *-ui*. These three terminations of the perfect taken as they appear in Romance are held to determine the class of primary verbs, just as the endings *-avi*, *-edi*, and *-ivi* have been shown to distinguish the secondary

verbs. So with *recevoir* there enters into the grammatical scheme of the four conjugations a historical
element which is not forthcoming in the first, second,
and fourth 'regular' conjugations.

We cannot enter here on the conditions underlying
the conjugation of the primary verbs, for this would
lead us from the province of general historical
grammar into that of specialised phonetics, and comparative etymology. Suffice it to say that *recevoir*
presents in its conjugation a less uniform compromise
than exists in the three other paradigms between
fidelity to etymology and compliance with the force of
analogy. The alteration of the stem of the verb from
*recev-*, as it appears in the infinitive, present participle,
and first and second persons plural of the present indicative, to *reç-* in the singular of the indicative, the
preterite, the imperfect subjunctive, and past participle,
the forms *reçoiv-* of the subjunctive present, and
*recevr-* of the future, all show how many different
factors were brought into play in the gradual elaboration of the Latin *reci'père*, till, after passing through
Romance and Old French, it was crystallised in the
modern forms of the French verb *recevoir*. The Latin
*reci'pio* gave *reçoi*, to which in the written language *s*
was added by confusion with the second person. In
*reci'pio* the accent is on the short *i* before *p*. Hence
the thickening of that *i* into *oi*, but when the tonic
accent was pushed onward to the termination, as in
*reci̅pie'bam*, the short *i*, free from the accentual stress,
was lightened into an *e* mute. Hence the subsidiary

stem *recev-*.   This process was carried a step further in the future; for when its flexion *-ai* was added to the infinitive *recevoir*, the syllable *-oir* lost in its turn its accent to the final *-ai*, leading to the intermediate form *receverai*.   It is now *recevrai*.   As in the preceding paradigms, the terminations that cannot be traced back to the corresponding forms of *recipjo* in Romance were introduced by analogy with the verbs of another conjugation.

VENDRE, ORDINARY PARADIGM OF THE FOURTH CONJUGATION.—The fourth conjugation of modern grammarians is made up of a medley of verbs, some of which, ending originally in *-ivi* or *-edi* in the Romance perfect, should be classified as secondary verbs, while others, the ' irregular' ones, ending in the Romance perfect in *-i, -si*, or *-ui* should be classed as primary.

The *s* which appears in the second person singular of the imperative is not etymological, and is not found in Old French.   It crept in after the thirteenth century in analogy with the second person of the indicative present.   But down to the seventeenth century, it was permissible to omit the *s* in that person, while poets preserved the further liberty of not writing the spurious *s* of the first person (cf. *je croi*, poetical and etymological for the *je crois* of prose).   Classical *ve'nditus* could not give the modern past participle *vendu*.   Romance *vendu'tu* must be assumed, or analogy appealed to (cf. Romance *battu'tu*, French *battu*).

SOME INTERROGATIVE FORMS OF VERBS.—In *aimé-je,*

*puissé-je*, interrogative for *j'aime*, *que je puisse*, the acute does not mark the close vowel sound of *e*, but it stands as a visible sign that the tonic accent should be laid on the syllable, because it is against the *génie de la langue* to have two mute syllables in succession at the end of any word.

The *t* written between hyphens in *aime-t-il, aima-t-il*, is the *t* of the third person in Latin which has survived in pronunciation owing to its being caught up between two vowels and essential to the sense.

THE DIPHTHONG OI OR AI IN THE IMPERFECT.—The wavering between *oi* and *ai*, first in pronunciation and then in writing, persisted down to the eighteenth century. Voltaire was the first to write *ai* where that sound was pronounced, not only in the imperfect of verbs, but also in adjectives like *français* instead of the older *françois*.

THE AUXILIARY ÊTRE IN THE CONJUGATION OF IN-TRANSITIVE VERBS.—Latin formed its perfect in the passive with the help of the auxiliary *esse*, saying *amatus sum*, and further, in deponent verbs, *profectus sum*. The latter being mostly intransitive, the auxiliary was quite naturally transmitted through Romance to some of the French intransitive verbs. *Je suis né* corresponds to *natus sum*; *je suis venu* to the Romance *ventus sum*, taking the place of classical *veni* when it was no longer able to express an indefinite past. (Cf. impers. *ventum est*.)

THE AUXILIARY ÊTRE IN THE CONJUGATION OF REFLECTIVE VERBS.—Reflective force could be given to a Latin verb in two different ways. The passive could be used : the history of the Latin passive shows that in its origin it cannot be distinguished from the reflective. Or else the reflective pronoun *se* with the verb in the active was taken advantage of. French preferred this latter formation. It borrowed the Latin reflective pronoun *se* and completed it by using reflectively the ordinary pronouns. Some verbs, which in themselves do not convey a reflective idea, such as *mourir*, received the reflective pronoun as expressing the progressivity of the action. *Je me meurs* means 'I am dying by degrees,' 'I am pining away'; *je meurs*, 'I am actually dying.' (Cf. s'en aller.) The deponent verbs of Latin forming their perfect with *sum* (cf. *ultus sum, pollicitus sum*) handed their auxiliary down to the French reflective conjugation, however illogical it may seem to an English boy to say *je me suis frappé* in the sense of 'I have struck myself.

IMPERSONAL VERBS.—These verbs are called impersonal because their pronoun stands in no definite personal meaning, it is merely a grammatical subject derived from Latin *illud*, and used for form's sake. An analytical language like French could ill dispense altogether with a subject pronoun even in its impersonal verbs.

VERBS WITH E MUTE IN THE PENULTIMATE SYLLABLE.— When we were dealing with the feminine of adjectives we explained such forms as *secret*, fem. *secrète*, and *sujet*, fem. *sujette*, where the accent grave is used in the first instance, and the *t* is doubled in the other instance, with one and the same purpose in view. That was a case of arbitrariness in spelling sanctioned by usage. In dealing with interrogative verb forms, we explained on grounds of accentual stress the forms *aimé-je*, etc. The rules affecting verbs with *e* mute in the penultimate syllable, so far as they determine the spelling only, repeat the arbitrariness apparent in *secrète*, as compared with *sujette*. But, whether *è* is used, or whether the *l* or the *t* is doubled, there is, as in *aimé-je*, an accentual working which the modifications alluded to in the spelling endeavour clumsily to mark.

In *acheter*, for instance, the accent is on the last syllable, but as soon as I say *j'achète* the tonic accent is thrown back on the syllable which was mute in the infinitive. French cannot say *j'a'chete* any more than it can say *ai'me-je*, so it says *j'achète* and *achete'r*, just as Latin said *a'mo* and *ama're*, and just as Old French said *j'ai'me* (which might be spelt *j'ème* or *j'emme*), and *ame'r* with a return in the absence of the accent to the pure vowel sound of the root. In that way all French verbs with an *e* mute in the penultimate, which either take *è* or double the consonant before the mute terminations *-e*, *-es*, *-ent* are shown to stand in a line with the general principles underlying the history of the language,

Verbs with *é* in the penultimate like *accélérer* change the closed *e* into an open *e* before a mute ending on the same principle as *léger* in the feminine becomes *légère*.

DOUBLE FORMS IN BÉNIR AND FLEURIR.—Latin past participle *benedictus* gave regularly in Old French *benir*, fem. *benite*.  In a Roman Catholic country like France this past participle is more frequently used in the two phrases *eau bénite, pain bénit* than in any other phrase.  Hence the modern language has preserved the *t* in those two instances.  In all other uses of the past participle the *t* is dropped, as in *fini* from *finitum*, etc.

The Latin *florere*, Romance *floreskere*, gave to French the infinitive *florir*.  Alongside of it a fresh verb *fleurir* was formed from the noun *fleur*, and was naturally used to express blossoming in its literal sense.  The older *florir* came then to be used only in a metaphorical sense.  At present it survives only in *florissant, je florissais*, etc. (metaphorical).

SO-CALLED PRINCIPAL PARTS AND DERIVED PARTS IN VERBS.—Grammars are accustomed to prefix to the regular conjugations a table of what they call the primary tenses or principal parts of the verb along with the derived parts or secondary tenses.  There is in this a faulty practice which may be grounded upon logic, but does not rest upon fact.  It is misleading, for instance, to say that from the present participle is formed the plural of the present indicative by changing *-ant* into *-ons, -ez, -ent*.  The French people never sat in solemn conclave to decide, that, as they needed certain linguistic conveniences called tenses and moods, they would lay down certain principal parts, and then carry out certain deliberate changes in their endings. French is not an artificial language like Volapük, and no tense was ever formed from another in the way indicated by our friends the formal grammarians. Their plan may be a convenient aid to memory, but its utility is far out-weighed by the misleading idea it impresses upon the mind of the pupil.[1]

[1] For a full treatment of the contents of chapters xii., xiii., and xiv. see, in addition to authorities already quoted, *Meissner's Philology of the French Language*, and *Brachet's Historical Grammar of the French Language* (translated by G. W. Kitchin).

The *Cours Supérieur de Grammaire Française*, by Brachet and Dussouchet (Hachette & Co.), is an excellent practical grammar on a historical basis, and should be read as a complement to *Eugène's Comparative French Grammar*.

The material left by the eminent French philologist Arsène Darmesteter is now being given to the public by Professor E. Muret of Geneva University, in the shape of a *Cours de Grammaire Historique de la Langue Française*. The first volume, dealing with phonetics, has appeared. This work marks a great advance on that of Brachet, and should be preferred. It will be complete in four parts, namely, phonetics, morphology, word formation, and historical syntax.

# CHAPTER XIV.

## THE SO-CALLED IRREGULAR VERB.

As languages in their development work up to no outer rule or standard, there can be no question in verbs of breaking the rule or of irregularity. In Latin already there was great dissimilitude in the inner phonetics of verbs, and French, though in a lesser degree, has inherited that characteristic. The so-called irregularity is seldom forthcoming in the actual terminations or flexions where the operation of analogy brought about almost complete uniformity. It is not often found either in the root, which remains, on the whole, a fixed phonetic quantity (accentual workings excepted, as in *je lève* compared with *lever*). The seat of the irregularity lies mostly between the root and the flexion. We have seen already, when discussing the formation of the feminine in adjectives, that certain letters and sounds of the Latin prototype, lost in the masculine form, reappeared in the feminine (cf. *malin, maligne*; *absous, absoute*). The cause of this is obvious; the sounds, and the signs marking them, which provided for the oral and written passage from the root to the flexion, were, by a wise instinct of economy and ease, used for the same purpose in the younger language. But they underwent many changes of their own.

PRIMARY VERBS.—The so-called irregular verbs of Modern French correspond roughly to that class of verbs in Romance which we have described as primary. While we found that all the secondary verbs were accented on the penultimate, primary verbs had their accent, in the first person singular of the perfect, on the stem (cf. *ama'vi* with *mo'nŭi* and *le'gi*). We have already given the flexions which in the perfect constitute the character of primary verbs, namely, *-si*, *-i*, and *-ui*. Some confusion of these three types was brought about by the working of analogy among themselves. For instance, a large number of verbs which formed their perfect originally in *-i* passed in Romance into the *-si* class : *prehendo* had no longer *prehendi* then, but *prensi* ; *occido* instead of remaining *occidi* became *occisi*. Besides the classical *veni*, there arose the subsidiary form *ve'nui* in analogy to the classical *te'nui*. The classical form *bi'bi* was superseded in Romance by *be'bui*. For *rece'pi* there stood *rece'pui*, etc. Later, when the *s* of the ending *-si* had been driven out as standing between two vowels, the differences between the three classes we have recognised in primary verbs according to their perfects were further obliterated, so that they can hardly be recognised at present as forming three distinct compact groups, without a reference to Old French to fill in the gaps. For that reason we shall not be able to give a connected history of the French primary verbs. We shall content ourselves with giving their three types as differentiated in principle, and then we shall have some remarks to make upon some verbs taken singly.

First Class of Primary Verbs.—The only modern representatives of this class are *voir*, *venir*, and *tenir*.

### TYPE OF PERFECT, Char. -I.

#### INDICATIVE. (PRETERITE.)

| *Rom.* | *Old Fr.* | *Mod. Fr.* |
| --- | --- | --- |
| vi'di | vi(t) | vis |
| vide'sti | ve(d)i's | vis |
| vi'dit | vit | vit |
| vidi'mus | ve(d)i'mes | viımes |
| vide'stis | ve(d)i'stes | vites |
| vi'dĕrunt [1] | vi'(d)rent | virent |

#### SUBJUNCTIVE. (IMPERFECT.)

| *Rom.* | *Old Fr.* | *Mod. Fr.* |
| --- | --- | --- |
| vide'sse | ve(d)i'sse | visse |
| vide'sses | ve(d)i'sses | visses |
| vide'sset | ve'(d)i'st | vit |
| videss-' | ve(d)issie'ns | vissions |
| videss-' | ve(d)issie'z | vissiez |
| vide'ssent | ve(d)i'ssent | vissent |

Second Class of Primary Verbs.—To this belong the verbs *dire*, *mettre*, *rire*, *faire*, etc.

### TYPE OF PERFECT, Char. -SI.

#### INDICATIVE. (PRETERITE.)

| *Rom.* | *Old Fr.* | *Mod. Fr.* |
| --- | --- | --- |
| pre'si (prensi) | pris | pris |
| prese'sti | presi's | pris |
| pre'sit | prist | prit |
| presi'mus | presi'mes | prîmes |
| prese'stis | presi'stes | prîtes |
| pre'sĕrunt | pri'strent | prirent |

#### SUBJUNCTIVE. (IMPERFECT.)

| *Rom.* | *Old Fr.* | *Mod. Fr.* |
| --- | --- | --- |
| prese'sse (prensissem) | pre(s)i'sse | prisse |
| etc. | etc. | etc. |

---

[1] See No. 12, p. 247.

THIRD CLASS OF PRIMARY VERBS.—In this class the preterite forms of the verbs are accented on the termination because they have deviated from their original accentuation under the influence of the corresponding forms of the auxiliary verb *fŭ'i* (perfect of *esse*). The Latin verb *debé're* was accented in Romance[1] *debu'isti, debu'imus, debu'istis*, after *fu'esti, fu'imus, fu'estis*. The loss of the *b* reduced in time the whole form to one accented syllable, with the flexion as a mere appendage. In Modern French this class is represented by *devoir, valoir, vouloir*, etc. In Romance the past participle in this class ended in -*ūtum*, giving *debu'tum* (Modern French *dû*) instead of classical *deb'ĭtum*. We discover here the origin of the *u* forthcoming in the past participle of *rendre, recevoir*, etc. When the verb-forms in this class are reduced to one syllable (apparently the stem syllable), faulty accentuation of the termination has none the less taken place, and contraction has ensued.

TYPES OF PERFECT, CHAR. -UI.

INDICATIVE. (PRETERITE)

| *Rom.* | *Old Fr.* | *Mod. Fr.* |
|---|---|---|
| de(b)ūī' | dūī | dus |
| de(b)ūī'sti | dus | dus |
| de(b)ūī't | dut | dut |
| de(b)ūī'mus | dumes | dûmes |
| de(b)ūī'stis | dutes | dûtes · |
| do'(b)verunt | durent | durent |

To detect the attraction, compare with the same tenses of *être* and *avoir*, towards which they have gravitated.

---

[1] Against No. 10, p. 246.

VERBS WITH A MIXED PERFECT.—These are *naître*, *vaincre*, and *vivre*; also the verbs ending in *-aindre*, *-eindre*, *-oindre*, with the compounds of *-duire*. In these, analogy with verbs similar in form or akin in meaning brought about confusion in the etymological processes.

The larger number of so-called irregular verbs belonged in Old French to the third class of primary verbs. The defective verbs of Modern French are merely archaic forms preserved from verbs that were fully conjugated in the Middle Ages. They are survivals generally forthcoming only in well-established phrases, with which they are inseparably incorporated; and their tendency is to be driven out more and more by neological formations.

REMARKS ON SOME SINGLE VERB FORMS.—1. The future of *acquérir* is from the old infinitive *querre*, *j'acquerrai*. Similarly the old infinitive *courre* is represented in the future *je courrai*.

2. The verb *faillir* has almost died out in the three persons singular of the indicative present. It subsists, however, in *le cœur me faut* (neological, *le cœur me manque*), etc.

3. The past participle of *férir* (modern *frapper*) is still used in the past participle *féru*, meaning 'infatuated.'

4. Though the verb *gésir* is spelt with a single *s*, it is pronounced as if there were a double *s*. *Il gisait* is pronounced *gi(s)sait*, Romance *jake'bat*.

5. The verb *ouïr* was still used in the future by Malherbe in verse. The past participle is now only used in legal parlance. The future, the preterite, and the past participle of *choir* were still in use in the 17th century.

6. *Savoir* has in the present participle *savant* and *sachant*. The former is used as an adjective only, and was formed directly from the stem *sav-*. *Sachant* is from Romance *sabja'nte*.

7. *Souloir*, from Latin *solēre*, may still be found in the imperfect.

8. *Valoir* has two present participles, *valant* and *vaillant*. The latter is used literally in the phrase *n'avoir pas un sou vaillant*. Elsewhere it is metaphorical in the sense of ' valorous.'

9. *Vouloir* also had formerly two present participles, *voulant* and *veuillant*. The latter appears still in *bienveillant* and *malveillant*.

10. *Imboire*, a compound of *boire*, is used only in the past participle *imbu*, Romance *imbū'tu*.

11. The simple verb *paître* has neither preterite nor past participle, because confusion with the same tenses of *pouvoir* would be unavoidable, but the compound *repaître* has the two forms in question.

### CLASSIFICATION OF IRREGULAR VERBS.

1. Inf. in -er. { aller / envoyer } Secondary verbs, class : *-avi* in Romance.

| *Romance.* | *Old French.* | *Modern French.* |
| --- | --- | --- |
| Inf.  ala're | aller | aller |
| Pret. ala'ï | alâi | allai |
| Inf.  inde-via're | entveier | envoyer |
| Pret. inde-viaï | entveiâi | envoyai |

| | | |
|---|---|---|
| | dormir | |
| | mentir | |
| | partir | |
| | sortir | |
| | servir | Secondary verbs, class: |
| | sentir | -ivi in Romance. |
| | se repentir | |
| 2. Inf. in -ir. | bouillir | |
| | vêtir | |
| (Weak verbs of the second conjugation.) | acquérir | |
| | faillir | |
| | saillir | |
| | ouvrir | Originally primary |
| | couvrir | verbs. In Romance, |
| | offrir | secondary verbs, class: |
| | souffrir | -ivi. |
| | cueillir | |
| | fuir | |
| (Weak verbs of the second conjugation.) | mourir | Primary verbs, class: |
| | courir | -ui in Romance |
| Inf. in -ir. | tenir | Primary verbs, classes: |
| | venir | -i and -ui in Romance. |

EXAMPLES.

| | *Romance.* | *Old French.* | *Modern French.* |
|---|---|---|---|
| Inf. | parti're | partir | partir |
| Pret. | parti'ï | parti | partis |
| Inf. | mori're | morir | mourir |
| Pret. | morŭï' | morui | mourus |
| Inf. | co'rrere | corre | [courir][1] |
| Pret. | — | — | [courus] |
| Inf. | veni're | venir | venir |
| Pret. | ve'ni | vin | vins |

---

[1] The forms in square brackets are *weak* forms, disregarding the law of Ionic accentuation on the same syllable as in Latin.

3. Inf. in ·oir.
$\left\{\begin{array}{l}\text{pouvoir}\\\text{mouvoir}\\\text{pleuvoir}\\\text{savoir}\\\text{valoir}\\\text{vouloir}\\\text{devoir}\\\text{·cevoir}\end{array}\right\}$
Primary verbs, class: ·ui iu Rom.

Inf. in ·oir.
$\left\{\begin{array}{l}\text{falloir, secondary verb, class : ·ivi}\\\text{seoir, primary verb, class: ·si}\\\text{voir, primary verb, class : ·i}\end{array}\right\}$ in Rom.

$\left.\begin{array}{l}\text{pourvoir}\\\text{déchoir}\end{array}\right\}$ Compounds of voir and choir.

### EXAMPLES.

| *Romance.* | *Old French.* | *Modern French.* |
|---|---|---|
| Inf. pote're | pooir | pouvoir |
| Pret. potûi' | poi | pus |
| Inf. move're | movoir | mouvoir |
| Pret. movûi' | mui | mus |
| Inf. sape're | savoir | savoir |
| Pret. sapûi' | soi | sus |
| Inf. vale're | valoir | valoir |
| Pret. valûi' | valui | valus |
| Inf. vole're | voloir | vouloir |
| Pret. vo'l | voil | [voulus] |
| Iuf. debe're | devoir | devoir |
| Pret. debûi' | dui | dus |
| Inf. vede're | veoir | voir |
| Pret. ve'di | vi | vis |

U

<table>
<tr><td rowspan="12">4. Inf. in re.</td><td>nuire<br>plaire<br>taire<br>boire<br>croire<br>coudre<br>moudre<br>connaître<br>paraître<br>paître<br>croître</td><td>Primary verbs, class:<br>-ui in Rom.</td></tr>
</table>

|  |  |
|---|---|
| nuire<br>plaire<br>taire<br>boire<br>croire<br>coudre<br>moudre<br>connaître<br>paraître<br>paître<br>croître | Primary verbs, class:<br>-ui in Rom. |
| -duire<br>-struire, -truire<br>cuire<br>luire<br>écrire<br>dire, -dire<br>faire, -fire<br>rire<br>traire<br>lire<br>conclure<br>plaindre<br>-soudre<br>mettre<br>prendre | Primary verbs, class:<br>-si in Rom. |
| suivre | Primary verb, class:<br>-i in Rom. |
| naître<br>vivre<br>vaincre | Primary verbs, mixed<br>class in Rom. |

4. Inf. in -re.

## EXAMPLES.

| | Romance. | Old French. | Modern French. |
|---|---|---|---|
| Inf. | noke're, no'kre | nuisir, nuire | nuire |
| Pret. | nocūī' | nui | [nuisis] |
| Inf. | plake're, pla'kcre | plaisir, plaire | plaire |
| Pret. | plakūī' | ploi | plus |

| Inf. be'bere | beivre | boire |
| Pret. bebūī' | bui | bus |
| Inf. cre'dere | croire | croire |
| Pret. credūī' | crui | crus |
| Inf. conno'skere | conoistre | connaître |
| Pret. connovūī' | conui | connus |
| Inf. cre'skere | creistre | croître |
| Pret. crevūī' | crui | crûs |
| Inf. du'kere | duire | -duire |
| Pret. du'ksi | duis | [-duisis] |
| Inf. scri'bere | escrivre | écrire |
| Pret. scri'psi | escris | [écrivis] |
| Inf. di'kere | dire | dire |
| Pret. di'ksi | dis | dis |
| Inf. fa'kere | faire | faire |
| Pret. fe'ki | fi | fis |
| Inf. tra'kere | traire | traire |
| Pret. tra'ksi | trais | ... |
| Inf. le'gere | lire | lire |
| Pret. le'gi, legui | lis, lui | lus |
| Inf. plae'ngere | plaindre | plaindre |
| Pret. pla'nksi | plains | [plaignis] |
| Inf. me'ttere | metre | mettre |
| Pret. mi'si | mis | mis |
| Inf. pre'ndre | prendre | prendre |
| Pret. pre'si | pris | pris |
| Inf. na'skere | naistre | naître |
| Pret. nask-' | nasqui | naquis |
| Inf. vi'vere | vivre | vivre |
| Pret. vesk-' | vesqui | vécus |
| Inf. vēē'nkere | veincre | vaincre |
| Pret. venk-' | venqui | vainquis |

Some of the Romance forms given in the preceding
table of verbs have not been actually found in documents. They are re-constituted hypothetically. There
is, throughout the conjugation of primary verbs, a

tendency towards the secondary verb form, either in the passage from Archaic Latin to Romance, or from Romance to Old French, or from Old French to Modern French.

The *s* which appears at the end of the Modern French preterite is spurious, except in the primary verbs ending in *-si*, where it is rightfully preserved. Some primary verbs had perfects of different classes; for instance, *fakere* had *feci*, *feki*, and *fesi* in Romance, *legere* had *legsi* and *legui*. *Venire* had *veni* and *venui*, while *tenere* besides *tenui* had *teni*. In many primary verbs in which Old French formed the etymological (also called strong) preterite, recognisable by the reduction of the verb form to the stem syllable, a weak preterite in Modern French was formed, recognisable by the addition to the stem of a terminational syllable, which was introduced in analogy to the forms of secondary verbs. Such is the case with Modern French *(con)duisis*, compared with the Old French preterite *(con)duis* in which the termination is absorbed into the stem syllable. Compare also Old French *voil* with Modern *voulus*; Old French *nui* with Modern *nuisis*; Old French *escris* with Modern *écrivis*; Old French *plains* with Modern *plaignis*. In some instances when a weak preterite failed to take the place of a strong preterite the tense disappeared altogether, as happened to the preterite of *traire*, from *tra'kere*. The three mixed perfects transmitted to French, though belonging to verbs primary in principle, have all weak preterites in Old and in Modern French.

# CHAPTER XV.



SYNTAX.—Starting from imperfect Romance foundations, as Old French did in the Middle Ages, it was not possible to develop syntax very considerably, yet the French syntax that prevailed from the Renaissance period was already in all its essential features contained in Old French. But syntax, in a language like French, which has its origin in a highly-developed form of human speech, could not but be subjected to learned and scholarly influences such as are less visible in the case of English for instance, which has not behind it a mother-tongue endowed with a high literary development. This amounts to saying that while popular influence was paramount in shaping the material of the French tongue, the matter stood differently with regard to its syntax.

Yet scholars did help also in the coining of single words, and they did so very clumsily, for when mediæval writers who knew Latin, and to a greater degree the humanists of the Renaissance after them, introduced words directly from Latin into their French writings, they committed very much the same sort of mistake as when the writer of the *Reichenau Glossary*,

mistrusting the bareness of the Romance or Neo-Latin
forms, fitted on to them terminations of classical
reminiscence.  The Renaissance scholars who wrote in
French had no such mistrust of the capabilities of the
language, but the classical forms of Latin words were
so impressed upon their minds, as the only correct and
elegant ones, that they introduced large numbers of
classical Latin words into French by carrying out in
the terminations only so much change as was required
to make the words look and sound French.  Even if
they had been able to follow out the laws of proper
derivation, and had deliberately attempted to coin the
new words accordingly, they would have failed, because
the organic process of derivation from Latin had come
to an end and could not be revived.  In that way
words of learned formation in the French language
form a class of their own.  Being the outcome of
mechanical processes (as distinct from dynamic) of
derivation they run counter to the general principles
which, we have seen, underlay the popular formation.
They have the accentual stress on the last sounding
syllable without regard to the place in which it was in
Latin.  They preserve the short vowel which was
dropped in Romance.  They keep the consonant which
Romance dropped between two vowels.  In other
respects still they are imitations, not derivations.

EXAMPLES.

| *Romance.* | *French.* |
|---|---|
| fra'gilis | fragi'le |
| car(i)tas | charité |
| fra(g)ilis | fragile |

In the matter of syntax the action of the humanists was fully justified.   For this is a province where there is little scope for a right popular action, and the refinements of Latin syntax, essential to clear and complete literary expression in Modern French, could not penetrate the language through any other channel than scholarship.   The building up of syntax on the pattern of Latin can be traced with the greatest ease in the writers of the 16th century, such as Calvin, and in the earlier writers of the 17th, such as Descartes and Pascal.   In the second half of the 17th century the syntactical development is practically complete.   The deliberate imitation of Latin constructions is no longer visible.   French appears then in full possession of a syntax of its own, after rejecting all Latinisms which were at variance with the character of the language. From that time till the present the syntax of French has remained almost stationary.   And it could not well be otherwise when we consider what huge weight of authority was allowed to the classical French tongue. Now-a-days, through the seeking of new literary effects and the comparative disregard of regularity in language which characterise the writing of the period, the bonds of syntax are being somewhat loosened; care to preserve the beauty and purity received from the past is no longer so visible; and the forcing of the capabilities of syntax, with a view to effect, as well as the loosening of its stringency, with the same object, is distinctive of the times.

GALLICISMS.—Most Gallicisms have to be explained on other grounds than historical ones. They are mostly idiomatic phrases inextricably connected with the constitution of the language, and with the temperament of its speakers. But a large number of them are rooted in the historical development of French, or else they contain an allusion to ancient customs and manners by reference to which they can be explained.

A reference to the meaning of Latin *magis* (French *mais*) is enough to explain the Gallicism *n'en pouvoir mais*, in which *ne . . . mais* is old-fashioned for *ne . . . plus, ne . . . pas davantage*.

In *monter sur ses grands chevaux* a reference to etymology will be of no avail. The history of military customs has to be applied to.

Gallicisms are most frequent in colloquial French, in comedy, in popular satire, in songs, in familiar oratory and in letters. The more elevated or pathetic the tone becomes, the fewer are the Gallicisms. We shall give a few of those Gallicisms which can be explained historically or etymologically.

1. *Coiffé à la Titus, aux enfants d'Edouard, à la malcontent, à la turque*, etc., are phrases in which the words *manière, façon*, or *mode*, all feminine, have to be supplied: *coiffé à la manière turque*, etc. The same omission accounts for the phrases *Boucler les sacs à la diable, être fait à la diable* (*à la manière du diable*), etc. Cf. *je vous la donne en cent ; vous m'en donnez d'une*.

2. In such phrases as *Ce diable d'homme, coquine de femme!* the preposition *de* arises from the unwillingness

of French to allow the free use of a substantive as an attribute to another substantive. Cf. *La ville de Rome, le mot de bonheur.*

3. In *si j'étais que de vous* there survives an old exclamatory use of *que de* which is now otherwise extinct. Cf. Latin *quos ego ; quid de vobis dicam.* Cf. *comme si de rien n'était ; grenouilles de sauter*, etc.

4. In *cela ne laisse pas de nous inquiéter* the old meaning of *laisser* based on that of Lat. *laxare* is preserved (Eng. 'to leave off'). Now that this use of *laisser* is single, and that all similar uses have died out, an attraction in meaning to *manquer de* has established itself (*cela ne manque pas de nous inquiéter*).

The use of *penser* in the sense of *faillir* (*il pensa mourir*), and of *fus* in the sense of *allai* (*je fus à Paris le voir*) is a similar survival.

5. In such phrase as *il n'y voit pas* (he is blind), and *il n'y en a que pour les coquins* (idiom. Eng. 'rascals alone are *in it*') *y* and *en* may be viewed historically as expletive words which have crept in here from the numerous sentences in which they have a necessary grammatical function. But in the modern language they have become the most forcible part of such idioms. (Cf. also idiom. Eng. 'Well, he is going *it*').

6. The idiomatic use of an adjective, apparently as a substantive, but really in agreement with a noun that is not expressed, is quite frequent. At one time the noun alluded to was still present in the mind of the speaker. *La bailler bonne à quelqu'un,* also *la bailler belle à quel-*

*qu'un* (supply to the adjective the noun *histoire*) are equivalent to the English 'to stuff somebody.'

In *l'échapper belle, la manquer belle,* the noun *occasion* is understood. In the idiom *avoir beau,* it would appear that the masculine *coup* or *jeu* has to be understood. *Il a beau nous aider* meant at first, 'Now he has a rare opportunity of showing that he can help us,' a meaning which was gradually changed (by the ironical implication that help would not be forthcoming) to the modern sense: 'His help is vain.' Cf. *il ferait beau voir.*

7. *Monter sur ses grands chevaux* (to stand on one's dignity, to make a show of indignation) refers to the big war steeds on which the knights marched into battle.

*Faire pièce à quelqu'un* alludes to the practice, prevalent in the sixteenth and seventeenth centuries, of calling *pièce* a 'skit' or satirical play aimed at some personage objectionable in the opinion of the caricaturist. The phrase is now very much on a par with the English 'a Roland for an Oliver.'

*Avoir maille à partir avec quelqu'un* contains two words, one of which, namely, *maille* (a small coin, a farthing), has gone out of current use; while the other, *partir,* has no longer the sense of 'to divide.' The phrase has now acquired a more general sense than its origin implies (Eng. 'to have a crow to pick with somebody').

*Un homme de sac et de corde* is explained by the practice once prevalent of tying up a culprit in a bag the better to drown him.

*Prendre sans vert* brings to mind the French rural practice of wearing a green twig during the month of May. Failure to do this entailed a fine payable to those who combined to uphold the practice. (Eng. equivalent: 'to be caught napping').

*On en mettrait la main au feu* once applied to actual ordeal by fire; it is now only a literary phrase. It is an instance of the manner in which customs, after dying out as such, bequeathed to the literature of a subsequent age some most picturesque touches.

*Se faire blanc de son épée* alludes similarly to the ordeal by single combat, and *rompre en visière*, literally, 'to break one's lance in the visor of one's adversary,' points in modern figurative language to the actual practice in the tournaments of chivalry.

[illegible]
[illegible]
[illegible]
[illegible]
[illegible]
[illegible]

Avoir mauvaise grâce à
Grâce d'état
Le coup de grâce
De grâce
faire grâce de
Rendre grâces
Aller des mieux
Faire de [illegible] mieux
il qui mieux mieux
Le mieux de [illegible] de

Cure etymology of full words [illegible]
[illegible]
[illegible]
deux, même, chacun, élide mourrai
[illegible]
[illegible]
[illegible]
[illegible]
[illegible]
[illegible]

# INDEX

*See also Table of Contents and Chronological Tables.*

Printed by T. and A. CONSTABLE, Printers to Her Majesty, at the Edinburgh University Press.

www.ingramcontent.com/pod-product-compliance
Lightning Source LLC
Chambersburg PA
CBHW031134120726
47905CB00006B/1693